Democracy as Death

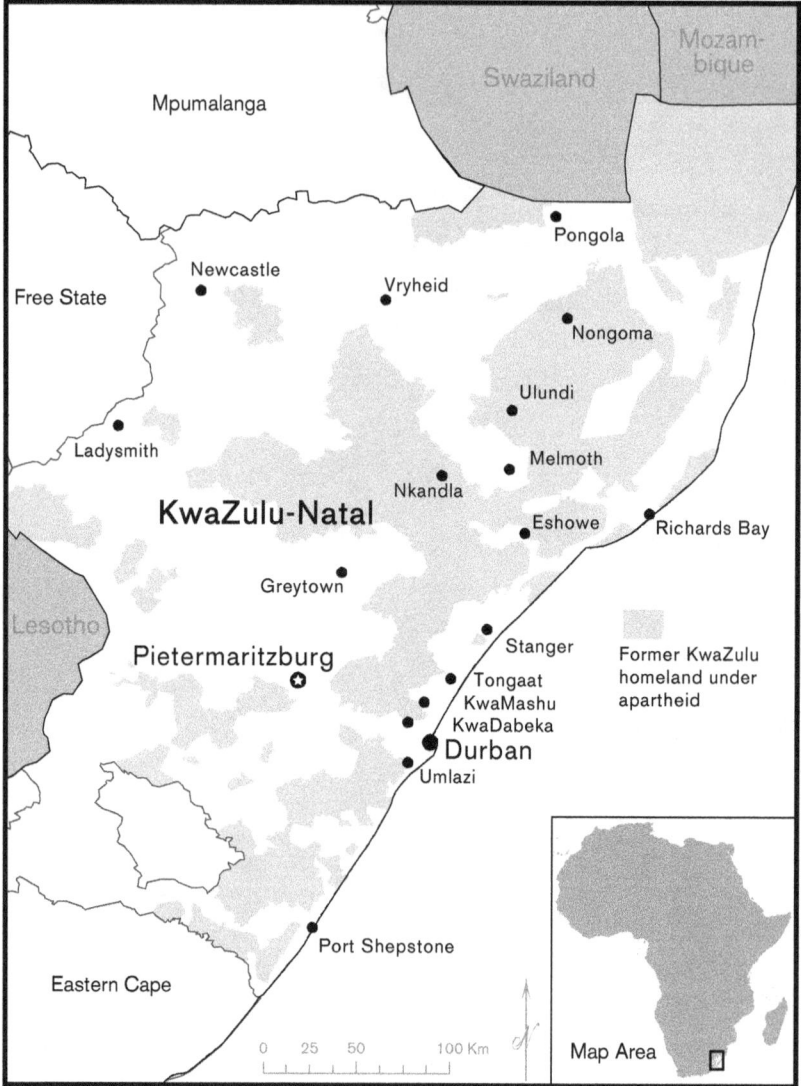

KwaZulu-Natal. Map by Lee Perlow.

Democracy as Death

The Moral Order of Anti-Liberal
Politics in South Africa

Jason Hickel

UNIVERSITY OF CALIFORNIA PRESS

University of California Press, one of the most distinguished university presses in the United States, enriches
lives around the world by advancing scholarship in the
humanities, social sciences, and natural sciences. Its
activities are supported by the UC Press Foundation and
by philanthropic contributions from individuals and
institutions. For more information, visit www.ucpress.edu.

University of California Press
Oakland, California

Library of Congress Cataloging-in-Publication Data

Hickel, Jason, 1982– author.
    Democracy as death : the moral order of anti-liberal
politics in South Africa / Jason Hickel.
      pages   cm
    Includes bibliographical references and index.
    ISBN 978-0-520-28422-7 (cloth : alk. paper)
    ISBN 978-0-520-28423-4 (pbk. : alk. paper)
    ISBN 978-0-520-95986-6 (ebook)
      1. Democracy—South Africa.   2. South Africa—Poli-
tics and government—1994–   I. Title.
    JQ1981.H53   2015
    320.968—dc23   2014035011

Contents

Illustrations

Map of KwaZulu-Natal *frontispiece*

TABLE

Partial list of bovine anatomical classifications typically used in rural Zululand / *160*

Acknowledgments

This book's central question came out of a series of conversations I had in 2004 with a friend of mine in Swaziland. Having completed my undergraduate degree in the United States, I had returned to Swaziland—where I was born and raised—to work for a local development organization. There I worked closely with Miso Dlamini, and he and I frequently discussed the democracy movement in Swaziland, which suffers intense repression at the hands of the monarchy. While he agreed with many of the monarchy's critics, he liked to point out that if Swaziland were to hold a referendum on the monarchy, the king would be upheld by a landslide, bolstered mainly by the country's rural majority. Not because people don't object to many of the king's policies—many do—but because the *principle* of the monarchy and the king's *ritual* importance remain salient in people's everyday lives and central to popular conceptions of collective well-being. Miso impressed on me that not all Swazis wanted Western-style liberal democracy and the particular types of freedom it seeks to inscribe. I had difficulty accepting his argument at the time, despite having lived in Swaziland's rural areas for many years, but it intrigued me.

These are the personal connections that tie me to my research, which ultimately seeks to understand the politics of my home region. But this book is not about Swaziland. When I chose my field site I wanted something a bit less familiar, yet similar enough in language and culture to allow me to build on my existing knowledge. KwaZulu-Natal, the

South African province immediately south of Swaziland, fit this bill. When I first moved there for fieldwork I intended to focus on the labor movement. I was curious to know why migrant workers from rural KwaZulu-Natal refused to join COSATU—the country's most powerful labor union confederation—when it seemed it would have been in their class interests to do so, preferring instead their own independent unions even though they are much less powerful and have access to fewer resources. I learned that their reason for this was that they rejected the politics of liberal democracy, which COSATU generally supports as a partner to the ruling African National Congress. So I ended up getting drawn back to my earlier conversations with Miso almost ineluctably, compelled once again by the question of why some groups of people reject the political values that Westerners often take for granted as universally desirable.

This book owes its being to a broad network of relationships and a series of long-standing conversations. It illustrates Michel Foucault's famous assertion that authors—as individuals—do not exist as such. My list begins with the Department of Anthropology at the University of Virginia, which provided a nourishing and challenging intellectual home for the dissertation work that served as the basis for this book. In particular I would like to thank my mentors and teachers Ira Bashkow, Richard Handler, Susan McKinnon, Wende Marshall, Hanan Sabea, Fred Damon, and Joseph Miller, all of whom had a formative impact on my intellectual development. Without their support this project would never have come to fruition. Coursework and conversations with other faculty who were at UVA while I was there—including Eve Danziger, Roy Wagner, Edith Turner, John Shepherd, Peter Metcalf, Robert Fatton, Cindy Hoehler-Fatton, Bob Swap, Chris Colvin, Adria LaViolette, Ellen Contini-Morava, and Dan Lefkowitz—provided a reservoir of knowledge and insight on which I have continued to draw. My fellow graduate students and other colleagues who were in the UVA orbit at the time provided a rich and exciting intellectual community, as well as long-standing friendships, especially Arsalan Khan, Roberto Armengol, David Flood, Harri Siikala, Clare Terni, Andrew Nelson, Claire Snell-Rood, Melissa Nelson, Rose Wellman, Jack Stoetzel, Todne Thomas, Alex Isaacson, Julian Hayter, Chris Hewlett, Sue Ann McCarty, Amy Nichols-Belo, Nadim Khoury, Betsy Mesard, Emily Filler, Omar Shaukat Ali, Justin Shaffner, Cassie Hays, Kristin Phillips, James Hoesterey, Bukky Gbadegesin, and many others. After I returned from the field I joined a writing group with Roberto and Harri, who helped me hone my argument in the early stages of its development. I also want to thank the students in the courses I taught at UVA—especially Stephanie DeWolfe, Greg Casar, Tai Ford, Ishraga Eltahir, Zach Cox, and Lolan Sagoe-Moses—who inspired me to frame my arguments in provocative and accessible ways.

I carried out the field research for this book in KwaZulu-Natal over a total of sixteen months between 2007 and 2011, including an intensive twelve-month period in 2008–9. The time I spent there was some of the most interesting and exciting of my life, made so by the people with whom I shared it. Robyn Hemmens was a constant source of help and encouragement when I first began to fumble my way around KwaZulu-Natal. Adriaan Diederichs treated me as a brother and offered tremendous support. My primary hosts in Durban—Richard and Elda Lyster—provided not only a welcoming home base and a rich source of friendship, but also served as living encyclopedias of South Africa's political history, in which each of them played inspiring roles. Xolani Dube, Rochelle Burgess, Rosa Lyster, the Holst family, and the Rapson/Von Maltitz family also made living in Durban delightful.

Thanks to Catherine Burns and Keith Breckenridge I found a warm intellectual home at the University of KwaZulu-Natal, where I regularly attended the excellent History and African Studies Seminar. I also want to thank Patrick Bond, Khadija Sharife, Ashwin Desai, Dennis Brutus, and the others who welcomed me into the scholarly community around the Center for Civil Society. Thanks also to Jeff Guy, who invited me to join his Tradition, Authority, and Power research group with Percy Ngonyama, Eva Jackson, Vukile Khumalo, Molly Margaretten, Mark Hunter, and Meghan Healy-Clancy—all of whom became good friends and taught me a great deal. Meghan's friendship in particular enriched my time in Durban, as did that of Mwelela Cele. Their passion for South African history inspired me to think much more historically about my ethnographic work than I might otherwise have done.

Much of the data in this book comes from interviews I conducted with workers in the KwaZulu-Natal sugar industry. For this dimension of my research I must thank Yasmeen Motala at the National Bargaining Council for the Sugar Industry, who worked hard to open doors for my research with the unions and employers alike. My fieldwork would not have been possible were it not for Yasmeen's generosity as a gatekeeper. For my research on COSATU I want to thank Comrades Ali Mdluli and Washington Silangwe, who granted me access to the Food and Allied Workers Union (FAWU), COSATU's agricultural extension, and introduced me to the labor movement more broadly. My research on National Union—the largest independent union in the sugar industry—was facilitated by Stefanos Nhleko, the union's Secretary General, who helped me get to know many of the union's members. For interviews with workers and shop stewards I travelled to most of the sugar mills and plantations across the province and spent a few intensive weeks living at the Pongola mill near the southern border of Swaziland. I want to thank Barry Lane and Brian Rapson, among others, for graciously granting me access to these otherwise restricted spaces.

For research on the townships in the Durban area I made regular trips to KwaMashu, Umlazi, KwaDabeka, and, to a lesser extent, Chesterville and Lamontville. I also took these opportunities to spend time in the hostel districts of each of these townships: A Section in Kwa-Mashu, T Section in Umlazi, and Kranskloof in KwaDabeka, where I conducted interviews with residents and community leaders. I want to thank the people who welcomed me into these communities. For research in rural areas I made extended trips to villages in the regions of Eshowe and Nkandla. In Eshowe, about 90 miles north of Durban, I spent my time in the village of Entenjani, where I benefitted from the hospitality and wisdom of Walter Cele, an elder and former village councilor under Inkatha who became one of my most helpful interlocutors. In Nkandla, some 180 miles north of Durban, I lived at the homestead of Mandlenkosi Buthelezi. During this time I grew close to Mandlenkosi's son, Jabulani, who proved to be a remarkable friend and research assistant. Muzi Hadebe and Lwazi Mjiyako both worked with me to polish my IsiZulu and were always willing to field even my most obscure questions. Gxabhasha Xulu, Moses Gasa, and Constance Mkhize also taught me a great deal; they are intellectuals in their own right, and I continue to regard myself as their student.

For documentary data I mined the archives of the National Bargaining Council and the Sugar Employers' Association in Mt. Edgecombe; human resources records at Amatikulu and Pongola mills; Killie Campbell Africana Library, the National Archives Repository, and the Local History Museum Archives in Durban; and the Historical Papers at the University of the Witwatersrand in Johannesburg. I want to thank all of the archivists who so patiently helped me in this endeavor, particularly Mwelela Cele and Nellie Somers.

This research was funded by a Wenner-Gren Dissertation Fieldwork Grant, a National Science Foundation Doctoral Dissertation Improvement Grant, and a Fulbright-Hays Doctoral Dissertation Research

Abroad Fellowship. The University of Virginia Graduate School of Arts and Sciences funded summer language study, preliminary archival research, and preliminary fieldwork. Heartfelt thanks go to Julie Lassetter and Karen Hall—the unsung heroes of the Anthropology Department at UVA while I was there—who helped with the administration of these grants. Writing was supported by a Charlotte W. Newombe Dissertation Fellowship from the Woodrow Wilson National Fellowship Foundation. I rewrote the dissertation and prepared the manuscript for publication while on a postdoctoral fellowship at the London School of Economics. My mentors Matthew Engelke, Deborah James, and Rita Astuti provided invaluable support during this period, and I benefited a great deal from conversations with Michael Scott, Charles Stafford, Laura Bear, Hans Steinmuller, Harry Walker, Nicholas Martin, Max Bolt, Jay Sundaresan, Tom Boylston, George St. Clair, Andrew Sanchez, Tom Grisaffi, Charlotte Bruckerman, Insa Koch, Cristina Inclan, Alice Pearson, Lewis Beardmore, and many others. I want to thank Yan Hinrichsen and Tom Hinrichsen, who continue to provide patient logistical support for all of us in the Anthropology Department at the London School of Economics. All of these people have made my time in London enlightening and enjoyable.

A special vote of thanks goes to those who were kind enough to read and comment on the manuscript or portions thereof, including Ira, Richard, Meghan, Charles, Arsalan, Matthew, Nicholas, Max, and David—who I mentioned above—as well as Joseph Hellweg, Timothy Gibbs, Alex Lichtenstein, Steve Lyon, and a number of anonymous reviewers. I presented various parts of this book's arguments in seminars and workshops at Yale University, Princeton University, the University of St. Andrews, the University of Chicago, Reed College, the University of Virginia, the University of KwaZulu-Natal, and the LSE, as well as at conferences hosted by the University of Oxford, University College London, the University of Birmingham, James Madison University, the Southern African Historical Society, the North Eastern Workshop on Southern Africa, and, of course, the American Anthropological Association. Thanks to Dan Segal, Bonnie Urciuoli, Elizabeth Dunn, Naomi Haynes, Brian Howell, Gareth Jones, Sharad Chari, Gerard Mare, Thembisa Waetjen, William Mazzarella, John Kelly, Carol Greenhouse, Paul Silverstein, Abby Neely, Ben Carton, William Beinart, Saul Dubow, Tim Allen, Catherine Boone, and many others who engaged with my work during these presentations. It has been a delight to work with Reed Malcolm, Stacy Eisenstark, and the rest of the team at the University of California Press, as well as Peter Dreyer, who managed the copyediting, and Lee Perlow and Anita Michalkiewicz, whose line drawings grace these pages. All of them have done a great deal to make this book much better than it otherwise would have been.

It goes without saying that any flaws that remain are my own—and there are no doubt many. I have come to learn that ethnographic writing is always incomplete. Representations are always also misrepresentations, conclusions are just interpretations, and generalizations always ride roughshod over the nuances of lived experience. I am painfully aware that the story that unfolds in this book could be told in a million different ways. I have had to choose but one, yet I can imagine many others. I trust that they will emerge in time from minds better than my own.

One last word remains. I want to offer my heartfelt thanks to Guddi Singh, not only for her useful advice on the manuscript, but also for so graciously extending the love, patience, and support I needed to complete it.

A Note on Translation and Transcription

I conducted all of the interviews for this study in either IsiZulu or English, depending on the preference and ability of each interviewee. All translations from IsiZulu to English are my own, unless otherwise noted. In the transcriptions I have retained IsiZulu words for significant concepts or categories that appear repeatedly throughout the book, or where particular words deserve scrutiny for other reasons. Some of the transcriptions reflect editorial changes that I made during the process of translation in order to enhance clarity and flow.

A Note on Translation and
Transcription

Abbreviations

AIDS	acquired immune deficiency syndrome
AMCU	Association of Mineworkers and Construction Union
ANC	African National Congress
COSATU	Congress of South African Trade Unions
EFF	Economic Freedom Fighters
FAWU	Food and Allied Workers Union
FOSATU	Federation of South African Trade Unions
GATT	General Agreement on Tariffs and Trade
GEAR	Growth, Employment, and Redistribution
GNP	gross national product
HIV	human immunodeficiency virus
IFP	Inkatha Freedom Party
IMF	International Monetary Fund
NFP	National Freedom Party
NDR	National Democratic Revolution
NPA	National Prosecuting Authority
RDP	Reconstruction and Development Program
UDF	United Democratic Front
WTO	World Trade Organization

The Question of Freedom

Democracy is not simply related to a set of institutions but is conceived in relation to a state of being: that of being *free*. It designates a certain category of people rather than a host of practices, possibilities, activities. One is free not when one acts freely, but when one most closely resembles a figure said to be in a state of freedom.

—Ivor Chipkin, "The South African Nation"

The revolution in South Africa that put an end to apartheid is widely celebrated as a triumph of liberal democracy. The images that captured the world's attention in 1994 tell a set-piece tale: after decades of difficult struggle, the black majority queued up in long, snaking lines to cast their ballots in defiance of the minority white administration, elected Nelson Mandela to the presidency of the country's first democratic government, and enshrined a constitution so progressive that it remains a model even for western European countries. When most people think about the liberation movement that preceded this moment, they tend to imagine the black majority united against the apartheid state, driven by the common goal of ushering forth a new era of liberalism. But in reality things were not quite that simple, and the battle lines were not so clearly drawn. As it turned out, not all black South Africans wanted to sign on to the vision of a liberal democratic future, and some were so repulsed by the prospect that they resorted to violence to defend themselves against it.

During the years leading up to and following the democratic transition, South Africa was torn apart by internal conflict. To the bewilderment of outside observers, instead of closing ranks against the apartheid regime, many Africans turned against each other in what the media sensationalized as "black-on-black" violence—a prolonged civil war that claimed the lives of some 20,000 people and left tens of thousands more internally displaced. Around Johannesburg the conflict appeared to pit Zulus against other African ethnic groups—Xhosas, Sothos, and so on—leading the media to cast the pogroms as motivated by tribalism.[1] But events in the eastern province of Natal (now known as Kwa-Zulu-Natal), the epicenter of the conflict, gave the lie to that theory, for antagonists on both sides self-identified as Zulu. There, the fault lines developed between the residents of planned urban townships, on the one hand, and migrant workers from rural Zululand who lived temporarily in adjacent settlements and labor hostels, on the other. Township residents generally supported the African National Congress (ANC), which symbolized the vanguard of the popular struggle for democracy. Rural migrants, by contrast, generally identified with an organization known as Inkatha and formed vigilante militias to sabotage the revolution that was developing in the townships.

While most of the violence of that turbulent period has subsided, the rural-urban divide remains a defining feature of popular politics in KwaZulu-Natal. I began fieldwork in 2007 with the purpose of understanding how these tensions play out in the labor movement, where it is common for migrant workers from rural areas to refuse affiliation with ANC-linked unions even when they are much more powerful than the alternatives. Interviewing workers in the sugar industry, I found that many migrants explained their resistance to the ANC on the basis that they rejected the version of democracy (*idemoklasi*) and rights (*amalungelo*) that the party promotes—or at least certain dimensions of it. While they embraced the principles of racial equality and universal franchise, they questioned the underlying idea that all individuals are autonomous and ontologically equal—especially in relation to gender and kinship hierarchies—and objected to what they perceived as a systematic attack on their values by the ANC and its allies.

Intrigued, I decided to expand my inquiry more broadly, speaking with migrants who resided in labor hostels around Durban. I found the same anti-democracy sentiment crop up with remarkable frequency. Migrants who retain deep ties to homesteads in rural areas of Kwa-Zulu-Natal—my definition of "rural migrant" as I use it in this book[2]—routinely complain that the ANC's democracy, and the party's platform of liberal rights, is "ruining" families and "killing" the country, causing misfortune on a massive scale that registers as declining marriage rates, rising unemployment, deepening poverty, and epidemic disease. My interlocutors were often explicit about this. One hostel-dweller in Kwa-Mashu whom I grew to know well told me: "There is a problem with democracy. Relationships are changing within families, and things are topsy-turvy. It has become like a curse in the ears of the ancestors and brings about misfortunes that can lead even to death." A resident of the hostel in Umlazi explained the matter to me by referring to *hlonipha,* the system of taboo and avoidance that governs respectful decorum across social hierarchies in rural areas: "The culture of the rural areas is based on *hlonipha* . . . But these days *hlonipha* is going down . . . This is why everything is falling apart in South Africa. It is because of democracy and the Bill of Rights."

Migrants' resistance to the ANC has softened somewhat since Jacob Zuma assumed the presidency in 2009, for they see him as embodying many of the values that they feel are otherwise under threat. Yet the anti-democracy stance persists, and operates as a powerful expression of what people think about how the process of "liberation" has unfolded in South Africa since 1994. Most of the migrants I engaged with were middle-aged males, since they predominated at the workplaces and hostels I visited. But I heard a similar critique just as often on the lips of female migrants, albeit with a slightly different twist.[3] Of course, not all migrants hold this view—some support aspects of the ANC's liberal project for various reasons—but it is a very common perspective. In many cases it determines party allegiance and voting behavior, but this is not always true; some migrants who reject liberalism nonetheless vote for the ANC or join ANC-linked unions—a trend that has picked up significantly in the Zuma era. While I seek to account for these complexities, the focus of this study is the cultural logic of the anti-democracy stance itself. Why do the principles of individual liberty and equal rights appear so repugnant to so many rural migrants? How do we think about the connections that they draw between democracy and death?

In the following chapters I demonstrate that this stance makes sense according to the logic of a moral order common in rural Zululand that sees kinship hierarchies in homesteads as essential to the ritual processes of what I call "fruition." Many rural migrants see the ANC's liberal policies as threatening these hierarchies and therefore undermining the conditions for good fortune, social reproduction, and even development—a fear that has heightened as neoliberal structural adjustment renders family livelihoods ever more precarious. Yet this commitment to hierarchy is not a timeless or primordial element of social life in the countryside, and nor is the homestead in which it is rooted. Both have developed through a difficult history of engagement with the tactics of state power in the realm of *kinship* and *houses*—tactics that have long treated rural areas and urban areas very differently. The differences that the apartheid state created between rural and urban homes shaped the liberation struggle during the 1980s and 1990s, and continue to inform popular politics in KwaZulu-Natal today. This is particularly true for migrant workers: in the process of traversing back and forth between rural and urban, migrants construct a vision of contrast that provides a powerful framework for their critique of liberal democracy.

But before I delve into these arguments let me zoom out to get a wider perspective on the question at hand—the issue of freedom.

ON "FREEDOM" AND DEMOCRACY

This book explores the politics of a group of people who regard many of the values of liberal democracy not as liberating but as morally repulsive and socially destructive. In this sense it speaks to a broader trend, with the recent rise of social movements such as right-wing nationalism in Europe and the Islamic Awakening (al-Sahwa al-Islamiyya) across the Middle East. This trend has troubled modernist narratives popular in the West, which imagined that globalization, by opening international markets and expanding networks of communication, would facilitate the flow of enlightened liberal ideals around the world. According to this view, people will choose to embrace these ideals so long as they are free to do so—free, that is, from the grip of dictators, patriarchs, and the repressive norms of culture or tradition. As it turns out, however, globalization has not only failed to produce a world of liberal cosmopolitans, in many cases, it has done the opposite, inspiring reactionary and often violent waves of what Brigit Meyer and Peter Geschiere (1999) have called "cultural closure" and generating new longings for illiberal forms of social order, often expressed as nostalgia for an idealized past that has fallen apart as a consequence of liberal modernity. Even when people are free to exercise their franchise, in many cases they choose to support illiberal political organizations. For example, when parliamentary elections were held in Egypt a year after the 2011 revolution, voters overwhelmingly favored the Muslim Brotherhood and the Salafis over their various liberal opponents.[4] The same has been true of the rise of Hamas in Palestine and, earlier, the Taliban in Afghanistan. All of these cases have left Western analysts groping for explanations.

How are we to think about social movements that reject liberal values in this manner? Many progressives and leftists—including myself, when I first began to grapple with this question—tend to resort to explanations such as rigged elections, lack of education on the part of the people, or intervention by external interests, believing, in other words, that people do not *actually* make those decisions freely. These explanations are not without merit, but I have come to find them inadequate on the grounds that they assume that there is something intrinsic to humans that *should* predispose them to desire liberal freedoms. They ignore the possibility that people might actually find liberalism to run counter to their conceptions of the good and their ideas about human flourishing. To paraphrase the words of Saba Mahmood (2005, xi), we cannot arrogantly assume that liberal forms of life necessarily exhaust ways of living meaningfully and richly in this world; we have to be able to parochialize our own political certainty on this matter.

I should be clear that by "liberalism" I do not mean the political ideology that stands as the opposite of "conservatism," as in the divide between the Democratic Party and the Republican Party in the United States. Rather, I mean the deeper set of ideas about personhood and freedom that are shared by people on both ends of this political spectrum and that ultimately underpin what we might refer to as modern Western culture. In lieu of trying to unpack this model in its entirety (see Asad 2003; Keane 2007; Mahmood 2005; and Taylor 1989 for efforts toward this end), I want to dwell briefly on the conception of liberation that lies at its core.

As Webb Keane has pointed out, ideas about modernity and historical progress in Europe and the United States are generally cast as a story of human liberation. "In this narrative," he writes,

> progress is not only a matter of improvements in technology, economic well-being, or health but is also, and perhaps above all, about human emancipation and *self-mastery*. If in the past, humans were in thrall to illegitimate rulers, rigid traditions, and unreal fetishes, as they become modern they realize the true character of human agency. Conversely, those who seem to persist in displacing their own agency onto such rulers, traditions, or fetishes are out of step with the times, anachronistic premoderns or anti-moderns. (Keane 2007, 6)

The long tradition of liberal thought—spanning thinkers as diverse as Heidegger, Voltaire, Emerson, and Nietzsche—holds that liberation (the emancipation of the individual) requires achieving distance of the self from the external world: the goal is to stand apart from the arbitrary authority of others and recognize one's own agency, and to stand apart from one's own experience and know it for what it truly is.

This conception of liberation provides the logic that drives democratization projects in the postcolonial world. According to the narrative promoted by institutions such as the World Bank, the U.S. military, and all kinds of NGOs, democracy liberates individuals by restoring their supposedly innate autonomy and allowing them to find their way toward enlightened rationality and political self-interest. The model of personhood at the core of this thinking was recognized by Alexis de Tocqueville in the nineteenth century. He observed that democratic societies—such as the United States—were built on assumptions about underlying human equality: all individuals partake of a singular, abstract humanity such that every person, regardless of their social position, is just as good as anyone else. Endowed with this "imaginary equality" of substance—even in the face of significant inequalities of income and opportunity—each person is free to reason for themselves and express their ideas without constraint, for all opinions are equally valid and all have equal access to truth (de Tocqueville 2000). Tocqueville recognized this as a culturally particular model of personhood that contrasted sharply with that in aristocratic societies like his native France. Today, democratization projects around the world take this form of personhood for granted as natural and seek to "restore" it to people whose oppressors have denied it to them, even if this requires violence, as in the U.S. invasion of Iraq in 2003.

Hierarchy becomes a particularly salient issue in this process, be it in the form of patriarchal kinship, ancestor cults, or feudalistic social forms based on the "clan" and "tribe." Democracy is supposed to break the hold of hierarchies over the individual and liberate a public sphere wherein people might realize their own agency. This idea motivates U.S. interventions in the Middle East and Africa, specifically. Take for instance a 2003 article by John Tierney in the *New York Times* titled "Iraqi Family Ties Complicate American Efforts for Change." Following the lead of conservative thinkers like Stanley Kurtz and Steve Sailer, Tierney blames Iraq's democracy deficit on patriarchal extended families and cousin marriage, which he says encourage cronyism, nepotism, feuding, and general political corruption. Tierney implies that liberal democracy will only be possible if Iraqis adopt "modern" kinship forms, such as the nuclear families and autonomous individualism that supposedly characterize the United States. These ideas hinge on a social evolutionary trajectory borrowed from nineteenth-century anthropology, specifically Henry Maine's theory of "the movement of progressive societies" from status to contract, from patriarchy to egalitarianism, and from group to individual—a process that gradually separates the domain of kinship from the domain of politics and economics. As Susan McKinnon (2013) has put it, Maine's framework remains the "essential blueprint for narratives of modernity."[5]

Why should hierarchy pose a moral problem for moderns? Because to surrender one's autonomy to superior beings—be they patriarchs or ancestors—is to misplace one's agency, to abdicate responsibility, and therefore to diminish one's freedom. In other words, in a manner not dissimilar to the fetish objects that Keane describes, hierarchy appears as a source of political self-betrayal. True liberation requires abstracting the self from social entanglements to achieve the disembedded, objectified personhood that lies at the root of Western conceptions of the rights-bearing individual, the critical political subject, and the disinterested participant of the public sphere (Keane 2007; Comaroff and Comaroff 1997; Warner 2002).[6] Individual autonomy along these lines is crucial to the process of enlightenment and self-realization that liberalism celebrates, whereby individuals come to realize and act upon their "true" desires, interests, and will (cf. Gray 1980).

According to this line of thinking, the individual and society are understood as fundamentally at odds. This assumption appears repeatedly in Western social science and liberal political movements alike (Sahlins 2008). In the founding myths that organize Marxian and Freudian scholarship, the individual is understood as natural and a priori, while society is understood as contrived—an assumption we might trace back to a sort of Hobbesian worldview.[7] In this schema, the individual has "inner" or "authentic" desires that exist prior to social norms and expectations, which are imagined as external constraints. As in Hegelian thought, the individual is regarded as the proper locus of reason, while "society" (or cultural values and beliefs), by overdetermining the desires of individuals, appears as a form of bondage—a form of false consciousness that precludes objective knowledge of the external world. The process of liberation involves excavating and asserting this creative autonomous will, as in the figure of the "strong poet" that Nietzsche championed against the "slave morality" of the masses.[8]

In Rousseau's words, man is born free but he is everywhere in chains. Following this logic, liberal democracy projects itself as a neutral political framework that removes the artificial restrictions of society and liberates individuals to realize and express their supposedly innate, natural autonomy. The concept of democracy—like that of human rights—bears the aura of the natural, the inevitable, and the universally good, and it takes the form of a redemptive project that extends the offer of transcendence.

These are the key ideas that came to underwrite the mainstream liberation struggle in South Africa. The National Democratic Revolution (NDR) that gained traction in the 1980s was committed to the principles of liberal democracy, supported the concept of individual rights, and stood against gender hierarchy and the notion of ascribed status (at least in theory; in reality the movement was deeply patriarchal and clientelistic, and this remains true of the ANC today).[9] In addition, since it was mobilized in part through labor unions and the South African Communist Party,[10] the movement drew on a reading of Marx that saw the revolutionary class as a class in and for itself, separated from contrived affiliations of clan or tribe and free from the fetishes of animism and ancestors. These values became crucial to the conception of freedom that underwrote the revolution: only people who matched up with these values—namely, urban individuals—could be considered revolutionary subjects. It was not always this way. The anti-apartheid movement had a history of including, and indeed relying on, rural activists (see, e.g., Delius 1989; Sitas 1996; Gibbs 2014). But by the 1980s the movement's vanguard began to reject people who hinged their beings on chiefdoms, patriarchs, and the will of ancestors, all of which were thought to restrict the moral and political autonomy of the subject. Like Marxist and modernist movements elsewhere in the world, it tended to regard peasants as intrinsically apolitical, too mired in "culture" to realize and act on their true political agency.[11]

Rural Zulus bore the brunt of this critique during the revolution. They were considered backward and counterrevolutionary because they failed to embody the values of the free, revolutionary subject (Chipkin 2003). Supposedly shackled by the false consciousness of tribalism and tied down by feudalistic hierarchies, rural Zulus appeared as obstacles to the achievement of liberal democracy. In its struggle for national liberation, then, the ANC crafted a story of rupture from a traditional past and progress into a modern future. In the process, they projected the negation of modern freedom onto rural Zulus, who came to embody the figure of the backward Other—a symbol freighted with ideas about hierarchical kinship, ancestor cults, and the absence of authentic agency. This furnished the logic that justified violence against the latter in the form of what Bruno Latour has called "purification," the separation of distinct ontological zones: free, rational human beings, on the one hand, and obstacles or traitors to the cause of freedom, on the other (Latour 1993, 10–11). Today the ANC continues this project of purification by pushing policies geared toward reforming the hierarchical family in a manner not dissimilar to the civilizing mission that characterized certain aspects of colonialism.

DEMOCRACY THROUGH THE LOOKING GLASS

The migrants I grew to know rejected this narrative outright, and many rejected the idea of liberal democracy along with it. This reaction opens up an interesting ethnographic opportunity. The temptation—to which many analysts have succumbed—is to dismiss this perspective on democracy not only because it runs against the grain of progressive politics and liberation narratives but because it runs against Euro-American assumptions about moral personhood and the social good. This tension is precisely where anthropology promises to find traction. Migrants' concerns jar us into recognizing the contingency of our assumptions about progressive politics; they help us see the democratic project with new eyes and understand things about it that we normally take for granted. One of the goals of this book is to leverage the perspectives of liberalism's subalterns to illuminate important truths about contemporary political economy.

To return to the question with which I opened this chapter: How do we make sense of the connection that many rural migrants draw between democracy and death? I first stumbled upon answers to these questions by thinking about ritual. In addition to learning the ropes of everyday life in rural Zululand, I also participated in the full spectrum of ritual activity—weddings, funerals, rites of passage, cleansing ceremonies, and countless cattle sacrifices. While each of these ceremonies has a different goal, all are geared toward establishing the proper order of persons and things and thereby establishing the conditions for health, reproduction, and good fortune, or what we might call "fruition" (van Dijk et al. 2000). According to my informants, the state of nature is one of sameness, disorder, and sterility, and fruition can only be realized by properly ordering the social world. As they see it, this requires the meticulous *differentiation* of social elements into sets of hierarchical oppositions—oppositions that are considered crucial to establishing a kind of integrated wholeness or unity. This is what ritual does (Bell

1992). To apply an insight from Roy Wagner's (1977) essay on "analogic kinship," the imperative to differentiate is experienced as a moral obligation, specifically by men. Without differences between categories of persons, society becomes unthinkable, and the morass of sameness appears as a kind of moral degeneracy.

A moral code known in IsiZulu as *umthetho* polices this hierarchical social order by governing the correct practice of ritual and enforcing the elaborate rules of respect, taboo, and avoidance mentioned by the hostel-dweller I quoted at the beginning of this chapter. The ancestors are said to mediate between *umthetho* and fruition. When *umthetho* is upheld and order is intact, they are pleased; they protect their descendants from the chaos of the surrounding world and deliver fertility and good fortune. When the order is breached, they "turn their backs," leaving their descendants at the mercy of *amashwa,* or "misfortunes," which register as glitches in productive and reproductive processes and manifest as failure, infertility, joblessness, illness, and death—the opposite of fruition. In Zululand, an entire industry of traditional healing operates according to this theory of *amashwa.* For example, if a man is unable to secure a job, or cannot find a wife, he might consult a diviner to help him identify the sources of his misfortune. More often than not, the diviner will assert that the patient's ancestors are angry with him for violating *umthetho* and have communicated as much by allowing misfortunes to beset him.

These ideas pertain not only to personal and family well-being. They also extend to the realm of politics: leaders are expected to govern in such a way as to ensure the conditions for fruition. Drawing on these ideas, many people object to the ANC's egalitarian project, specifically policies that permit abortion and homosexuality, support single mothers, promote female home-ownership, and grant equal rights to women and children—all of which alter the terrain of relatedness and reproduction. They see these policies—which they lump together under the rubric of "democracy"—as culturally retrograde: democracy undoes the ritual work of differentiating persons, dismantles the hierarchical structure of kinship, and returns the world to a state of sterile sameness. By equalizing all persons across boundaries of gender, generation, and genealogy, democracy threatens the foundations of fruition and dissolves the social differences essential to reproduction. Extending the theory of *amashwa* to the state of the nation, many regard democracy as causing rising rates of poverty, crime, sexual violence, HIV transmission, and unemployment—re/productive misfortune on a mass scale.[12]

This perspective has found traction in the realities of recent economic history. During the negotiations to end apartheid, the ANC made a number of moves that hampered its future power over economic policy. The party retreated from its position on nationalization, signed up to the GATT, and accepted an IMF deal that deregulated the financial sector and clamped down on wage increases.[13] The central bank, left in the hands of the old apartheid bosses, was insulated from democratic politics and its mandate limited to targeting inflation instead of employment or growth (Padayachee 2013). In 1996, the cabinet implemented a neoliberal economic policy framework that promoted privatization, reduced trade tariffs, and loosened financial controls, despite significant resistance from within the ranks of the unions that had given such force to the anti-apartheid struggle (Bond 2000). Instead of creating jobs, as its proponents claimed it would, this approach nearly doubled the unemployment rate, which now (in 2013) stands at 37 percent.[14] Of those who do have secure employment, many nonetheless live precarious lives: some two-thirds of full-time workers earn less than the poverty threshold (Barchiesi 2010). About 62 percent of the black population lives below the poverty line, while in the rural areas of the former homelands this figure rises to 79 percent.[15]

For people in rural Zululand, this translates into what some scholars have called a "crisis of social reproduction" (cf. Bezuidenhout and Fakier 2006; Fakier and Cock 2009; Hunter 2011; Von Holdt and Webster 2005). The rural homestead, which has long relied on migrant wage labor, can no longer operate as it did under late colonialism and most of apartheid. One crucial factor is that as men's access to income diminishes, they become increasingly unable to pay for bridewealth (*ilobolo*), to the point where marriage rates have plummeted over the past few decades (Hunter 2010). Without legitimate bridewealth transactions, it becomes almost impossible to create and sustain the kinship structure, hierarchical relationships, gender roles, and division of labor that defines the kind of homestead to which most aspire. To some extent, this process of change was well under way before the end of apartheid: formal employment began to decline during the 1980s—a consequence of both the National Party's early experiments with economic liberalization and the impact of international sanctions (see Habib and Padayachee 2000)—just at the same time that employers began to reject rural migrants in favor of higher-skilled, better-educated urban workers. But the conditions for homestead reproduction have become even more precarious since the ANC's turn to neoliberalism—a downward spiral that is all the more difficult to bear given the widespread optimism that accompanied the end of minority rule.

Yet most of my interlocutors had very little to say about neoliberalism. It was liberal democracy that worried them. To be charitable to this perspective, we might grant that it is not entirely incorrect. After all, liberal democracy and neoliberal economics draw a great deal from the same pool of values: both are promoted under the banner of individual freedom. So migrants are correct to point out that democracy is bringing decline, but only because the type of democracy that the ANC has established is complicit with a form of capitalism that leverages the logic of freedom to justify the financial and economic deregulation that has generated the crisis of social reproduction that they find so troubling. But my interlocutors rarely drew this connection themselves. For them, the crisis of social reproduction is a consequence of democracy's apparent attack on social differentiation and hierarchical kinship, and the new forms of personhood and desire that it has brought about.

This perspective may seem jarring, but that is exactly what enables us to gain critical distance from a number of very common assumptions about liberal democracy. The chapters that follow will show that rural migrants' critique of the ANC illuminates three in particular.

The first is that democracy is a project of freedom, that it removes "artificial" social restraints that prevent individuals from realizing their "natural" autonomy. In the discourse of migrants, democracy is understood as exactly the opposite: it extracts persons from their natural context of social encompassment and artificially reifies them as autonomous, disembedded monads with discrete individual interests. From this perspective, democracy does not liberate. It destroys. It dismantles the proper order of persons and erases the hierarchical differences that supply the conditions for human flourishing. Indeed, rural migrants perceive the *disciplinary* nature of democratic ideology. They realize that, far from being a neutral lifting of restrictions, democracy attempts to produce and standardize a particular state of being—the state of being an individual. This point resonates with Michel Foucault's (1975, 1991) argument that liberalism comprises a subject-making project. Liberal democracy does not abandon the will to govern but serves the interests of states seeking to manage their subjects more efficiently. Democracy conceives of citizens as subjects of individual responsibility, autonomy, agency, and choice, acts upon them through shaping and utilizing their freedom, and trains them to participate in their own governance (cf. Barry et al. 1996; Burchell et al. 1991; Englund 2006; Harvey 2005; Mitchell 1991; Rose 1996, 1999; Scott 1999).

The second assumption about liberal democracy that many migrants question is the idea that democracy signifies progress, modernity, and development. Against this narrative, they regard democracy as a signifier of decline, decay, and degeneration; it obliterates the principles of respect and taboo that govern social relations and reduces people to "raw," unrefined and uncultured creatures, more like primordial beasts than properly socialized human beings. And herein lies a fascinating reversal of trajectories: just as township residents regard rural migrants as backward on an evolutionary trajectory that runs from traditional to modern, rural migrants regard township residents as undoing culture and unraveling society toward a state of nature and of amoral, animalistic disorder. In this sense, migrants *also* sense a need to "purify"—to use Latour's term again—by separating the properly human from the subhuman or nonhuman. In sum, they see nothing normal or good or inevitable about egalitarian individualism. On the contrary, they want to *restore* hierarchies, and in this it appears that they have common cause with many of the other right-wing social movements that have sprung up around the world in reaction to the onslaught of cultural globalization (Friedman 2002; Kalb 2005; Meyer and Geschiere 1999). As it turns out, not everyone wants to be "free."

The third point worth making here is that while liberal democracy may individualize, it does not necessarily liberate people from hierarchy. It simply replaces one kind of hierarchy with another. It does not eliminate repression so much as alter its style. This critique is common among autonomists who argue that real democracy has never existed in modern state societies, where elite domination is simply dressed up in the guise of popular representation (see Graeber 2004, 2013). As we shall see, rural migrants articulate a similar argument. They claim that the new democratic regime leaves them feeling *less* represented in the political sphere and *less* in control of their destinies, not more. Indeed, migrants describe their own norms of homestead autonomy and representation-by-encompassment as more democratic than the ANC's version of democracy. In this sense, their politics questions the very basis of the dichotomy between liberalism and illiberalism: the liberal government relies on undemocratic forms of power, while its illiberal subalterns make demands for more democratic forms of representation (cf. Zibechi 2005).

What becomes clear here is that democracy is best analyzed, not as a universal political form (as international agencies such as USAID and the World Bank would have it), but as a malleable signifier replete with local meanings. This is consistent with existing literature in the anthropology of democracy (e.g., Comaroff and Comaroff 2000, 334; Gutmann 2002, 11; Verdery 1996). As Julia Paley, a leader in this field, has put it: "the meanings attributed to democracy in various contexts and struggles do not necessarily match hegemonic definitions in actually-existing systems or even normative liberal democracy ideals" (2002, 485). In South Africa, this is true of both the ANC and its detractors. This book is not about democracy itself but about the *ideas* about democracy that people leverage as they construct competing visions for the postapartheid order.

COLONIAL POWER AND THE POLITICS OF HOME

Space is fundamental in any exercise of power.

—Michel Foucault, "Space, Knowledge, and Power"

Both democracy and the social movements that reject it must be understood as culturally particular phenomena. Yet one has to be careful to avoid reifying these cultural orientations as somehow bounded and static, as the popular "clash of civilizations" schema does when it pits modern secular-liberal values against those of "non-Western cultures," be it according to an evolutionary model or simply as opposing typological categories (see, e.g., Huntington 1996; Tierney 2003). As with all instances of cultural reification, history offers the best antidote to this tendency. This leads me to a second main goal of this book, namely, to demonstrate the historical contingency of both liberal and anti-liberal politics in South Africa, and to show that both tendencies emerged from the exigencies of the colonial encounter.

The political conflict that has divided KwaZulu-Natal for most of the past few decades offers a useful entry into this issue. If we understand the conflict as developing between a moral order organized around principles of hierarchical difference and a moral order organized around principles of individual egalitarianism, then we must ask: How did these two cultural tendencies—these two divergent ideologies of personhood—emerge from within the same self-identifying ethnic group? These moral orientations are not timeless or essential, and nor do they represent two different ends of a teleological trajectory running from "traditional" to "modern," as many accounts of the conflict would have it. I argue that what appears to be most traditional about rural migrants' political perspective derives from their long and difficult engagement with colonial modernity as much as from anything that we might call indigenous. By the same token, the liberal ideas that underpinned the revolution did not just emerge from nowhere, as if humans were universally predisposed to recognizing their superiority over "traditional" ontologies. We have to be able to explain what made it possible for this ideology to gain mass traction in KwaZulu-Natal in the late twentieth century, and why it happened specifically in urban townships.

Taking a historical approach, I argue that the emergence of these two political cosmologies can be traced in part to the influence of Native Administration policies under colonialism and apartheid. The colonial state entrenched deep distinctions between rural and urban and governed each with different techniques, relying on indirect rule in rural areas and deploying direct rule in urban areas. Both strategies sought to control Africans by organizing domestic social life, but in different ways: indirect rule organized a hierarchical social order in rural spaces, and direct rule organized an egalitarian social order in urban spaces. These divergent domestic governmentalities created the conditions for the development of competing political visions that came to be rooted in ideas about the home. As we shall see, domestic dwellings operate as potent symbols at the center of popular politics in KwaZulu-Natal today.

Yet while the history of segregation helps us understand the tensions between the political logics of rural and urban, the two sides are not as dichotomous as this might lead us to assume. Rather, they inhabit a continuum characterized by syncretism and flows (cf. Amselle 1998), not least because of the migrant labor system that keeps workers moving back and forth between the two, as Peter Delius (1996) has pointed out. Since a basic understanding of this system is necessary to understanding many of the arguments I make in this book, a brief overview is in order.

Colonial administrators had to reconcile two competing aims when it came to governing South Africa: maintaining racial separateness while supplying a steady flow of cheap black labor to the cities for industry. This was the core contradiction that the apartheid system had to face. Strict segregation would not suffice, since it would keep African labor away from white-owned farms, mines, and factories. But integration was equally undesirable—not only because of fears of miscegenation but because it would produce an urbanized proletariat liable to coalesce around a unified class or national identity. To solve this problem, administrators developed a system of internal migrancy that maintained racial separateness while still ensuring access to labor. African residence was restricted to a set of rural "native reserves," or "homelands," such as KwaZulu. While Africans would support themselves primarily through subsistence agriculture, the state imposed taxes and manipulated the size and arability of the reserves so that they would have to seek additional income in the form of wages. Black males were ferried between the reserves and the cities for work according to a system of "pass laws" that determined how many Africans could enter white areas and how long they could stay. Under this system, Africans in urban areas were subject to a condition of forced impermanence—migrants in their own country—compelled to live in labor hostels and expelled back to their rural homesteads when they were no longer needed (Crush et al. 1991).

This carefully contrived system came with significant benefits. It allowed Europeans to pay African workers a "bachelor wage" below that which any settled proletarian would require to support a family, since subsistence activities in the rural reserves—managed by the unpaid labor of African women—subsidized the costs of maintenance and reproduction (Meillassoux 1975). In addition, once workers' bodies were used up, sick, or disabled, they could be ejected back to the reserves, where the cost of caring for them would fall on their wives and children. The state did not have to take responsibility for the provision of welfare and social services in the reserves, and it was therefore spared considerable expense (Wolpe 1972). Finally, and most important for the purposes of statecraft, preventing full proletarianization forestalled the development of a militant African working class, and the division of the reserves according to "tribe" prevented Africans from uniting in opposition to the colonial regime (Mamdani 1996). The objective of the migrant labor system, then, was to leverage uneven development as a strategy of control—to maintain the peasant status of Africans, to keep them "backward" and "prepolitical" (Hobsbawm 1958) so that they would not develop critical consciousness, and to do so while *still* using them as industrial laborers. The result was what scholars have called a "peasant-proletariat": industrial wage workers who inhabit the realm of the peasant.

In rural areas, Africans were governed by chiefs who—while appointed and controlled by the state—provided a semblance of legitimacy to colonial overrule and supplied leadership for much cheaper than it would cost to govern directly. This system, known as "indirect rule," was pioneered in Natal by Theophilis Shepstone well before Frederick Lugard's experiments in Nigeria, and became the blueprint for similar strategies across the colonial world (Guy 2013). The key to this strategy lay in the codification of "customary law," which bolstered patriarchal authority in the homestead as a way of extending the reach of state power. As early as 1878, the colony of Natal instated a set of customary rules known as the Natal Code of Native Law, which sought to expand the power of chiefs and patriarchs and control rural Africans by ossifying and stand-ardizing what were previously flexible systems of privilege and status into a rigidly hierarchical form (Welsh 1971; Mamdani 1996; Meyers 2008). Today, after more than a century of operation, the rules of the Code bear the aura of "tradition," and social life remains shot through with hierarchy. This is particularly true of the domestic context—the rural homestead—which was the primary focus of the Code.

As with the houses famously discussed by Pierre Bourdieu (1977, 1979), homesteads act like cosmological maps, inscribing in their spa-tial layout the hierarchical principles that organize social relations according to male/female, senior/junior, and sacred/common opposi-tions—oppositions that are organized according to the logic of encom-passment. Within this system, the senior unit represents the whole to its constitutive parts, so that persons are constituted as fractals of the rela-tionships that encompass them rather than as discrete individuals (cf. Wagner 1991). For rural Zulus, these arrangements need to be upheld in order to protect the conditions necessary for collective well-being. I argue that this morally charged domestic order organizes rural migrants' political consciousness and informs their resistance to liberal democ-racy. But their political consciousness does not emerge as an automatic entailment of domestic structure. Rather, it is mediated by what Paul Silverstein (2009) has termed "structural nostalgia." As migrants move back and forth between rural and urban, they come to fetishize an ideal vision of the ordered homestead that does not necessarily match the crumbling, contested reality of actually-existing homestead life (cf. Bank 1999). This vision serves as a powerful counterpoint to what they perceive as the dangerous disorder of urban sociality and provides a touchstone for their political discontent.

At this point I should open a brief parenthetical about the ethnonym "Zulu." By using this term I do not intend to reify a timeless cultural entity. On the contrary, I intend to emphasize its contingency. "Zulu-ness" is a recent construct that owes its being to a number of key forces, the most prominent of which has been indirect rule.[16] The ethnonym continues to enjoy widespread currency today, even though there are many IsiZulu-speaking people who resist it and claim alternative identi-ties in their clan histories. With this in mind, I use the term "rural Zulu" in this book to describe the people who were subject over most of the past century to pass laws that restricted them to the native reserve of KwaZulu, and who were governed by a system that sought to organize them under a single set of customary rules. In other words, my use of the term Zulu self-consciously refers to the colonial production of the category, which proceeds from the same strategies of governance that generated the urban-rural conflict that I examine in this book. As we shall see, Zuluness was never intended to function simply as an identity. It was intended to inscribe a hierarchical social structure and a set of moral commitments that would be useful to the state. It is this aspect of Zuluness that informs the politics of rural migrants today.

If the politics of rural migrants can be explained in part by looking at the history of colonial governance over domestic spaces, the same can be said of the politics of urban dwellers. Despite the best efforts of the state to maintain segregation, African populations did eventually take root in "white" urban areas, outside the purview of indirect rule. As these communities grew during the industrial boom of World War II, the state set out to regain control by forcibly relocating them into segregated planned townships where they could be "civilized" and domesticated. As part of this process, planners sought to resocialize urban Africans according to a model of European domesticity centered on the detached, nuclear single-family house headed by a male bread-winner. This project coercively restructured Zulu kinship by breaking the family into its nuclear components, reorganizing gender roles, legislating monogamy, and disembedding the individual. The "modernization" of the family was not a natural process of development, as many liberal theorists like to believe, but required extreme violence.

I argue that the forced relocations reoriented normative conceptions of family, gender, and authority, altered the ancestor cult and taboo system, and therefore contributed to changing conceptions of misfortune and causality. Having departed from the social structure of the homestead and its corresponding moral order, the new townships opened the door for new forms of consciousness, rendering the urban African population amenable to ideas about individual liberty, equal rights, and class politics in a way that their rural counterparts never were. The youth who were born and raised in this new cultural context overdetermined revolutionary discourse along these lines in the mid 1980s, and when the ANC assumed power in 1994, it normalized these values on a national scale under the banner of "democracy." Of course, townships have never been characterized by a purely liberal ethos—they are rife with their own hierarchies and mysticisms—and in most cases they have never been clearly bounded from rural cultures. Yet the township has nonetheless come to stand as the categorical opposite of the homestead—particularly in the eyes of migrants.

The point I wish to underline here has to do with the intimate but violent relationship between the colonial state and the domestic realms that Africans inhabited. With a view of the history of homesteads and townships, it becomes clear that colonial power exerted itself forcefully over the lives of Africans at the level of domestic organization. In Natal, colonialism's dual form of rule was a single technology of power (viz., domestic manipulation) with two distinct manifestations: "modern" township and "traditional" homestead. The key division between direct and indirect rule, then, was not only between the legal categories of "citizen" and "subject," as Mahmood Mamdani (1996) has claimed, but between two forms of social organization and their concomitant moral orders. The division, in short, was a cosmological one. Divergent modes of governmentality produced the conditions for the emergence of different political subjectivities that came into conflict in the 1980s when influx controls were abolished and rural/urban boundaries were broken down. These differences are real in important respects, even though they are by no means absolute. But they are also imagined—reified by both sides in the process of constructing the moral oppositions around which people organize their political visions.

In sum, the rural-urban tensions that mark popular politics in Kwa-Zulu-Natal can be understood as diagnostic of colonial power, as a product of the specific technologies of domination that Europeans exercised over Africans. As Partha Chatterjee has observed, popular politics are "conditioned by the functions and activities of modern governmental systems" (2004, 3). Just as colonialism in South Africa was a colonialism of the home, so too popular politics in South Africa are a politics of the home.[17]

A CRITIQUE

Postcolonial scholarship is committed, almost by definition, to engaging the universals—such as the abstract figure of the human or that of Reason—that were forged in eighteenth century Europe and that underlie the human sciences.

—Dipesh Chakrabarty, *Provincializing Europe*

The account I offer here both departs from and offers a critique of the ways that Western social science tends to explain anti-liberal movements.

Existing scholarship generally tries to excavate the rational economic and political interests of such movements—a tendency epitomized in the growing field of so-called terrorism studies.[18] One of this book's contributions is to criticize the model of interest that informs this literature. For this I draw on the insights of postcolonial theory and subaltern studies, which emphasize the importance of disrupting the Eurocentric epistemological categories that underwrite social scientific thought (cf. Guha 1983; Nandy 1983; Mudimbe 1988; Chakrabarty 1989, 2000; Chatterjee 1993; Bhabha 1994). Scholarly accounts of the Inkatha movement in the 1980s and 1990s provide an excellent case study, for they tend to gravitate toward familiar interpretations.

One thread of this scholarship focuses on identity politics in its various guises. As I have pointed out, some have read Zulu identity through the lens of primordial essentialism. Others, attempting to get past the evolutionary or racial typologies that primordialist accounts presuppose, rely instead on instrumentalist perspectives. One type of instrumentalist approach points to the role of political leaders such as Inkatha's Mangosuthu Buthelezi, who has cleverly manipulated symbols, myths, and memories of "Zulu tradition" in order to galvanize a mass base to underwrite his personal struggle for political power. Another type of instrumentalist approach focuses on the motives of everyday actors, suggesting that they appeal pragmatically to concepts of culture and ethnic solidarity in a strategic bid for a more secure hold on resources – such as wages and houses – in a context of scarcity. In both cases, "Zulu culture" is understood as a means to an end, invoked as a site of mass mobilization in competition for power and resources.

These explanations help us understand important things about how the conflict was mobilized. But they also have their limitations. By claiming that people invoke the idea of cultural difference instrumentally, they ignore the possibility that real cultural difference might actually be at stake (Handler 1994). These accounts make the perpetrators more comprehensible to us, and perhaps even more palatable, by claiming that they are ultimately driven by a rational, end-maximizing logic that we can relate to. This gloss relies on a universal model of human nature—what MacPherson (1962) has called "possessive individualism"—that presupposes the cultural logic of interest and agency that is native to Euro-American capitalism. But what is lost when we as analysts project our own common sense into a universal theory? When we dress up our own particular culture as generic human nature? Clifford Geertz's observation remains important here: "men unmodified by the customs of particular places do not in fact exist, have never existed, and most important, could not in the very nature of the case exist. . . . There is no such thing as human nature independent of culture" (1973, 35).

A second type of explanation for rural migrants' politics focuses on gender. Most accounts see migrant males as driven by an interest in preserving the system of patriarchal privilege that underwrites their power in rural areas. I shared this perspective when I first began my research; it appeared self-evident to me that migrants were defending hierarchy because it allows them to exploit the labor of women. The division between men and women appeared to me as a class antagonism in the Marxist sense, and to the extent that women supported the ideology of hierarchy—which I found they generally did—I decided it could be explained away as false consciousness. Operating within this framework, Marxist and feminist scholars seek to expose the power interests that lie behind hierarchical kinship rules, rituals, and belief systems.

This analytical move has been useful in denouncing the abuses of patriarchy in South Africa. One can validly argue, from an etic perspective, that hierarchies have extractive and oppressive entailments. But this does not explain why people might be for or against hierarchy. We have to be cautious that we do not simply rationalize institutions of social hierarchy according to our own cultural (and moral) logic, assuming that the only reason anyone might support such institutions is to extract some kind of personal gain. In addition to relying once again on a form of methodological individualism, this kind of explanation also presupposes a duality between individual and society (or culture): women are "dominated by" society, which is controlled by men who wield culture and tradition as instruments of false consciousness. This should sound familiar. Here again the idea of culture is reduced to a kind of ruse. The point I wish to emphasize is that the democratizing project and the social science that attempts to explain people's resistance to it *both* presuppose the liberal individual as the natural (or desired) state of human ontology and see hierarchy as a system of hegemony: of society over individuals, of elders over juniors, or of men over women.

While recognizing the value of existing accounts, this book seeks to recover the cultural logic behind a movement that has been largely misapprehended by Western intellectuals. I argue that because Western social scientific categories—be they from rational choice theory, structural-functionalism, or Marxist-feminist analysis—derive from a culturally specific model of the individual, they cannot be readily applied to the case of rural African migrants. I take my cue here from Marilyn Strathern (1988), who has shown that categories like "society," "agency," "domination," and "inequality" are deeply informed by Euro-American metaphors about property and commodities, and thus fail to explain behavior among people who constitute personhood and relationships differently (in her case, Melanesians). I aim to rethink notions of power, agency, and gender in the Zululand context, showing that people construct "interest" not as individual utility but in terms of collective well-being that hinges on the maintenance and reproduction of hierarchical relationships. In rural Zululand, most persons are not the autonomous individuals that much of social scientific theory would have us believe. Persons cannot be considered apart from the community of relationships in which they have their being—nor can their individual interests and properties be abstracted out (see Piot 1999, 17; Jackson and Karp 1990; Riesman 1986). If there are no individuals as such, then standard interest-based models of social behavior and social inequality break down.

As Chatterjee has put it, subaltern political motivations do "not fit into the grid of 'interests' and 'aggregation of interests' that constitute the world of bourgeois representative politics" (1993, 159). To write Eurocentric forms of personhood and interest into subaltern contexts is to do violence to the realities of local subjectivity, to force the Other into a familiar mold. Instead of imputing bourgeois motives to subaltern subjects, then, my approach takes seriously rural migrants' particular awareness of their own world and the cultural logic that frames their politics. Of course, none of this is to say that migrants do not act in rational, end-maximizing ways. They may well do so. My point is that, as with all people, their rationality and their ends are culturally situated (cf. Sahlins 1976). To paraphrase Daniel Rosenblatt (2003), without some idea of culture, we can only understand the political lives of others in terms of our own projects.

Rural African migrants are bent on defending hierarchy, yes. But their reasons for doing so are quite different from what Westerners might think. It is not about accumulating power in the sense that political theory assumes. To say that migrants are driven by an individual interest in power would be to exactly miss the important part of their perspective, which is a critique of the very paradigm within which we denounce patriarchy, a paradigm that posits the primacy of the possessive individual. I argue in the following chapters that migrants seek to defend their hierarchies *not* to retain their grip on power over women and minors but to defend an overarching moral order that, despite being contested and variable, is nonetheless regarded as crucial to collective well-being. Sometimes this defense is highly conscious, and at others it plays out according to unconscious symbolic schemes. In any case, in defending hierarchy they seek to restore a totality, not assert private, individual interests; or, to the extent that they *are* asserting private interests, they are doing so according to the logic of a totality that potentiates different conceptions of interest altogether. Indeed, it is self-interested individualism itself that migrants are reacting against.

A POSITION

I want to acknowledge up front that the critique I have outlined above runs the risk of appearing politically problematic. It appears to undermine the democratic project that brought about the end of colonialism in South Africa, and seems to grant legitimacy to the forms of patriarchal conservatism that resist the principles of liberalism. I want to be clear that I am not articulating an argument against the project of democracy and individual rights. I do not intend to trivialize the freedoms that the liberation struggle has won, or to hail Inkatha against the ANC. I concur with the accounts that have painted Buthelezi as corrupt and power-hungry, and denounce him for accepting the military support of the apartheid state and for manipulating the discontent of his constituents for his own political ends. But these claims are not new; they have been the subject of many books. I am not interested in Buthelezi and Inkatha as such, which in any case is quickly falling out of favor in KwaZulu-Natal. Rather, I am interested instead in the reasons for which so many rural migrants express discontent with the ANC's democracy. It is their sense of moral panic that interests me. I seek to understand the cultural order within which their anti-liberal politics make sense to them.

To the extent that this endeavor requires an empathetic perspective on rural Zulu forms of social hierarchy, I also run the risk of appearing to undermine the Marxist-feminist critique that was so central to the liberation struggle, and which has led to some of the most progressive gender legislation in the world (Walsh 2010). Questioning the assumptions that lie at the heart of critical theory creates a difficult conundrum, since it appears to undercut the foundations upon which progressive politics rely. As Strathern has put it, "academic radicalism often appears to result in otherwise conservative action or nonaction. Radical politics, in turn, has to be conceptually conservative. That is, its job is to operationalize already understood concepts or categories" (1988, 27). In other words, by pointing out the cultural contingencies of political values (such as "rights," "exploitation," etc.), radical scholarship often seems to undermine radical politics. This is the question that plagues subaltern studies and has brought the group to a point of palpable political ambivalence (cf. Chibber 2013). A similar conundrum haunts postmodern liberalism more broadly: do we promote the project of human rights, or do we deconstruct the assumptions at the center of that project? How do we negotiate the tension between the political project of progressivism (which depends on claims about transcendental values) and the intellectual project of deconstruction (which questions all values identified as transcendental)?[19]

I do not wish to minimize the role of democratic politics in ending apartheid and introducing equal rights. Rather, I want to make the democratic project strange, to see it with new eyes, to render it unfamiliar by illuminating it from the perspective of its others. This process is not only analytically important, it also yields incisive critiques of the modernizing project—and of individualism and neoliberalism—that come not from the Right or from the Left, but from a discourse that, because it lies beyond the logic of this political plane entirely, has access to truly radical insights. Such scrutiny is crucial to ensuring that the bourgeois values of South Africa's National Democratic Revolution do not assume the status of cultural hegemony, as the ideology of apartheid did before it. We do not have to accept the whole package, of course—the patriarchy, the apparent misogyny, and so on—but we can find in the subaltern perspectives that I highlight in this book the seeds of an important critique from the voices of those who have been subjugated by modernity.

RETHINKING FREEDOM AND AGENCY

This brings me full circle, back to the question of freedom with which I began. I noted above that the theory of personhood that lies at the center of both progressive politics and social science sees the individual as the locus of authentic desire and will, and sees society as a series of repressive constraints and inhibitions. This tradition seeks to excavate the agency of the subject and celebrate its capacity for resistance against repressive external forces such as social norms (see Abu-Lughod 1990). This is particularly true of politics and scholarship since the emergence of the New

Left in the late 1960s, when the figure of the authentic individual subverting the normative constraints of mass society gained popular traction and came to inform thinkers who otherwise inhabited opposite ends of the political spectrum, such as Herbert Marcuse and Milton Friedman.[20] The assumption here is that the subject somehow precedes power relations, and that those power relations are somehow external to it.

This assumption is incorrect. The subject does not precede power relations (or society, or social norms), but is in fact *formed through* those relations. Michel Foucault and Judith Butler are often credited for pointing this out, but it is an observation that is nearly as old as anthropology itself: persons do not exist outside of culture. The same can be said of desire: desire is always the product of discipline and socialization. If this is the case, then the idea of agency has to be completely rethought (cf. Mahmood 2005). The subject's capacity for agency does not inhere in some authentic inner self or a prior substratum of personhood. To paraphrase Geertz, there is no "backstage" to which a person can retreat to cast off the constraints of social norms and act on some hidden kernel of desire. In this sense, there can be no resistance against norms that is not also at the same time normative. Rather, the subject's capacity for agency is a product of the processes—such as the disciplinary power of social norms—that produce the subject in the first place.

If this is true, then it means we need to relativize our understanding of norms. We have to accept that cultural artifacts such as hierarchical kinship, beliefs about ancestors, and ritual activity are no more norm-like, restrictive, or repressive than liberal individualism, nuclear families, and gender egalitarianism. It also means that we need to relativize our understanding of agency. We have to accept that a subject's capacity for particular forms of resistance is an effect of governmentality, as I argue in the following chapters. But why should we think of resistance as the only expression of agency? Following Mahmood (2005, 29), we need to broaden our definition of agency to encompass all the capacities and skills sedimented in persons through specific disciplines or operations of power that enable them to undertake particular kinds of moral actions. As Charles Taylor has argued, human agency is what is possible within some given moral orientation, rather than, as the liberal and social scientific positions would have it, some absolute freedom from orientations (1989, 33).

This broader definition of agency makes it possible to think of the anti-liberal politics of rural migrants without stigmatizing them as backward, reactionary, counterrevolutionary, and so on. In other words, it allows us to stop thinking of them as unfree. Mahmood's (2005, 31) words are worth quoting here: "How do we conceive of individual freedom in a context where the distinction between the subject's own desires and socially prescribed performances cannot be easily presumed, and where submission to certain forms of (external) authority is a condition for achieving the subject's potentiality?" Indeed, in the Zululand case, it appears that people seek to reestablish the conditions for what they consider to be justice, well-being, and full human flourishing by *reconstituting* hierarchies rather than by seeking to abolish them. Once again, this reassertion of hierarchy seems to be part of a broader trend, which I argue has something to do with the impact that neoliberal economic policy has had over the past decades. As unemployment skyrockets and livelihoods become increasingly precarious, people appear to long for and fetishize older forms of law and order, such as sharia in the Islamic Middle East and *umthetho* in rural KwaZulu-Natal (cf. Comaroff and Comaroff 2006). In this sense, the decay brought on by liberal *economic* policy has sparked a reaction against liberal *social* policy. Neoliberalism heralds the death of liberalism.

OVERVIEW OF THE CHAPTERS

The chapters that follow can be divided roughly into two parts. The first three offer an historical ethnography of the main forces that have shaped KwaZulu-Natal's political landscape.

Chapter 1 traces the ANC-Inkatha conflict as it played out in Natal, providing the necessary background for understanding contemporary politics in the region. While scholars have usefully explained the realpolitik dimensions of this conflict, I argue that we still need to unpack the culturally distinctive values and desires that rural migrants draw on. This is a tricky argument to make in South Africa, where social analysts are wary of overemphasizing otherness. While I acknowledge these concerns, I build a case for taking cultural difference seriously, while still foregrounding the relationship between culture and history.

Chapter 2 shifts attention to the rural homesteads to which migrants are tied. I look at the structure of kinship and domestic space in homesteads with emphasis on the principles that organize hierarchy, and I trace the history of these forms through indirect rule and the codification of customary law under colonialism. I show how migrant workers construct an idealized vision of the hierarchical homestead that contrasts starkly with the apparently dangerous disorder of urban sociality—a form of structural nostalgia that organizes their political discontent. Yet while homestead culture is an *idea* in this respect—conditioned by colonialism and based on an overdrawn dichotomy with townships—I argue that it nonetheless informs common understandings about personhood, misfortune, and causality.

Chapter 3 moves from the homestead to its symbolic antithesis, the township—the space wherein the mass democratic movement gained traction in KwaZulu-Natal. I show that the values that underpinned the revolution were in large part the product of the apartheid state's efforts to control urban Africans through social engineering in planned townships, which transformed kinship structure and the ancestor cult in a manner that allowed for liberal ideas about personhood and causality to take root. This history helps us understand why people in KwaZulu-Natal—and particularly migrants—imagine there to be such a rigid moral opposition between township and homestead, despite the fact that the two forms exist on a relatively fluid continuum.

If the first three chapters offer a sort of bird's-eye view, the next three provide a much richer feeling of the social field, zooming in on family dramas and personal narratives. In chapter 4, I explore the aversion that migrants have to the ANC's democratic project. I argue that they interpret "democracy"—and township culture—as socially destructive because it appears to dismantle hierarchies and obliterate the social differences that they hold to be crucial to fruition, particularly in a context where neoliberal policy has led to a crisis of social reproduction. This critique is organized largely around houses: migrants from the Zululand countryside regard township houses—with their stand-alone four-room plan—as inverting the physical (and moral) order of the homestead. To them, the house becomes the material embodiment of all that is immoral about liberalism.

Chapter 5 explores the sacrificial rites that families in rural Zululand perform in their attempts to restore hierarchies and reestablish the conditions for social reproduction. I focus specifically on mortuary ritual, which leverages the symbolic dimensions of bovine anatomy to reorder kinship, reincorporate the wild ghosts of lost ancestors, and cure families of misfortunes. This ritual work reestablishes a moral terrain that helps mitigate the abjection that defines rural KwaZulu-Natal: people seek to build the foundations for a prosperous future not by rejecting the past but by returning to it to establish good relationships with the dead. These rituals offer a poignant call for justice from a people who have been excluded from the promises of liberation.

Chapter 6 goes back to the townships to explore the story of a woman who tries to make sense of why her family's fortunes have taken a turn for the worse. Her narrative reflects a deep sense of disappointment with modernity that has many urban residents nostalgic for the social order of the 1960s townships at the same time as they seek to learn the ancestral rituals that they once denounced as backward, spurring a resurgence of "tradition" in townships as a reaction to neoliberal decay. These trends illustrate the syncretism and flow that links urban and rural worlds, and they help explain the surprising outpouring of support in urban areas for Jacob Zuma.

The concluding chapter pulls together and reflects on some of the main threads of the book's argument. I build on this to return to the question of freedom by exploring the apparent tension between reason and culture—a dialectic that troubles scholarly debates in South Africa and gets refracted through the dilemmas faced by the country's constitutional legal system.

1

A Divided Revolution

In . . . the domain of peasant politics . . . beliefs and actions
did not fit into the grid of "interests" and "aggregation of
interests" that constituted the world of bourgeois representative politics . . . The specific determinants of the domain of
peasant political activity remained incomprehensible from the
standpoint of bourgeois politics.

—Partha Chatterjee, *The Nation and Its Fragments*

I sat with Sicelo in a café above Essenwood Road at midmorning on a
sunny weekday. From our table by the window we could hear Durban
bustling below, and the noise provided welcome relief during the silences
that occasionally cut through our conversation. It was an emotionally
exhausting exchange, for me almost as much as for him. I had been sur-
prised a few days earlier when he agreed to share his story of growing up
in the Natal Midlands in the 1980s and 1990s, when the region was torn
apart by civil war. Getting firsthand accounts of that period of violence—*udlame,* as most call it—is difficult; people are generally willing
to offer analyses of the conflict in abstract terms when asked, but rarely
will they share stories of their own experiences or involvement—the
trauma just runs too deep, and most people would rather try to forget it.
And yet Sicelo sat across from me and tried to convey what it was like.
As I listened to his narrative I realized that I was unprepared to understand the horror that was wrought on the lives of the people who were
caught up in the violence of *udlame.* It struck me that the difficulty of
writing an anthropology of conflict lies in the balance between the
impulse to explain or theorize violence and the need to create space for
the grief and outrage of the people who have been damaged by it.

Sicelo's family had been supporters of the ANC-led revolution along
with most of the people in their township, which is situated just a few
kilometers west of Pietermaritzburg. As a result, they had been targeted
by Inkatha-supporting vigilantes (*amabangalala*) who were determined

to purge the area of "comrades"—the term they used for ANC members in reference to their allegedly communist inclinations. Sicelo's older brothers had been recruited into a neighborhood watch unit and were tasked with patrolling the area at night, ready to sound the alarm against any attackers. When there was reason to suspect an impending assault, the township's residents would sleep outside in riverbeds or in the bush, knowing that Inkatha vigilantes would attempt to burn their houses down in hope of killing any occupants inside. Sicelo recalled passing countless nights in this manner, sleeping fully dressed and ready to get up and run at a moment's notice, slowly growing accustomed to the nauseating smell of burning houses, the sound of gunfire shrieking through the darkness, and the occasional police helicopter sent out to aid the attackers. Young men in the community—even boys as young as ten—eventually took up arms and organized counterattacks to defend their families and secure vengeance for the dead, lending a blood-feud character to the conflict. Sicelo's generation was devastated by these clashes, and by 1990 his community had mostly abandoned the area in order to seek refuge with relatives in safer settlements.

Nearly everyone in KwaZulu-Natal who was alive during that period has similar stories to tell; it would be difficult to overestimate how destructive this conflict was to so many communities. For most people, this was their experience of the revolution. Instead of the unified front against the colonial oppressor that young revolutionaries had dreamed of, they found themselves locked in battle with their own neighbors, caught in cycles of terror and violence that turned communities into killing fields and wrought untold suffering on hundreds of thousands of people. In most of the world this story has been almost entirely forgotten, obscured behind the celebratory narrative of South Africa's liberation. Not because people want to forget the conflict, but because it seems to make so little sense—because it seems too difficult to explain. Yet understanding how this conflict unfolded is key to understanding contemporary politics in KwaZulu-Natal.

A SCHISM FORMS

Tensions in Natal first began to emerge in 1979, the year Inkatha formally split with the ANC. When Mangosuthu Buthelezi first founded Inkatha four years earlier, it enjoyed the backing of ANC President Oliver Tambo as a front for the banned resistance movement.[1] As a so-called "cultural organization," Inkatha was permitted to operate because it appeared to dovetail with the state's project of encouraging "tribal identity" for divide-and-rule purposes (Marks 1986). But as Buthelezi began to use Inkatha to leverage his own personal power base, the ANC publicly denied association with him, much to his bitter dismay. After an incident where Inkatha dispatched a vigilante group to intimidate striking students back into school, ANC leaders in London issued a stinging rebuke that denounced Buthelezi as a collaborator in the crime of apartheid.[2] From that point on, Buthelezi adopted a platform that departed markedly from that of the ANC: he stood against the idea of socialism as a method of economic reform, he opposed the tactic of boycotts, divestment, sanctions, and strikes on the grounds that it would reduce employment and ultimately hurt workers, and he supported the "homeland" system because it gave him political power over a large segment of the black population. These conservative positions earned him the support of the apartheid regime and its backers—including Ronald Reagan and Margaret Thatcher—and made him a well-known figure on the international stage during the Cold War era.

After the ANC split with Inkatha, township residents in Natal began to rally around civic organizations that focused on local problems, protesting the rising costs of rent, utilities, and transportation and resisting the "Bantu education" system that was designed to keep Africans marginalized and exploited. Many of these townships were formally under the jurisdiction of the KwaZulu Legislative Authority, which was controlled by Inkatha, so Inkatha ultimately became the target of civic protests. Activists accused the organization of collaborating with the apartheid regime through the homeland system. Another point of tension was the fact that students in these townships were forced to submit to the Inkatha curriculum, which included a series of textbooks—known as "Ubuntu-Botho"—that peddled blatant Inkatha propaganda and explicitly promoted submission to authority, praised the Zulu Royal Family, and celebrated the seniority of elder men over minors and women (Mdluli 1987). In many cases students were even required to join the Inkatha Youth Brigade and wear Inkatha uniforms. But perhaps the most heated issue was the fact that townships around Durban had been earmarked for incorporation into the KwaZulu homeland, as a way for the apartheid government to displace the costs of maintaining them. This meant that township residents stood to lose their coveted "Section 10" rights, which guaranteed them access to employment in white urban areas.

When the United Democratic Front (UDF) formed in 1983—a powerful coalition of township activist groups and churches led by such luminaries as Allan Boesak and Albertina Sisulu—it became a key player in organizing resistance around these issues (Seekings 2000). Inkatha authorities found themselves under pressure to suppress a rising tide of discontent leveled against them, which they did by targeting activists and terrorizing township residents.

Just as revolutionary activism was mounting in the townships, it also began to gain traction in the labor movement. After a long period of quiescence following the Sharpeville massacre and the banning of resistance organizations in 1960, the labor movement resurged in the early 1970s with the rolling strikes that gripped Durban when over 100,000 workers downed tools in what became the broadest display of resistance in more than a decade.[3] A number of trade unions formed in the wake of the Durban strikes, but they refrained from overt involvement in liberation politics for fear of falling foul of stringent apartheid laws.[4] Throughout most of the 1970s, the unions remained committed to a philosophy of mobilization known as "workerism," which focused solely on factory-floor issues—such as wages, hours, and working conditions—that immediately affected workers' lives and well-being. In 1979 these unions banded together under an umbrella organization known as FOSATU (Federation of South African Trade Unions). FOSATU reaffirmed a commitment to the ideals of workerism and eschewed involvement with the broader goals of nationalist struggle, partially because they feared that association with the ANC would invite government repression, but also because the leaders of the workerist movement—many of them white Marxist intellectuals[5]—emphasized the *class* character of apartheid accumulation and sought to nourish clear working-class identities with the goal of galvanizing socialist revolution. FOSATU refused to align with the nationalist bourgeoisie and criticized the ANC for lacking a clearly defined commitment to working-class issues (see Foster 1982; Nash 1999).

FOSATU's commitment to workerism allowed it to bring workers of various cultural backgrounds—both urban and rural—together under the same umbrella regardless of their political faction. Indeed, migrant workers from rural areas, many of whom supported Inkatha, were particularly important to the success of the union movement in its early years. Union leaders focused their efforts on migrants because they were easy to organize given their concentration in all-male hostels and the fact that they occupied the most menial, underpaid jobs. Because this demographic was so important, FOSATU elected to cooperate with Inkatha—albeit uneasily—on purely pragmatic grounds. Jay Naidoo,

an organizer who had worked in the predominantly rural sugar industry, explained to me in an interview that "FOSATU would stick to factory-floor issues and Inkatha would be the dominant player in the political issues." In other words, the union was content to ignore Inkatha
and its conservative political agenda so long as it could focus on class-
based organization.

Under this arrangement, rural migrant workers could be members of
Inkatha *at the same time* as they were members of FOSATU unions.
FOSATU unions made no demands on workers' political orientation;
instead, organizers put aside their own (often radical) politics and
focused on the bread-and-butter issues that concerned workers on the
factory floor—an agenda that workers were happy to support. As
Naidoo put it to me: "[Even though] I was an anti-Inkatha person . . .
the reality was that the majority of the workers in the sugar industry
were Inkatha, and strongly Inkatha. So I was very careful not to raise the
issue of political affiliation . . . I was careful not to disclose my political
background." Naidoo recalled that

> In making the choice, workers said "on the factory floor [FOSATU] is the
> leader; in the community Inkatha is the leader . . . [FOSATU] has done noth-
> ing to undermine us as workers; we are not asking them to join Inkatha—
> they can have their own political views—but when it comes to union democ-
> racy they have been our strongest proponents." . . . That's the choice they
> made. Because they knew us. They knew we were committed to the cause of
> workers on the factory floor . . . so even though Inkatha was against us,
> workers stayed.

This arrangement began to change during the early 1980s. Some of
FOSATU's most influential leaders—particularly Jay Naidoo and Chris
Dlamini, the Federation's national president and another leading figure
from the sugar scene—eventually decided to shift FOSATU's stance and
link it up with the ANC and the broader liberation movement that was
taking root in the townships, moving the union's politics closer to their
own.[6] This decision made sense given a gradual demographic shift in
the workforce from rural migrant workers to settled urban workers—a
shift propelled by firms that were beginning to seek better-educated and
better-skilled labor.[7] This shift paved the way for increasing collaboration between workers and the township activists led by the UDF, culminating in the mass stayaways of November 1984—an event that transformed the nature of the resistance movement. According to FOSATU
leader Thami Mali, this was "the first time in South African history
that trade unions and militant organizations acted in such dramatic

concert."[8] Building on the momentum from the stayaway, the following year FOSATU's member unions gathered to inaugurate a new confederation under the banner of the Congress of South African Trade Unions (COSATU). The birth of COSATU changed the style of working-class politics, heralding a new form of unionism with overt ties to the nationalist movement and committed to political agitation beyond the factory floor—a strategy known at the time as "popularism," "political unionism," or, given its association with the National Democratic Revolution, "NDR unionism."

The relationship between the two fronts—between township and shop floor—was solidified in 1988 when COSATU formally joined the UDF. The movement's leaders reasoned that, because apartheid was predicated on a relationship between racial domination and class exploitation, effective resistance would require an alliance between the nationalist movement (battling racial oppression) and the workers' movement (battling class exploitation) (Chipkin 2004:317–8). Yet these two interest groups received unequal priority, for COSATU operated on the policy of "two-stage revolution" that had been promoted by the Communist International in the Soviet Union. This policy held that because the industrial proletariat in developing countries is not normally mature enough to overthrow colonial capitalism by itself, workers should form alliances with the indigenous bourgeoisie and pursue national emancipation as a first stage of the revolution, and only later, in a second stage, move toward socialism (Drew 2000).[9] In other words, the class-based struggle in South Africa was relegated to the waiting room of history, and the National Democratic Revolution took precedence.

The abandonment of the workerist tradition and the ascendency of political unionism created a deep rift in the labor movement, drawing out latent antagonisms between workers who had previously coexisted quite happily. The lines were drawn primarily between residents of urban townships, who identified with the National Democratic Revolution, and rural migrants, who rejected it—the same divisions that were eventually replicated in the liberation struggle at large. COSATU-affiliated unions quickly became primary sites for mobilizing grassroots resistance against the apartheid regime. Many union organizers, some of whom were also politically active in their township communities, worked to conscientize members to understand the importance of the liberation struggle. One COSATU shop steward I spoke to remembered how he sought to bring the two movements together:

I would push [democratic revolution] in the communities, and I would push it in the working class. We were involved in the working class and we were involved in the communities—so we were using both powers. I would invite workers to come to the community meetings. And some of the issues we were not happy about in the communities we would discuss on the shop floor. So [the movement] became a mixture of everything. I forced the working class to go and attend the UDF meetings and listen to the political people and help them realize that we must have a democratic country.[10]

This approach made it difficult to organize workers from rural Zululand who did not support the goals of National Democratic Revolution, and many of them defected to join Inkatha-friendly unions (Chipkin 2004; Hickel 2012). The largest of these were National Union,[11] which grew out of the sugar industry and boasted some 25,000 members at its peak, and the United Workers Union of South Africa,[12] which was formed by Buthelezi as an Inkatha-friendly counterweight to COSATU.[13] Buthelezi's union was a cynical ploy backed by the apartheid state to divide the labor movement and ended up collapsing a few years after it was formed, but National Union remains a strong player in KwaZulu-Natal, particularly among workers from rural Zululand. National Union claims to have taken up the mantle of workerism that FOSATU abandoned in 1985 in order to maintain a space where workers can organize for their rights on the shop floor without having to affiliate with the ANC and assent to its particular values.[14]

This narrative gives a sense for how the tensions formed that eventually divided the liberation struggle in Natal. The first high-profile incidents of violence took place shortly after the UDF was founded. That year some five hundred Inkatha vigilantes stormed the University of Zululand on the North Coast to clamp down on student support for the UDF, killing four people in what became known as the Ongoye Massacre. This set off a series of violent clashes between Inkatha and UDF-affiliated civic associations in the Midlands, particularly around Pietermaritzburg and Hammarsdale. By 1985, these tensions had deepened into large-scale battles involving thousands of militants: Inkatha had begun to launch aggressive invasions of UDF-supporting townships, and UDF supporters responded by attacking Inkatha members in neighboring hostels. The newspapers listed new killings nearly every day. In Imbali, Inkatha vigilantes assassinated a number of leaders of the Congress of South African Students,[15] a radical organization aligned with the ANC. In KwaMakhuta, vigilantes waylaid a prayer meeting at the home of a UDF official and executed thirteen women and children. In 1986, after the formation of COSATU, Inkatha agents began to target and execute activist union leaders, and COSATU agents responded in kind. In the first few days of 1988, Inkatha vigilantes burned thirty-five houses in Mpumalanga township. That same year, in the township of Trust Feeds, Inkatha attacked a funeral procession and massacred eleven mourners after days of trying to force the UDF out of the area.[16]

By 1990, after the unbanning of the ANC, the conflict had escalated to the point of outright warfare. In the area southwest of Pietermaritzburg a contingent of as many as twelve thousand armed Zulu warriors, many of them dressed in traditional regalia, descended on townships that supported the UDF—Vulindlela, Caluza, and Ashdown—looting and burning more than three thousand houses in what became known as the Seven Days War. By the time the assault ended a week later, hundreds of people had been killed and over thirty thousand residents had fled for refuge in Edendale, forced to seek shelter in church halls and emergency camps. Two years later more than two hundred Inkatha vigilantes launched an attack on Boipatong township from KwaMadala hostel near Johannesburg, slaughtering forty-six residents, including seventeen women, and destroying some fifty homes. Smaller-scale incidents during this period were orchestrated by powerful warlords loyal to one or the other party, who operated out of settlements near Durban and Pietermaritzburg.[17] The buildup to the national elections in 1994 brought on yet another surge of violence, resulting in nearly seven hundred fatalities in March and April of that year alone. A month before the elections, ANC security guards massacred nineteen Inkatha supporters who were taking part in a large protest march outside Shell House, the ANC headquarters in Johannesburg.[18]

The violence did not cease after the elections, which Inkatha contested at the last minute as the Inkatha Freedom Party (IFP). In perhaps the most notorious incident of postapartheid political violence, an IFP chief in Shobashobane orchestrated the murders of eighteen ANC youth on Christmas day of 1995. While most of the outright violence has subsided over the past decade, tensions remain high to this day, resurging predictably during election seasons when the ANC and Inkatha battle it out at the polls across rural Zululand.[19]

As this list of key events illustrates, Inkatha was the primary aggressor in this conflict, claiming roughly four times as many lives as the ANC.[20] UDF and ANC supporters were not just passive victims, how-

FIGURE 1. An Inkatha rally at Ulundi in 1991. Photo by Ian Berry (Magnum Photos).

ever, even if their violence was never perpetrated on the scale that Inkatha was able to mobilize. Township activists regarded rural migrant Zulus as stooges of the apartheid regime, complicit with the cynical structures of indirect rule and collaborators in the state's plan to divide the Africa population and forestall the rise of national or class consciousness. These perceptions were not unfounded, given that the state security establishment covertly funded and trained Inkatha and contingents of rural Zulu warriors in order to destabilize the anti-apartheid movement. This motivated township activists to seek out and assassinate paid informers, appointed politicians, and other "counterrevolutionary" individuals whom they deemed collusive with the state's attempts to sabotage the revolution. Many of these attacks were orchestrated in revenge for Inkatha's pogroms in the townships or in order to coerce compliance with boycotts and strikes (without which the revolution could not have succeeded), and focused specifically on the labor hostels that housed tens of thousands of rural Zulus in the vicinity of urban areas—evocative symbols of the apartheid-era migrancy system. Attacks by ANC supporters fueled Inkatha's sense of being under siege and supplied fodder for the apartheid state to discredit the ANC as a "terrorist" organization.

EXPLAINING THE CIVIL WAR

This period of civil warfare poses questions that have puzzled scholars and analysts for decades. Why did Africans fall into such bitter conflict at precisely the moment when the world expected heightened racial solidarities against the apartheid regime? Why did rural migrant workers refuse to align with the National Democratic Revolution when it seems it would have been in their interests to do so? And what motivated them to go so far as to attempt to sabotage the movement?

Scholars have gone a long way toward explaining the various drivers of this conflict. Perhaps the most obvious reason has to do with the rivalry between the ANC and Inkatha that followed the rupture in 1979 between Buthelezi and the leadership of the ANC in exile—a personal fallout that set the parties against each other in an aggressive struggle for power (Hart 2002; Morris and Hindson 1992; Waetjen 1999). This leadership-level conflict activated animosities between loyal members of the two parties that spread throughout the province and eventually divided almost every African community into one or the other camp (Kramer 2007). Most accounts that emphasize this theme focus on the power that Inkatha's big-men leaders used to coerce people to support them (see Aitchison 1989; Sutcliffe and Wellings 1988; Minnaar 1992). Inkatha cultivated a close relationship with the Native Authority structures in rural KwaZulu and in the migrant workers' hostels; indeed, in many cases the two organizations were indistinguishable. Inkatha-affiliated chiefs, headmen, and warlord leaders of informal settlements would often refuse to allocate land and services to their subjects unless they agreed to join the party's ranks. This system of conditional patronage is often invoked as the reason for Inkatha's high membership numbers and success in Natal during the 1994 elections; the claim is that people were *coerced* into voting for Inkatha—that they would never do so voluntarily.

Scholars have also focused on the role of ethnic nationalism in the conflict.[21] Some have seen migrant Zulus as driven by a sort of primordial tribalism. Others begin from a more instrumentalist perspective, and emphasize how Buthelezi, in his scramble to accumulate power, has skillfully manipulated rural Zulus by reviving and appealing to an ancient historical tradition rooted in the Zulu monarchy, to which, as the uncle of King Zwelithini, he has very close ties (Marks 1986; Mare and Hamilton 1987; Hamilton 1998; Waetjen 2004). According to this approach, Buthelezi built up the ranks of Inkatha by mobilizing a new and very powerful form of ethnic identity. Realizing that he had lost the struggle for power within the nation at large, Buthelezi resigned himself to claiming power within a nation ethnically defined, and went on to dominate the politics of the KwaZulu homeland. By collaborating with the ideology of apartheid, he and other opportunistic homeland elites were able to advance a pro-capitalist, petit-bourgeois agenda that lined their pockets but granted very little to the constituents they mobilized under the banner of the Zulu nation (Southall 1986).

Yet Buthelezi is not the only one guilty of manipulating migrants—and Inkatha—for his own political ends. In the 1990s, journalists exposed how the apartheid state had been using Inkatha as a proxy force against the UDF and the ANC, channeling South African Police funds to organize Inkatha rallies and to train, arm, and transport Inkatha *izimpi* (warriors).[22] In the most extreme instance of this, President Botha conspired directly with Buthelezi to have the South African Defense Force train Inkatha paramilitary troops as counterinsurgents in the Caprivi Strip of northeast Namibia. Operation Marion, as it was called, returned over two hundred trainees to Natal in September 1986 with the objective of destroying the UDF/ANC and their supporters (Meyers 2008:5off.). The United States—and specifically the conservative Heritage Foundation—also contributed funds to build Inkatha as a Cold War ally, a bulwark against the "terrorism" and "communism" presumably fomented by the ANC (Adam and Moodley 1992:491). Much of the violence during the 1980s and 1990s can be directly attributed to these forces.

The apartheid state also co-opted a number of other key African institutions in the political field. As I mentioned above, Inkatha's trade union wing was set up with state money—upwards of R1.5 million at the time—on the condition that the union would maintain a pro-capitalist line and refrain from antagonizing employers (Myers 2008:52). The state also created Joint Management Councils to link the South African military and police establishment with local government structures in KwaZulu in order to fend off the forces of revolution (De Haas and Zulu 1994:442; McLean 1994; Zulu 1992). These various organs were used deliberately to engender antagonism between hostel-dwellers and township residents in Natal. One way they did this was by fabricating and circulating rumors. In Soweto, for example, police distributed forged pamphlets designed to appear as ANC directives calling on township residents to incinerate the hostels and drive "the Zulus" from the city. When hostel residents saw these pamphlets they defended themselves with preemptive attacks on the township.[23]

The goal of this covert campaign was not only to divide the African population and to create a proxy for state violence, but also to fabricate a narrative that would justify the continuation of apartheid policies. Political leaders pointed to black-on-black conflict as evidence that in the absence of white rule, Africans would descend into savage tribal warfare.

Another clue to the conflict lies in the history of the labor movement that I described above. As FOSATU linked up with the popular struggle in the townships it began to focus more on urban workers and left rural migrants largely marginalized and alienated from the political process (Sitas 1996). To make matters worse, organizers gradually abandoned hostels for townships as their primary sites of mobilization, particularly after influx controls were abolished in 1986 and large numbers of unemployed migrants took up residence in the hostels. Mahmood Mamdani has argued that the exclusion of migrants from the new resistance movement left them "available for organization" by Inkatha and its affiliated unions, which "tried to harvest their alienation from township militancy" (1996:255). Migrants' sense of alienation was made worse when the ANC proposed to gender integrate hostels and convert them into family units for settled urban workers. Mamdani suggests that migrants saw this as an attack on their urban patch—their ticket to the incomes they needed to support their rural families. Taking advantage of this growing discontent, Inkatha began to organize in the hostels and managed to shore up a solid political base among rural migrants. Some hostels eventually became the equivalent of military barracks for Inkatha's warriors, fortresses from which Inkatha launched attacks against surrounding township communities.[24]

According to Mamdani, then, rural migrants—having been abandoned by the unions—needed a new form of political organization, which they found in the Native Authority system (a product of indirect rule) that governed both their hostels and the rural areas to which they were linked. This was particularly important given increasing competition over living space and jobs at the time, which heightened migrants' sense of economic insecurity (Olivier 1992). Desperate for access to a diminishing resource base that was increasingly controlled by township dwellers, migrants coalesced into an interest group defined by the identity marker that seemed most readily available: ethnicity. Buoyed by their power in the Native Authority, hostel headmen drew on the idiom of customary law to shift the discourse of resistance from class-based interest to ethnically defined rights, with which they could leverage greater traction with the apartheid state.

Each of these explanations illuminates important dimensions of the ANC-Inkatha conflict. Yet if we focus only on the self-perpetuating logic of party rivalry, the instrumentalization of ethnic identity by political leaders, and the covert manipulation of factional tensions by the state, we run the risk of papering over the real political differences that are at stake in the conflict.[25] What gets lost in these kinds of explanations is the perspectives of migrants themselves, who come across as mere pawns in a game orchestrated by dominant power interests. It is not enough to say that the people who took up arms against ANC members in the townships were manipulated by malicious political leaders, or subject to a form of ethnic false consciousness. We also need to consider the vernacular interests that motivated them as conscious political agents.

Mamdani's account makes important strides in this direction. He sees rural migrants as rational decision-makers with agendas that we can make sense of and relate to. Yet his narrative implies that if the agents of the National Democratic Revolution had made a better effort to integrate rural migrants, they could have proceeded amicably together into the postapartheid dispensation. To the extent that migrants diverge from the values of their counterparts in the township (by appealing to the customary, for example), Mamdani claims that they do so as rational actors bidding for a more secure hold on a dwindling resource base. This perspective misses two crucial points: first, that NDR-linked unions were often *actively hostile* toward migrant workers (i.e., the very ideology of National Democratic Revolution itself necessitated their exclusion); and second, that migrant workers had their own, sui generis reasons for disliking the popular struggle and mobilizing against it (i.e., even if the NDR unions had not abandoned the hostels, migrants would still have rejected the movement).

HIERARCHY AND POLITICAL CONSCIOUSNESS

The interviews that I conducted with rural migrants who were active in the labor movement in the 1980s and 1990s suggest a different story.[26] Never once did my interlocutors point to resource competition or ethnic identity as key issues; instead, workers explained—almost without exception—that they refused to join the NDR union movement because they did not want to be involved with "politics" (*amapolitiki*). By this they meant that they did not want to participate in the tactics of the liberation struggle—strikes, stayaways, and so on—because doing so would compromise their wages and work security. During the 1980s and 1990s, migrants were known for having a conservative approach to work: they sought to earn as much money as they could while in the city, spend as little as possible on basic necessities, and then send the rest back home to "build the homestead" (Bonner and Ndima 2009). For them, the obligation to build the homestead was more important than political transformation; indeed, the sacrifices demanded by the struggle undermined their ability to fulfill their domestic responsibilities. "We are not dealing with the politics!" one migrant told me; "When COSATU came, they tried to implement that here . . . but we didn't want to bring politics into the workplace." And according to another: "We knew that thing of politics wouldn't help us." ANC cadres from the townships regarded this position as indefensible—they saw migrants as a weak link in the chain of solidarity.

The refusal to participate in "politics" also signified a rejection of the specifically liberal politics of the ANC and its vision of equal rights within an egalitarian social order. This became a divisive issue with the rise of COSATU in the late 1980s. The shift to popularism, or NDR unionism, was propelled in part by the entry of young men into leadership positions in the labor movement who had been radicalized by the student riots of 1976. They considered themselves independent from their parents and self-consciously cast off the authority of conservative elders as part of their political radicalism. They believed that their parents' generation was overly submissive to and respectful of apartheid authorities. Indeed, they often took it upon themselves to chastise—and sometimes physically attack—elders who failed to uphold boycotts, strikes, and other tactical maneuvers. Rural workers I interviewed claimed that they objected to this behavior as deeply "disrespectful" and considered it an inversion of the natural order of generational hierarchy. As one put it to me: "For us Zulus, children do have rights, yet you can't take a child and make him equal to his father. But the ANC doesn't believe in this culture. They want to destroy the culture of the Zulus."

A number of scholars have picked up on this point. Ivor Chipkin reports the words of migrant workers who expressed their dissatisfaction with the township youths by referring to the value of "respect":

> Discipline is very important. If you are a child growing up [in a Zulu household] you are not used to speak[ing] with your father. You always speak with your mama. Township residents do not impress me. Respect is unknown amongst them. Sometimes you hear that comrades have assaulted the father of a house. That is not human; it's very barbaric. It is an insult to humanity.

Nature doesn't allow that a child can beat an elderly person, under no circumstances. [cited in Chipkin 2004:330]

Adding to this sentiment, some of the male migrants I interviewed also indicated that they had been concerned about COSATU's commitment to a certain theory of gender equality. One or two objected to the fact that some of COSATU's shop stewards and organizers were women, or that women were encouraged to participate as decision-makers in the union's proceedings. But most had no problem with women taking these responsibilities; rather they took issue with what they saw as COSATU's attempt to promote the idea of men and women as ontologically equivalent beings. As one of my interviewees put it: "In our culture a woman has rights, maybe even better than a man, but you can't take a woman as equal to her husband."

If rural workers were upset at NDR unionists for undermining generational hierarchies and gender differences, NDR unionists were equally upset at rural workers for upholding them. As the labor movement shifted to embrace the NDR agenda it promoted a particular approach to freedom that stood against the notion of hierarchy, as in the encompassment of one subject by another. The NDR unions had their own particular kinds of hierarchies, of course; indeed, many were organized according to rigid ladders of command that gave leaders at the top an extraordinary amount of power. Still, the basic principle was that being a revolutionary subject meant being an autonomous individual freed from the constraints of elders, clans, tribes, chiefdoms, and other authorities who trumped the agency of their subordinates. One woman from Durban who was a labor organizer during the transition told me:

> In the rural areas people do not have solidarity. Even when they want to have a [political] meeting they must go via their chiefs and headmen, and if permission is not granted then they cannot do anything. And when they meet they must report to the chief what the meeting was about, which is wrong.

Drawing on Marxist thought, the NDR unions placed a premium on escaping the strictures of false consciousness and empowering each individual to think and act of their own will and initiative. The NDR unions could not accommodate rural workers who seemed to value submission to authority and who appeared to defer to the wishes of their elders, chiefs, and headmen.

A second dimension of the NDR approach to freedom was that it rejected as irrational and fetishistic the belief that one's fortune hinges on the will of the ancestors, and that angering the ancestors could result in consequences such as poverty, sickness, and unemployment. This belief remains widely held among migrants. "Let's say you are here in the working place and you get an accident for no reason," one migrant from Hlabisa explained to me. "You need to go to a *sangoma* [diviner] to check what you have done wrong. Then you must do exactly what they tell. The problem is that you are not communicating with *amadlozi* [ancestors], so they leave you and misfortunes come up." These beliefs are not exclusive to migrants, of course; some COSATU members hold similar views. But in its official discourse COSATU has always insisted on a materialist analysis of causality and a class analysis of fortune. Today COSATU seeks to promote "proper" revolutionary conscious-ness by conducting training sessions designed not only to politicize workers on issues of gender, class, and rights, but also to push people to understand social relations within a secular model of agency and cau-sality—to shed false consciousness in favor of objective knowledge. I attended a number of these sessions. During one, the COSATU training consultant—a longtime member of the Communist Party—accused rural Zulu workers of false consciousness in the following terms:

> This thing of understanding misfortune to be the consequence of broken relationships with the ancestors or witchcraft . . . it is a religion they hold as part of their culture. . . . [But] you can't just sit and slaughter goats and hope you get a job; that is not responsible. You should not hang all of your hopes on the ancestors. . . . We have to build people's consciousness about how to act on the objective conditions they are in . . . We need programs to dispel these beliefs about witchcraft. It all centers around education. . . . People must realize that they are architects of their own destinies.

During the period of political transition, the (culturally marked) image of the peasant came to stand in contrast to the ideal national subject, which NDR unions conflated with the (unmarked) image of the "modern" urban individual. "Freedom" became associated with a determinate cultural state, namely, that of being liberated from the arbi-trary authority of kinship hierarchies and fully conscious of the objec-tive conditions of the external world (see Chipkin 2004:335; 2007). Migrants, by contrast, were considered *unfree,* and as such were regarded as obstacles to revolutionary change. COSATU organizers often denounced rural Zulus as traditionalists committed to moribund cultural values that run counter to the developmentalist trajectory that underwrites the modern nation-building project.

COSATU's reasoning followed the logic of Eric Hobsbawm's argu-ment that peasant-proletarians are "prepolitical"—people whose actions are organized along the "archaic," "anachronistic" axes of kinship and clan, and involve spirits, ancestors, witches, *umuthi,* and other supernatural agents as actors alongside humans (Hobsbawm 1959). In Hobsbawm's formulation, these "primitive rebels" have yet to come to terms with the secular logic of power and class; "[capitalism] comes to them from outside, insidiously, by the operation of economic forces which they do not understand" (1959:2). COSATU relies on a similar logic, and has traditionally regarded peasants as lacking revolutionary potential. In this they follow Marx, who assumed that capitalist development is a necessary precondition for secular political consciousness.[27] One COSATU organizer—a woman from Lamontville—complained to me that "[i]n rural areas people are still blank. . . . To organize them is like teaching a child. You have to make them understand politics, teach them basic things about their rights. . . . How can you teach someone about politics when they cannot even express themselves? We have to open their eyes."

Not surprisingly, most workers from rural Zululand find COSATU's discourse profoundly alienating, which is why they have sought refuge in workerist unions like National Union, where they are not patronized and stigmatized. Zeblon Mbatha, the longtime president of National Union, suggested to me in an interview that COSATU's historicist narrative renders it incapable of organizing rural Zulus, complaining: "They say a person from the rural areas is ignorant and cannot think." It was not just that rural migrants were ignored by the NDR unionists, as Mamdani would have it; they were actively rejected, and—inasmuch as they were considered an obstacle to the revolution—often became the object of violence.[28]

These tensions came to a head in 1985 after the formation of COSATU. The workerist tradition that had been championed by FOSATU beforehand had maintained a public domain where rural migrants could engage with workplace issues in a democratic fashion that did not exclude them on the basis of their kinship structure, cultural values, and epistemology. As Chipkin (2004:327) has put it, being a member of a workerist union "did not imply a transformation of their souls, of their beings. It was not necessary for them to become secular [and, I would add, liberal] individuals . . . they did not have to become 'modern' in order to become democrats" and join a revolutionary struggle aimed at achieving a social order with which they did not identify. The open, politically nonaligned democratic space and shop-floor focus of workerist unions allowed workers to act *as if* they were a class in and for themselves, while retaining other commitments at the same time. When FOSATU abandoned workerism in favor of NDR unionism, that inclusive domain was replaced with a project that privileged and actively sought to reproduce the modern political subject. The illiberal perspectives that were tolerated under the workerist movement were suddenly drawn out into the open and made the object of reform. This helps explain the fact that COSATU managed to gain immense traction among workers from urban townships but struggled (and continues to struggle) to acquire majority representation at centers in rural Zululand.

For rural migrants, the transformation of the labor movement was not simply an inconvenience, it ran straight against their moral vision of the proper order of things. Liberalism was not only abstractly anathema to their most cherished social values, but actually dangerous. Inkatha did not produce this discontent, as some have claimed (e.g., Aitchison 1989; Gwala 1989), but *tapped into it* by reaffirming the importance of "traditional" Zulu values and defending these on the national political stage. As a political organization, Inkatha bears a dual structure: a Western-educated, bourgeois leadership, on the one hand, and membership base comprised of peasants and peasant-proletarians, on the other. The former attempted to appropriate and claimed to represent the moral outrage of the latter in its cynical bid to secure power in the field of national politics.

A CRITIQUE OF CRITICAL THEORY

Evolutionism, functionalism, diffusionism—whatever the method, all repress otherness in the name of sameness, reduce the different to the already known, and thus fundamentally escape the task of making sense of other worlds.

—V. Y. Mudimbe, *The Invention of Africa*

If we accept that rural migrants are motivated to defend the principles of hierarchy and social difference, the next question becomes: Why? My answer—and the ethnographic evidence I marshal to back it up—unfolds in the following chapters. Readers who are eager to begin the ethnography may wish to skip straight to Chapter 2, for I devote the remaining pages of the present chapter to assessing some of the existing theories that have set out to explain the politics of hierarchy in South Africa. I argue that while these accounts can teach us a great deal about the issue, they tend to rely on a set of assumptions about human behavior that we need to question. To do so we need a theory of culture, which in South Africa proves a tricky terrain to negotiate. This discussion may seem to be a bit of a detour, but it provides important background for the broader argument that I develop in the conclusion of the book.

The dominant view about the rural Zulu defense of hierarchy holds that migrant males are interested in maintaining patriarchal social order because it allows them to control the labor of women and minors and thus maximize their status and power in rural areas. This arrangement came under attack in the late 1980s when the UDF and ANC began to demand that hostels be either abolished or converted into family units as part of a multi-pronged tactic of reform: to dismantle the exploitative migrant labor system that colonialism had created, to urbanize and modernize rural Zulus, to undermine Inkatha's power base, and to end the oppression of women in the rural areas to which they were confined (see Bazilla 1991). According to Glen Elder (2003), migrants resisted out of fear that once their wives and families moved to urban areas they would no longer be subject to the patriarchal power of homestead heads and chiefs under customary law. By contrast, Inkatha fought in favor of hostels remaining as temporary accommodations for single males—as urban extensions of the rural homestead—and worked hard, in Elder's words, to invoke "an idyllic rural past with a hierarchical cultural order where old age was respected and a 'traditional' sexual division of labor prevailed" (Elder 2003:931; see also Hassim 1993).

The underlying claim here is that rural Zulu culture—characterized specifically by kinship hierarchy, or patriarchy—is rigged in the interests of elder males. Migrants seek to protect this cultural order because it serves their material interests.

This approach participates in a long and noble tradition of Marxist-feminist critical theory in South African social science—a tradition that has been crucial to the critique of colonialism and capitalism in the region. Yet nonetheless some of the assumptions it makes require a bit of scrutiny. Let me offer a few examples to illustrate what I mean. In a highly influential 1990 anthology on gender in South Africa, the historian Jeff Guy deploys a materialist framework to confront gender in rural Zulu society as a class divide. Guy interprets "precapitalist" gender relations as fundamentally "based upon the control of women's labor power by men" (1990:33). His argument hinges on the institution of *ilobolo,* bridewealth in cattle. He recognizes that the transfer of bridewealth from a groom to his affines is contingent on the bride fulfilling specific productive and reproductive duties. If she abdicates these duties, the transaction can be reversed. Guy therefore reads *ilobolo* as the effective transfer of labor power between male homestead heads who vie to appropriate "surplus value" in the form of female labor and fertility. Guy notices that the division of labor within the precapitalist homestead was structured, not only by gender, but by generation as well. To be a woman, a child, or an unmarried man (the subordinate class) was to be "propertyless," subject to the superiority of married male homestead heads (the dominant class) who accumulated the surplus value produced by their dependents.

James Ferguson (1985) tells a similar story about gender in nearby Lesotho. He shows that in Basotho culture, cattle operate as a special type of commodity: they can only be controlled by men, they cannot be exchanged for cash, and they represent the highest form of social prestige. Ferguson argues that this "bovine mystique" operates as a class ideology that serves the interests of married men by allowing them to accumulate wealth in a form that cannot be accessed by their wives, and can be used to develop networks of patronage that enhance their social standing. Women, by contrast, do everything they can to subvert the bovine mystique by praising men who accumulate cash instead of cattle, since cash is a form of household wealth that women can make claims on. Similarly, junior men also attempt to subvert the mystique by accumulating wealth in commodities other than livestock, which—unlike cattle—cannot be claimed by their in-laws as part of their bridewealth dues. Ferguson's stated purpose is to debunk the notion that people across cultures operate according to predictable models of economic rationality, but—ironically—he leaves us with a picture of Basotho society wherein individuals strategically manipulate cultural resources to maximize their material interests. Culture, from this Bourdieuian practice-theory perspective, becomes a terrain manipulated by competing individuals and interest groups, and ends up serving the interests of the dominant class.

One final example. Benedict Carton (2000) reads the Zulu rebellion of 1906 as a struggle of radical young men against a system of patriarchal authority whereby "a small number of homestead heads shielded their power from rivals," "contained assertive young men," and "narrowed the life prospects of youth" (3). In this narrative, youths challenged the rigid system of hierarchy that subordinated them to their elders—overbearing patriarchs who exercised arbitrary authority over wives and youth and sought "commercial advantage in marrying off their daughters" (40). To Carton, elders perpetuate the ancestor cult to legitimate the patriarchal order and to mystify and naturalize their power (39). In this reading, hierarchy is intrinsically bad inasmuch as it denies juniors their individual autonomy. The assumption is that youths will automatically object to hierarchy, that they possess a natural inclination to rebel against the cultural constraints imposed by their elders. Patriarchy here appears as a means for thwarting the "interests" of youth, which are assumed to be naturally opposed to those of patriarchs as if across a class divide. In sum, Carton gives us an epic battle between the assertive individual and an overbearing hierarchical society—a favorite Western metanarrative written back into early twentieth-century Zulu history.

Each of these accounts leverages Marxist class analysis to critique the hierarchical order of gender and generation in rural African society. Culture appears as a form of ideology that the dominant class (elders, males) invokes and perpetuates to maintain the upper hand over the subordinate class (juniors, women). Culture is controlled by elder males and reflective of their interests just as the superstructure reflects the interests of the bourgeoisie in capitalist society.

In African anthropology, this perspective became popular with the Manchester School as a counterpoint to the structural-functionalist approaches that had previously dominated the field. Structural functionalists saw social institutions—such as kinship rules, rituals, and belief systems—as functioning to keep individuals together in groups by overriding their natural tendency to fragment. Where structural-functionalists saw cohesion, Marxist scholars pointed to conflict, seeking to expose the power interests and inequalities that lay behind what appeared to be social unity and solidarity.[29] For them, kinship rules, rituals, and religious beliefs are not about holding people together, but reflect the cunning attempts by a dominant class to accumulate power at the expense of other groups. Yet, despite their obvious differences, these two schools of thought share crucial common ground. Both presuppose a fundamental antagonism between the individual and society, and see society as an artificial force that overrides individuals' natural desire for autonomy—the standard liberal metanarrative that I outlined in the previous chapter. The difference is that structural-functionalists see this as basically good, whereas Marxists see it as basically bad, for it impinges on individual freedom and agency and constrains people's capacity for critical thought.

This is exactly the framework that informs the ANC's critique of rural Zulus described above. It comes at them from two sides: from the dominant political party as well as from Western social scientists.

There is another assumption in the Marxist approach that is worth drawing out. These types of accounts tend to turn on a theory of exploitation that relies on the concept of alienation. Women and juniors are alienated from their labor power, and male elders accumulate wealth and prestige by expropriating the surplus value that they generate. Comaroff and Comaroff (1990) epitomize this approach when they argue that the agricultural labor of Tswana wives generates goods—such as beer and livestock—which men then alienate (or "steal") and circulate as gifts to enhance their prestige in the public sphere. The role of women's labor gets covered up, and men use women's surplus for their own interests, which are assumed to be incompatible with the interests of the women they exploit. As Marilyn Strathern (1990) has pointed out, the concept of expropriation here relies on the assumption that each individual *owns,* or ought to own, the things that they produce, a conceit of Western possessive individualism that believes persons to be the natural proprietors of their will, their energies, and their labor power.[30] This view of personhood and the dichotomous person-thing relationship is closely associated with the rise of industrial capitalism in Europe, to which the Marxist critique is internal. Strathern accuses Marxist analysts of importing capitalist notions of class, interest, and power—categories that derive from a distinctly Western social science—into contexts where they might not apply.

Strathern's work has not been taken up much by scholars of South Africa. If we were to apply her insights, we might say that to see patriarchs pitted against women and youth in a class-like battle over surplus value is to erase the cultural specificity of the rural Zulu family, the relationships that constitute it, and emic ideas about labor, property, and power. I do not mean to say that hierarchy is embraced by women and youth without conflict, or that problematic forms of domination and exploitation do not exist. I mean only to say that we cannot assume that these dynamics conform to our expectations (indeed, to use terms like "domination" and "exploitation" throws us off track from the start, because they are freighted with assumptions from specific moral traditions; there is no neutral or objective language with which to speak about power). Existing accounts tend to smuggle in Eurocentric notions of personhood, interest, and possession, and they take for granted the very categories that most need to be explained, namely, "man" and "woman," and the relationship between them. We need to be able to elucidate the distinctive nature of the sociality in question in order to understand precisely how "interest" operates for rural Zulus, which requires ethnographic work. Strathern reminds us that "the task is not to imagine one can replace exogenous concepts by indigenous counterparts, but to convey the complexity of the indigenous concepts in reference to the particular context in which they are produced" (1990:8).

This statement captures the burden that motivates the following chapters, which seek to take seriously the categories and concerns that migrants themselves point to when describing their political motivations. Hierarchy is central to rural migrants' political aspirations, yes. But why? What does hierarchy mean to them? Why do they feel so compelled to defend it? What are the consequences of its violation?

THE POLITICS OF CULTURE

When I initially began my field research, I set out to do a Marxist analysis not dissimilar to the ones I have outlined above. I wanted to know why rural migrant workers in KwaZulu-Natal—specifically in the sugar industry—continue so vehemently to resist recruitment by COSATU unions. I hypothesized that some form of mystification or false consciousness was at play—a form of cultural hegemony complicit with capital, or the cynical machinations of managers well-versed in industrial psychology, cramping workers' ability to perceive and act on their own class interests. My assumption was that the political agenda of class struggle and National Democratic Revolution—which COSATU embodies—is somehow in line with the natural interests of workers. But as I delved into the ethnography I began to recognize the importance of suspending the categories of Marxist analysis in order to think more seriously—in the tradition of Boasian anthropology—about the culturally particular meanings that frame rural migrants' political interests. In the process, I discovered that the concerns that motivate migrants do not fit easily within the paradigm of interests that organizes so much of Western social science and critical theory, which assumes a model of personhood and possessive individualism that simply does not operate in rural Zululand. Put simply, I realized the analytical importance of acknowledging cultural difference.

This is a tricky position to take in South Africa. To many in South African academia—and in the ANC—theorizing the reactionary politics of rural migrants as consistent with some kind of cultural orientation smacks of collusion with the ideology of apartheid. Apartheid administrators explicitly sought to forestall the rise of political radicalism, class consciousness, and Pan-African ideology among rural Africans by forcibly "tribalizing" them, effectively inflating and reinscribing cultural difference as a tactic of control in the classic tradition of divide-and-rule governance. In addition, administrators sought to maintain the "mystification" of rural Africans by keeping them tied to social orders that left little room for Marxist ideas about class, oppression, and exploitation, and whose cosmologies diverted attention away from materialist conceptions of causality. As if having read Marx, segregationists sought to forestall the march of History by preventing rural Africans from becoming a proper proletariat. And they did so under the rubric of promoting and upholding culture.[31]

What is more, the element of so-called traditional culture that they most sought to take advantage of was in fact hierarchy. The long tradition of Marxist scholarship in South Africa has played a crucial role in illuminating and denouncing this scandal. Scholars have shown how the apartheid system of native reserves and pass laws was organized for the optimally efficient exploitation of African labor. Harold Wolpe (1972) argued that the cunning articulation of (white, urban) capitalist with (black, rural) precapitalist modes of production allowed industries to pay male migrant workers a fraction of the cost of their social reproduction, which was subsidized by the unpaid labor of African females in rural homesteads. In other words, as Belinda Bozzoli (1983) has pointed out, this system only worked because of the hierarchical social organization of rural areas, which prevented women from accessing resources, mobility, and power. Women, according to Bozzoli, were doubly exploited under apartheid, subject to a "patchwork quilt of patriarchies" that ultimately served the interests of white capital. In short, Wolpe and Bozzoli argued that the patriarchal order of rural African society was manipulated by the architects of apartheid in the service of capital accumulation. These perspectives were crucial to the resistance movement at the time, which saw the "traditional" aspects of rural Zulu society as serving the interests of apartheid capital.

Given this history, it is hardly surprising that there is something sticky about the culture concept in the context of South Africa. Focusing on culture and difference skirts too close to the discourses that underwrote racial segregation (Kuper 1999). This is partly due to the fact that anthropology was once complicit with the project of segregation and apartheid. One of the region's early instantiations of the discipline evolved in the 1920s from the Afrikaans *volkekunde* school, which drew heavily on the "culturalist" tendencies of German and

American anthropology as well as the "organismic" approach of Malinowski. Among the most influential of the *volkekunde* ethnologists were Max Eiselen and P. J. Coertze, who emphasized the uniqueness of each so-called cultural group, conceived as distinct, unchanging, and clearly bounded units (Pauw 1980:319). Native groups were defined according to particular cultural characteristics in what Richard Handler (1988) calls "cultural objectification," the process by which culture is cast as a "thing," a natural object bounded in space, homogeneous in essence, historically continuous and characterizable by the properties and traits that it bears.

The *volkekunde* school used this theory to justify segregation under colonialism and apartheid, insisting that the boundaries of cultural difference in South Africa corresponded with groups of humans distinct enough to approximate different species. Indeed, many *volkekunde* theorists considered culture to be genetically determined. During apartheid, proponents of this approach went on to organize projects aimed overtly at promoting state ideologies of ethnic purity. Eiselen was a close associate of Hendrik Verwoerd, the principal architect of apartheid in his role as minister of native affairs in the 1950s and later as prime minister. Afrikaans universities funneled their graduates in "applied anthropology" into various branches of the government—including the Department of Native Administration and the South African Defense Force—where they helped manage and control indigenous peoples (Gordon and Spiegel 1993:85; Hammond-Tooke 1997:4). The creation of Bantustans and the philosophy of "separate development" evolved directly from *volkekunde* anthropology. *Volkekunde* theories were essential to apartheid ideology on two fronts: the insistence on cultural difference among Africans in service of intra-African segregation as an element of divide-and-rule policy; and the construction of the Afrikaans community according to ideas about ethnic and racial purity.

British social anthropologists of the region—specifically Max Gluckmann—reacted strongly against the use of anthropology for racist ends. They criticized the *volkekunde* school for its "preoccupation with individual cultures" (Gluckman 1975), for reifying culture as historically continuous, and for assuming cultures to be "unique, bounded, unchangeable, and all-determining" units (West 1979). The British school were not interested in mapping the characteristics of "ethnic" units. They focused instead on studying issues like labor, migrancy, and marriage in the context of the broader political and economic system. Led by Isaac Schapera, who drew on the social-structural approach of Radcliffe-Brown, the

British school rejected essentialist theories and insisted that, rather than being overdetermined by culture, individuals could strategically "use" cultural resources to maximize their interests. They emphasized the "universality of humanity," the "unity of mankind," and "reasonable man" theory in approaching the study of culture. B. A. Pauw (1980) called this approach "methodological individualism" or "neo-utilitarianism." They saw this stance as crucial to liberal politics and the development of a nonracist state; emphasizing shared human reason and historical change was important to challenging the foundations of racial segregation.

With apartheid still very fresh in the nation's collective memory, social analysts today remain wary of discussing cultural difference for these same reasons. In addition, for a self-consciously developing country like South Africa, to claim that the nation's people operate according to anything other than universal modes of practical rationality not only gainsays any hope of modernity but seems to paint a future of perennial parochialism or even backwardness—the very image that Africans are trying to escape. Progressive politics depends on a theory of universal human nature organized around the construct of the rational, agential individual.

The problem of culture in South African anthropology mirrors similar debates that have taken place within the discipline more broadly. Edward Said (1978), an influential critic of the term, saw culture as the product of Western observations and writings that inscribe exotic, orientalizing fantasies about the other, which contributed to their oppression under colonialism. Some of Said's perspectives were echoed in James Clifford and George Marcus's influential 1986 book *Writing Culture,* which questioned whether the cultural order depicted in ethnographic texts is found in lived reality or fabricated by the observer. Preceding these studies, Talal Asad (1973) looked at the possibility that the apparently timeless customs that anthropologists encountered in the colonial world were themselves largely shaped by the colonial project— an argument later reiterated by Terence Ranger (1984) and Leroy Vail (1989)—and pointed out that anthropologists tended to efface this relationship in their textual representations. With these critiques in mind, it makes sense that Lila Abu-Lughod (1991) calls on anthropologists to work "against culture," promoting a "tactical humanism" that emphasizes the universals of everyday life. Her politically pragmatic approach recalls the concerns of Gluckman and other British social anthropologists who sought to navigate the pitfalls of doing anthropology under apartheid.

But the possibility that culture is the product of both colonial and anthropological inventions, and used to reinforce relationships of oppression and domination, is only one of the political problems that the concept presents for South African scholars. The other pertains to the age-old dialectic between structure and agency. This tension exactly mirrors that between society and the individual, respectively, which runs through the history of Western social science (Barnett and Silverman 1979; Sahlins 2008). In the Hegelian tradition (which influenced key elements of the liberation struggle in South Africa),[32] to be free is to be self-determining, to escape the social norms that condition the will of individuals. Rationality—in the universal mold—is the root of self-determination, since it allows individuals to arrive at an objective perspective on their world and to distinguish between real interests and conditioned desires. This is precisely the logic that motivates Marx's notion of "consciousness"—the ability of a class to exist "in and for itself," to exercise agential will unencumbered by the mystifications of society. For Hegel, Marx, and most of social science, the social determination of the subject—the sway of "culture" over "reason"—is considered a form of bondage. Culture appears to stifle freedom of the will. This is the perspective that Marxist intellectuals contributed to the South African revolution; resistance, for them, depended on leveraging Reason to surmount the constraints of culture, which they recognized as a cynical tool of colonial governance.

In anthropology, this dialectic has been dramatized in the debate between Marshall Sahlins (1985) and Gannanath Obeyesekere (1992). Obeyesekere criticizes Sahlins's famous interpretation of the murder of Captain Cook on the grounds that it denies that the Hawaiians had the agency to reason outside the strictures of structure, casting them as predestined to act out a set-piece cosmological drama. In contrast—like Gluckman and Abu-Lughod—Obeyesekere advances the notion of "practical rationality" and argues that Hawaiians had the capacity to rationally navigate the multivocal cosmological order that they inhabited. For Obeyesekere, the Hawaiians were not bound to the prescriptions of a rigid, determinative structure. In short, while Sahlins emphasizes cultural and epistemological difference when it comes to explaining human behavior, Obeyesekere emphasizes pragmatic, utilitarian, problem-solving rationality as a counterweight to the exoticizing tendencies of the Western anthropological imagination.

But culture and reason need not—and should not—be understood as dichotomous. As Ruth Benedict pointed out, all people are rational, but reason is always culturally situated: there is no standpoint external to culture from where the individual might operate with objective rationality. Culture provides "the raw material" for reason and agency; culture enables human creativity and expression rather than constraining it. For Benedict, the project of ethnography is to make even apparently bizarre practices comprehensible—not according to some universal rationality, but according to internally coherent, patterned frameworks of values, goals, and desires. In Daniel Rosenblatt's words, "The Boasian claim is not that the world is composed of a collection of distinct peoples (each of whom has some "essence"), but that despite a complex history of migrations, diffusions, and intermixing, the different aspects of life in a community are often characterized by the recurrence of similar patterns and themes" (2004:465).

This is very different from the idea of culture that the *volkekunde* ethnologists peddled. Recognizing this important distinction is crucial to any political anthropology, for, to quote Rosenblatt again, "Without some idea of culture, we can only understand their struggles in terms of our projects" (2003:2–3). This is very close to the perspective that informs postcolonial theory and subaltern studies, whose proponents denounce Marxist and nationalist historiographies of anti-colonial resistance as projecting Eurocentric categories of interest and motivation onto non-Western peoples, a process that amounts to something like epistemological colonialism. Dipesh Chakrabarty, for one, argues that Marxists tend to assume that workers all over the world, irrespective of their specific cultural location, experience capitalist production in the same way: "their propositions end up conferring on working classes in all historical situations a uniform, homogenized, extrahistorical subjectivity" (1989:223).[33] The downside of throwing out the culture concept is that we are left assuming a model of personhood that we project as generic and universal, even though it is actually particular to a specific tradition.

We cannot assume that all activists hold—or should hold—interests premised on orthodox revolutionary ideology. It is vital to investigate the cultural bases of activism and to search out the pillars that frame people's political consciousness (see, e.g., Lan 1985; Comaroff 1985; Atkins 1993; Moodie 1994; Delius 1996; Bank 1994; Ashforth 2005; White 2012). If we find that their politics do not follow what Chakrabarty has called "the logic of secular-rational calculations inherent in the modern conception of the political" (2000:12), we must reject the notion that this form of consciousness is "prepolitical," along with the modernist narrative that underwrites that claim. Instead, we should think of subaltern epistemologies as stretching the category of the political beyond the boundaries assigned to it in Western thought. We need to take the distinctive political consciousness of rural migrant workers seriously, as a fundamental part of South African modernity rather than as a backward vestige of the past or a cynical form of false consciousness, accepting that they act in the world on their own terms and that their representations are not merely symbolic of some deeper secular or material reality.

Of course, to circle back to the issue at hand, none of this is to say that rural Zulu culture—and its hierarchical social order—was not manipulated by the colonial state in the interests of capitalism. It was, as I shall demonstrate in the following chapter; and it still is (cf. Comaroff and Comaroff 2009). But that does not make it any less real to the people who inhabit it.

2

The Habitus of the Homestead

Because tradition owes its present form to, and derives its
meaning from, modernity as much as from anything local or
"indigenous," it becomes analytically impossible to separate
the two. Where does the "traditional" end and the "modern"
begin?

—Charles Piot, *Remotely Global*

When migrant workers from Zululand criticize liberal democracy in
South Africa, they often illustrate their discontent by contrasting the
culture of urban townships—from where the ANC draws the bulk of its
support—with the rural homesteads from which they hail. Most of the
migrants I interviewed claimed that the ANC was slowly destroying the
amasiko ("customs") and *imithetho* ("rules") that order social hierarchies and structure everyday behavior within the homestead.

In 2009 I had a long conversation with a migrant worker in Eston—
I'll call him Sipho—who made this point in a particularly compelling
way. "The ANC has turned everything upside down," he lamented.
"Because of democracy, now the women and the men are becoming the
same, the ancestors are displeased, and many misfortunes are coming
upon us." "But you see, in the homestead," he continued, "things are
carefully ordered, people are not the same; there are different places for
different people." To dramatize his point he picked up a scrap of paper
from the table, asked me for my pen and began to draw, tracing about
a dozen small circles neatly organized around a bigger circle—a sche-
matic diagram of the homestead from above, depicting round houses
clustered around a central cattle byre. "In the homestead," he explained,
"there is a great house and there are two sides: a right side, which is
more important, and a left side, which is less important . . . ," and he
went on to explicate the organization of rural domestic space in rigorous detail, delineating the order of hierarchy and noting the different

statuses and roles that men, women, and various dependents occupy in this context.

Of course, no homestead looks as perfect as the model that Sipho drew for me, and nor do domestic social relations play out as smoothly as he implied. Sipho was articulating a romantic ideal—shared by many migrant workers like him—of how the homestead should properly operate, and was using that ideal to leverage a critique of the ANC. The construct of the homestead carries powerful political implications in South Africa today; it serves to anchor the values that mark migrants off from their counterparts in urban townships and provides the touchstone for their discontent with the ANC regime. The ideal homestead—envisioned as embattled and besieged by the postapartheid dispensation—becomes something of a fetish around which migrants mobilize their anti-liberal politics, a material construct that objectifies the moral order that they seek to uphold against the incursions of "democracy." To the extent that migrants represent this moral order in the shorthand language of ethnicity, the homestead serves as the symbolic centerpiece of authentic "Zuluness."

This chapter drives at two overriding arguments. First, I seek to explain how an idealized representation of the homestead has come to dominate Zulu migrants' moral imaginations. I want to trouble common tropes that cast the homestead—like migrants do—as "traditional," static, or essential, and show instead that the homestead's present form derives in part from a deep history of cultural inventions that British colonizers manipulated in their efforts to control Natal Africans through indirect rule. Specifically, I look at how the 1878 Natal Code of Native Law sought to ossify what were previously diverse and flexible systems of kinship and domestic organization into a single, rigidly hierarchical form, which—after more than a century of operation—continues to structure people's ideals about domestic order. Furthermore, I argue that these ideals are cultivated and reproduced as a product of the migrant labor system itself, which keeps migrant workers away from their rural homes for the vast majority of the year. Given their distance from the messy, tumultuous workings of everyday homestead life, migrants construct an idealized vision of hierarchy, holism, and fruition as a foil against the individualism, fragmentation, and decay that they believe characterizes urban townships. The homestead, then, is largely the product of migrants' "structural nostalgia" (Silverstein 2009), a powerful longing for the order of a threatened past, an order they work to actualize during the rituals associated with returning home.

Still, invention or not, the notion of the ideal homestead is deeply compelling for the migrant men that I grew to know, as well as for their partners and families: it shapes their everyday experiences and weaves through the moral fabric of their lives, the second argument in this chapter.

The basic moral principle of rural Zulu social life hinges on the production of hierarchical difference. Just as the structure of the ideal homestead inscribes distinctions between genders, generations, and statuses, so a complex code of taboos polices hierarchical gradients and marks off social differences. Within this system, the production of social difference is understood as crucial for fruition and collective well-being, and the collapse of social difference is understood as inducing dangerous, contagious sterility. Violations of this code are thought to hobble productive and reproductive processes and leave people vulnerable to misfortunes such as crop failure, infertility, miscarriage, poverty, illness, and joblessness. This view motivates migrants to defend the order of rural society against the ANC's egalitarian project, which they believe causes national misfortune by dismantling hierarchies.

A HOMEBOUND DIASPORA

As I developed relationships with migrant workers in the Durban area, some invited me to accompany them when they returned home to their families in rural Zululand during holidays. This was only ever possible with male migrants, I found, since it would have been considered inappropriate for me to make a similar journey with a woman—a reality that no doubt colored my observations. I visited many homesteads across the region, but spent the majority of my time living in two chiefdoms north of the Thukela River: Entenjani, east of the town of Eshowe; and Mayese, in the western reaches of Nkandla district. The journey to central Zululand requires travelling by *kombi*—or minibus taxi—from the bustling ranks of central Durban north along the N2 highway. A glimmering example of South Africa's transport infrastructure, the highway flies through the sprawling townships of Inanda and KwaMashu, skirts the opulent suburbs of Umhlanga and Ballito, traverses the coastline's beautiful beaches, and heads off into a landscape of rolling hills carpeted with thick stands of sugarcane that stretch to the horizons. After crossing the Thukela River, the southern boundary of Zululand, a number of subsidiary roads branch off to the west, exit the cane fields, and eventually trickle as gravel tracks into territories formerly part of the KwaZulu homeland under apartheid. There the impressive infrastructure of the coastal corridor gives way to a patchwork of economically depressed chiefdoms where often the only signs of "development" are district centers marked by a municipal office, a primary school, and a traditional courthouse that doubles as a community hall. Dusty outposts like these function as the hubs of a vast web of capillary paths that connect far-flung homesteads across the rugged terrain of rural Zululand.

Homesteads in this region do not cluster into anything dense enough to be considered a village in the strict sense. Independent of each other and surrounded by their agricultural fields, homesteads are typically spaced at least a few hundred meters apart. Indeed, to many outside observers, homesteads appear as small villages unto themselves, since they often incorporate dozens of houses and scores of residents into a multigenerational community. With circular mud-and-thatch huts, no plumbing or electricity, and ubiquitous livestock, rural Zulu homesteads present a bucolic image. Add to this the chieftaincy system, a vibrant ancestor cult, and frequent ritual activity, and it becomes evident why Zulu homesteads function in the mainstream urban imaginary as holdovers from a "traditional" precolonial past. But appearances deceive. If popular—and even scholarly—renditions of the Zulu homestead have tended toward the static, the work of South African historians has done a great deal to complicate this image.

The homestead was at the very center of the colonial project in Natal and has been shaped by a long history of social engineering and cynical interventions by European administrators. Colonial demands for taxes, land, and labor significantly affected the internal organization of African domestic life. The notorious "hut tax" was imposed on homesteads in 1849 to line colonial coffers and draw African men out into the labor market, which transformed the gender division of labor, undermined the authority of fathers over their sons, and partially monetized the bridewealth system.[1] In addition, beginning in the early twentieth century, Natal administrators coercively relocated Africans into designated "native locations" or "reserves" that were so resource-poor and overcrowded that residents had to seek wages to supplement subsistence agriculture— another strategy to generate cheap labor for European settlers. In this sense, the creation of the reserve system operated very much like the process of "enclosure" that transformed the countryside of fifteenth- and six-teenth-century Europe (Marx 1867; Polanyi 1944). The difference was that the colonial state sought to *prevent* rural Africans from becoming full proletarians, choosing instead to keep them tied to rural reserves while drawing able-bodied men out as migrant workers on fixed-term contracts and sending them back when they were no longer needed.

This system of labor migrancy remains entrenched to this day, even without the dreaded "pass laws" that limited Africans' access to urban areas during apartheid. Many migrants return home only once or twice a year, depending on how far away they have to travel. The men of the Buthelezi family with whom I stayed in Nkandla worked in Durban and Johannesburg, far enough away to limit their visits home to Christmas, Easter, and one additional special occasion—such as a ritual ceremony—a year. I travelled from Durban to Nkandla with Buthelezi men on many such occasions. After four to five hours on the road, mostly corrugated gravel, the dusty *kombi* would drop us outside the municipal office in the Mayese valley. Gathering our bags and whatever supplies we had brought for the family, we would begin the steep climb up the escarpment rising from the Umfolozi River toward the homestead, greeting friends in their homes along the way, herding goats up the footpath ahead of us, and dispatching eager young boys to carry the news of our arrival up the mountain on feet faster than our own.

The moment of arrival was always thick with excitement. The family would gather by the entrance to the homestead in the dusk to welcome the migrants home while children jostled for the chance to carry their bags to the "great house," where the adults—after exchanging greetings, news, and brief stories—would eventually make their way. Once inside, the men and their sons would line up kneeling along the right side and their wives and daughters would kneel on the left side, all situated in order of rank. The senior wife—who appeared to be in her seventies— would gather the cash remittances that the men had brought home with them, place them at the shrine at the back of the room and lead prayers to the ancestors, dedicating the money to their keeping and asking them to use it for the development of the homestead, adding wives and children and cattle. Money that is not dedicated to the ancestors in this manner is liable to become unproductive and "slippery," leaving its earner more impoverished than before. The arrival ceremony, then, is intended to realign the migrants with the moral coordinates of the homestead and connect their wealth to the well-being of the family.[2]

THE FRACTAL HOME

Kinship in rural Zululand pivots on the homestead unit (*umuzi*). While ethnographers of the past have gone to great lengths to find clans, lineages, and lineage segments in Zulu society, these categories have never accurately reflected social reality. Only recently have anthropologists, influenced by house-society theory, accepted that the homestead—and not the lineage—forms the central kinship construct around which daily life revolves, and flexibly enough to incorporate people not related by biology or marriage (Kuper 1982a, 1982b). Agnatically related homesteads form another important kinship category, the *umndeni,* which the anthropologist W. D. Hammond-Tooke (1984) glosses as an "agnatic cluster."[3] The *umndeni* comprises homesteads that share a proximate common ancestor—usually a grandfather or great-grandfather, for descent is rarely traced back beyond three or four generations—and interact for important ceremonies such as marriage and mortuary rites. Ceremonial feasting is important to familial belonging: members of an *umndeni* refer to one another as "relatives with whom we eat," in contrast to other agnatic clusters that do not share in this ritual conviviality, even though they might share the same clan name (*isibongo*) (cf. Ngubane 1977).

Like the "house societies" theorized by Lévi-Strauss ([1984]1987), homesteads embody two intertwined realities: a domestic residential site, and the social group associated with it. As with the dwellings famously discussed by Tambiah (1969), Bourdieu (1977, 1979), and Mueggler (2001), homesteads provide the basic organizational blueprint for the kinship system, and embody the enduring principles of social and cosmological order. As the anthropologist Adam Kuper observes, the homestead "provides a physical crystallization of family history, and maps the nodes of contemporary social networks. In its layout it models ritual values and ideas about the organization of the world . . . a symbolic representation of the principles of the socio-cosmic system" (1993:472–3). While homesteads vary quite dramatically in form, they all share a common set of symbolic categories and a basic spatial logic that organizes houses concentrically around a cattle byre, in what the archeologist Thomas Huffman (2001) has termed the "central cattle pattern."[4]

Today, most rural Zulus recognize an ideal homestead model—like the one that Sipho drew for me—which they attempt to approximate as best they can, depending on their financial resources, the materials they have at their disposal, and the practical constraints of their land (see figure 2). Because the internal logic of this model is so essential to understanding migrants' political subjectivity, I shall explore it here in some detail. The description I present derives from my observations of home-

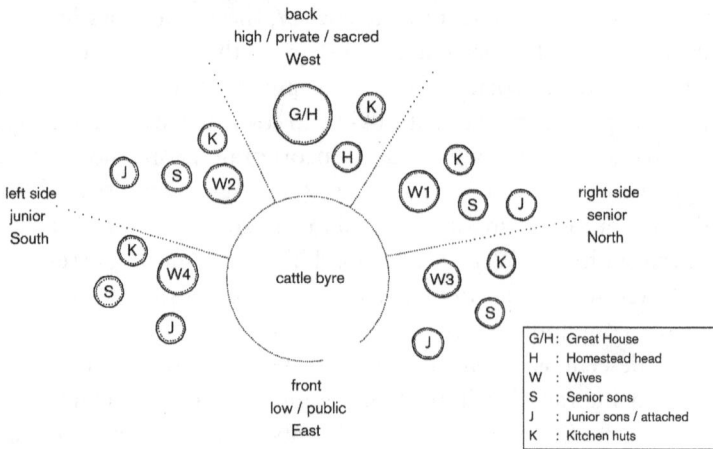

FIGURE 2. Layout of an ideal-typical Zulu homestead. Compare to similar images in Raum 1973, Kuper 1993, and Huffman 2001. I have used straight lines to demarcate the ranked segments of the homestead, though no physical separation exists in reality. Drawing by Anita Michalkiewicz.

steads in Nkandla, specifically from extended experience living in the Buthelezi homestead, which was relatively affluent compared to others (see figures 3 and 4). That said, I include only those aspects that are generalizable across the dozens of homesteads I visited throughout the Zululand region.

According to the orthodox model, homesteads are oriented so that one enters through a gate at the downslope side and looks up into the compound. A circular cattle byre, usually fenced off with thick, knotty branches, occupies the very center of the yard. While primarily used to house cattle, the byre also serves as a community meeting place for men and as the site of ritual sacrifices, and it often contains the graves of the homestead's ancestors. Directly above the byre, on the same axis, the great house (*indlunkulu*) sits at the top or apex of the homestead, facing downslope and ideally toward the rising sun in the east. The great house represents both the homestead's founder (*umnumzana*) and his mother, and is referred to as the anthropomorphic "head" of the homestead. The great house contains the primary site of ancestral mediation, a sort of shrine at its back known as *umsamo,* where elders burn incense to communicate with dead relatives and ask for protection and good fortune for the family. The *umsamo* sometimes holds a wooden chest that contains the family's valuables, as well as the family's ritual spear, which is often an heirloom passed down by preceding generations. The spear is usually named after the father of the homestead head, and is sometimes stored by piercing it into the thatch above the *umsamo*—an evocative symbol of fertility, as we shall see later.

When homesteads are polygynous, they are always divided into two distinct "sides," a right side and a left side. The right side (*isibayesikhulu*)[5] is superior to its "twin," the left side (*ikhohlwa*).[6] The first wife—the homestead's most senior—constructs her house at the top of the right side, slightly below the great house, while the second wife constructs her house at the top of the left side. The first and second wives operate as the heads of their respective sides, which become like ranked "houses" in the Lévi-Straussian sense *within* the larger homestead unit—fractal replications of the primary form. While the second wife is junior to the first, she remains functionally independent as the head of the left side. If the homestead is wealthy enough to have additional wives, they fall under the direct authority of the first two and attach to their respective sides. For example, the third wife falls under the authority of the first wife, and builds her house—*umnawekosana*[7]—lower on the right side; and the fourth wife falls under the authority of the second wife and builds her house—*umnawekhohlwa*[8]—lower on the left side. A fifth wife would attach to the side of the first wife, a sixth wife would attach to the side of the second wife, and so on. All junior wives are considered "rafters"[9] of the principal houses to which they are attached, and exchange tribute[10] with their seniors in the form of sacrificial meat.

The physical house (*indlu*) of each wife symbolizes the "uterine family"[11] that she produces—her sons and daughters, her sons' wives, and her sons' children. The uterine family is a consanguineous unit headed by both the wife and her eldest son, who represents the father to his uterine siblings. Each uterine house contains an *umsamo* that mediates a wife's access to her own agnatic ancestors. All homestead property (fields, cattle, tools, food, etc.) is possessed, managed, and inherited under the auspices of the uterine families associated with these houses. Bearing as eponyms the personal names of the wives they objectify, these houses are nested as fractals within their respective sides, which nest in turn within the homestead. The status of each house is indexed by its location within the homestead landscape, both spatially and temporally: houses located on the periphery of the settlement represent persons and families that are temporally more distant from the progenitor than those nearer the center. In addition, homesteads develop according to a pattern of rank and seniority expressed through right/left and high/

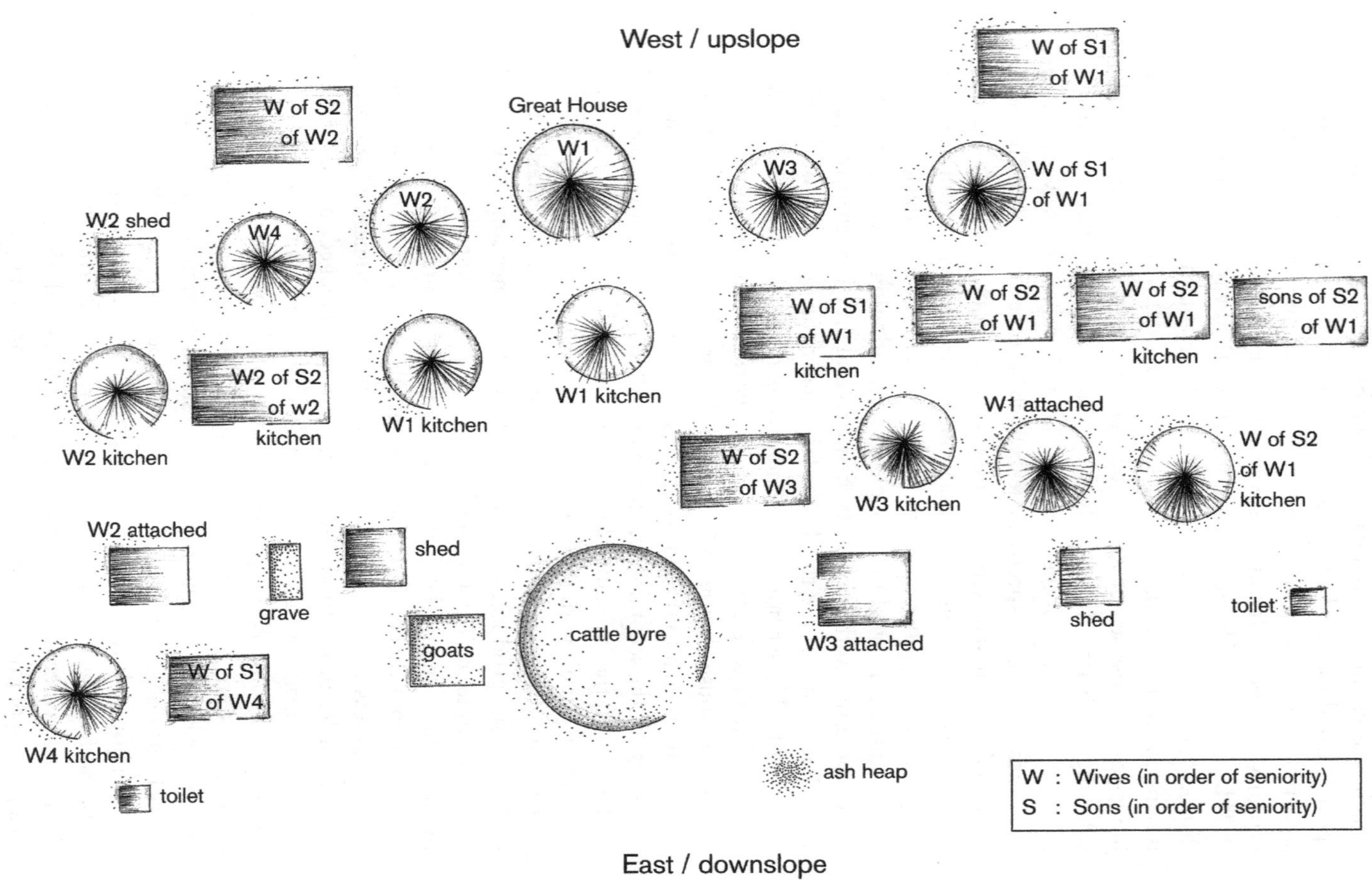

West / upslope

East / downslope

W of S1 of W1

W of S1 of W1

W of S1 of W1

sons of S2 of W1

W of S2 of W1

W of S2 of W1

W of S2 of W1 kitchen

W of S1 of W1 kitchen

W of S2 of W1 kitchen

W3

W1 attached

W3 kitchen

toilet

Great House

W1

W1 kitchen

W of S2 of W3

W3 attached

shed

ash heap

cattle byre

W2

W1 kitchen

W of S2 of W2

W4

W2 of S2 of w2 kitchen

shed

goats

grave

W2 shed

W2 kitchen

W2 attached

W of S1 of W4

W4 kitchen

toilet

W : Wives (in order of seniority)

S : Sons (in order of seniority)

FIGURE 3. Layout of a homestead near Nkandla, in 2009. Drawing by Anita Michalkiewicz. Compare this with the "orthodox" model depicted in fig. 2.

low oppositions: the right side always bears higher status than the left, and houses nearer the apex bear higher status than those below them. As a homestead expands, accretions grow outward in a manner that leaves the original center intact and discrete—a testament to the precedence of the progenitor.

These same basic principles also organize space within the great house, since, as we have seen, the homestead follows a fractal logic whereby the basic form of the whole is mimicked in its constitutive parts (cf. Eglash 1999). The great house is always constructed in the traditional manner, round with a thatched roof, even while other houses in the homestead may use rectilinear forms and tin roofs to signal modernity (see White 2010).[12] As in the homestead, the back/front opposition in the great house operates as a gradient of seniority and privacy (see figure 5). The back of the house—the *umsamo*—is marked as private/sacred and reserved for seniors and close kin, while the front, near the door, is considered public/common and suitable for juniors, children, and visitors. In addition, just as in the homestead, the right side of the house is superior to the left. In the house, however, this opposition has a gendered dimension: the right side is coded male, and the left female.[13] When people gather inside, seniors sit toward the back—men on the right and women on the left—while juniors and children gather nearer the door, also on the right or left according to their gender. These dualistic oppositions are oriented around a central hearth, which is coded female/wives. This inverts the gendered symbolism of the broader homestead, which is organized around a cattle byre coded male/agnates.

Homestead development follows a recognizable pattern of growth, climax, and eventual fragmentation. Each homestead begins with only a great house and a cattle byre. Additional houses are constructed as the head marries new wives, as his wives bear children, and as his sons bear grandchildren. As sons reach puberty, they construct their own bachelor houses[14] on the side to which they are attached. After marrying, every young man establishes his own virilocal residence with his wife, usually next to his mother's house. As their families grow and they gradually accumulate resources, married sons hive off to found their own neolocal homesteads, installing their mothers—should they be widowed—in the great house. In this way, each uterine house eventually becomes an independent homestead. These satellite homesteads remain ranked according to the same order that ranked them as uterine houses, and they continue to recognize the authority of the original homestead, which they treat as a sacred ritual site. Older homesteads,

FIGURE 4. Photograph of the same Nkandla homestead, taken at dawn from the northern approach. Photo by author.

then, contract as daughters leave for marriage and as the families of married sons relocate. At a patriarch's death, his widows leave to join the homesteads of their sons, his body is buried in the byre of his first wife's eldest son, and the homestead is left to decay until nothing remains beneath the overgrowth but foundations and graves.

It is worth making an important point about gender within this moving system. Rural Zulu kinship is often considered to be patriarchal, but this is not technically accurate. Women are far more central to the system than it might appear at first glance. While gendered oppositions are ranked in favor of men by default, women are not *categorically* inferior to men. The place of women depends on their generational position and their ranking vis-à-vis other wives, which changes over time. Elder women—particularly those who have begun menopause—can come to enjoy significant power as heads of houses and sides.[15] And of course in her later years, the mother of the homestead head often exercises greater ritual authority than her son does, for she is closer to the ancestors. We can see this "hidden" power of women at key points of the spatial order. The most obvious example is in the great house (which is often referred to as *kwagogo*, "the place of the grandmother"), but it is evident in other ways as well. While the homestead is organized around a male core (the byre), its fractal houses are organized around a female core (the hearth). We could see this as an expression of how the male work of cattle and politics encompasses the female work of cooking and child rearing. But

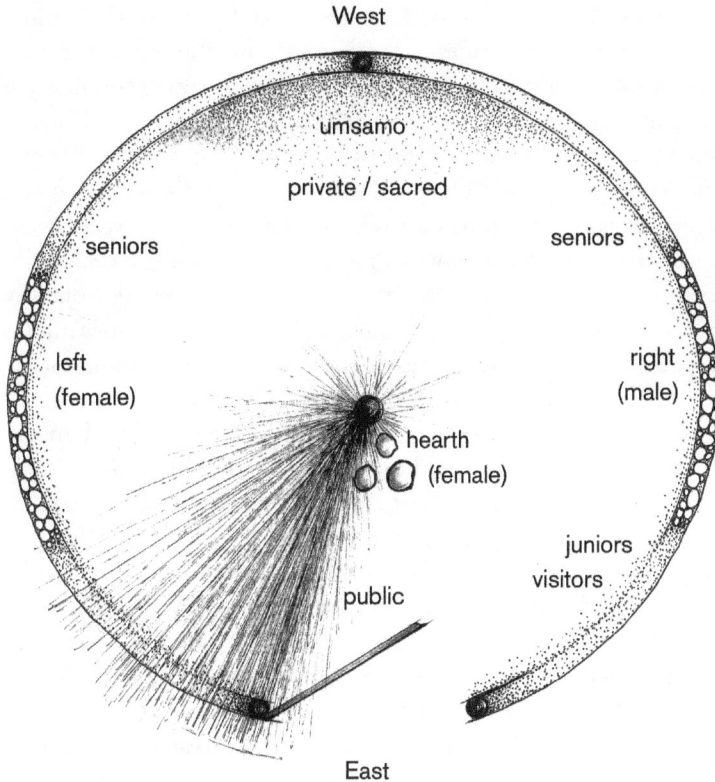

FIGURE 5. Layout of the interior of a Zulu round house. Drawing by Anita Michalkiewicz.

I would argue for a different view, namely, that the work of cooking food and raising children is the basis on which the work of cattle and politics occurs. As I shall show later, the *domesticating* work of women provides the basic metaphor for processes of healing and fruition.

ENCOMPASSING OPPOSITIONS

The homestead inculcates into its inhabitants a commonsense world of taxonomic principles that bear the aura of objectivity and consensus through reference to the material realities of architecture. Human hierarchy is mapped onto domestic space, and vice versa, so that each series authenticates the other. This self-referential relationship between signifier and signified creates the convincing illusion that each series is natural and motivated, producing—as Bourdieu would put it—"the naturaliza-tion of its own arbitrariness" (1977:164). By traversing the morally loaded precincts of the domestic realm, children grow from their young-est ages into an awareness of the significance of a spatialized hierarchy, which they internalize as a kind of embodied knowledge. The home-stead, then, operates as a blueprint for the gendered system of hierarchy that organizes the social whole. Whenever someone enters a house, for instance, they make their way to a position appropriate to their rank and gender; any breach of this pattern is considered a moral violation. Of course, it bears pointing out that this system of hierarchy does not persist in a static state. Rather, it is a dynamic process: hierarchies shift and alternate during the course of homestead reproduction, and they are pro-duced—as we shall see—through processes of ritual and exchange.

Hierarchy in the homestead context is not organized in the Western sense of hierarchy at all. It is not conceived of as a ladder of command, or as a relationship among discrete entities according to a linear chain of authority. Instead, hierarchy operates as the principle by which per-sons are related to one another as *parts* of an encompassing *whole,* as described by Louis Dumont: "The hierarchical relation is, very gener-ally, that between a whole (or set) and an element of this whole (or set): the element belongs to the set and is in this sense consubstantial or iden-tical with it; at the same time, the element is distinct from the set or stands in opposition to it" ([1966] 1980:240).

Hierarchical rank operates, not as graded authority, but as degree of encompassment: "that which encompasses is more important than that which is encompassed, just as a whole is more important than its parts" (Dumont [1966] 1980:76). But while an encompassed part exists as consubstantial with its encompassing whole, it also differs from it at the same time. Dumont calls this "the encompassing of the contrary." The relationship of difference according to the logic of encompassment is one neither of polarity nor of complementarity, but of mutual constitu-tion that refers to a broader totality. In rural Zululand, differences of gender, generation, and rank are never strictly oppositional—as much of the literature on hierarchy in southern Africa assumes—because the junior elements of the system are *constitutive* of the senior elements.

In rural homesteads this plays out according to the fractal logic of houses on two scales: a nesting scale and a ranking scale. Take the smallest unit in a homestead: the house of a homestead head's son's wife. That house would be encompassed by a uterine house (the son's mother's); each uterine house would be encompassed by the side of the homestead to which it is attached; each side would be encompassed by the homestead as a whole; and each homestead would be encompassed by the homestead from which it derived. Given this logic, it is said that to make an offering at the *umsamo* of the great house is tantamount to making offerings at the *umsamo* of each of the uterine houses; but of course the reverse does not apply. In addition to this nesting scale, the houses at each of these levels are also ordered according to a ranking scale, again through the logic of encompassment. For instance, the sons of a uterine house are ranked with the senior son encompassing the others; the uterine houses on each side of the homestead are ranked with the senior wife encompassing the junior wives attached to her; the two sides of the homestead are ranked with the right side encompassing the left side; and agnatically related homesteads are ranked in the same way they were as uterine houses within the homestead of their progenitor.

These rankings have nothing to do with wealth. Indeed, I encountered a number of extended families wherein higher-ranking people were materially worse off than their lower-ranking counterparts. Rather, seniority is marked by ritual precedence. And this same order of precedence carries on after death. One diviner in Entenjani explained this principle to me as follows:

> When you speak with the ancestors, you cannot speak directly to the highest ones. You must first speak with your [deceased] mother, and your mother will speak with your father, and your father speaks to his mother, and his mother speaks to your grandfather. This is the same way that you give food that you have prepared. Your mother gives food to your father, your father gives it to his mother, and his mother gives it to your grandfather.

Within this system, synecdoche becomes the primary principle of representation: a senior element represents the beneficence of the whole to the parts it encompasses, and represents the interests of its parts to the whole. As we shall see later, this is how many rural Zulus think democracy should operate and forms part of the reason for which they so avidly resist liberalism. As they see it, the regime of encompassment guarantees them the attention of authority in a very intimate way, while liberal democracy, they claim, renders them hopelessly removed from remote persons of power who have no reason to care about their needs.

The principle of synecdoche applies also to the notion of the person. Far from being regarded as autonomous individuals with discrete interests, persons are fractals of the relationships that encompass them; as parts of a whole, each person shares the substance of the larger corporate group. This is meant literally—it is not simply a quaint metaphor for closeness. For instance, if witches manage to steal *insila* ("body substance") from one member of a family—say, by snatching hair clippings or scraping oils off the pillar of a round house—they can use it to harm any of the relatives encompassed by that person. Or if one member of a family displeases the ancestors, they might punish her by allowing misfortunes to visit any of her relatives. More fascinating still, if a man is stabbed in a violent encounter, his descendants will suffer sharp pains in their bodies, sometimes for generations down the line. Such things would be unthinkable within the logic of liberal personhood, obsessed as it is with individual autonomy and personal responsibility. Yet people in rural Zululand go through life knowing that everything they do and everything that happens to them carries ramifications that ripple through the fabric of the homestead, with effects that reach even to the dead and the unborn.

HISTORICIZING THE HOMESTEAD

It is tempting to regard the homestead system, with its clear logic and elegant structure, as static and timeless. But this would be incorrect. The social order I have sketched out above owes its existence to the long encounter with imperial rule as much as to anything "indigenous." While the central cattle pattern extends deep into the archeological record of the region (Mack et al. 1991), it has not always been the only—or even the predominant—form of domestic organization. Certain eighteenth-century forms, the most common of which is known among archaeologists as the "Type B" homestead, appear to have lacked the inscribed hierarchies that define the central cattle pattern. Some evidence suggests that the latter achieved ubiquity during the expansion of the Zulu kingdom in the late eighteenth and early nineteenth centuries (Hall 1984), as Shaka and other kings drew self-consciously on the hierarchical logic that informs the central cattle pattern in order to consolidate the Zulu state and organize rank and tribute among their vassals (Kuper 1993; Bjerk 2006). In other words, the eventual dominance of the central cattle pattern had to do with its use as a tool of statecraft.

But it was not only the Zulu monarchy that used the hierarchical homestead as an instrument of imperial control. Secretary of Native Affairs Theophilis Shepstone reproduced it as the locus of indirect rule in the mid-nineteenth century.[16] As early as 1878—decades before

Lugard—colonial Natal instated a lengthy set of customary rules known as the Natal Code of Native Law, which was extended and made legally binding in 1891.[17] The purpose was to standardize otherwise diffuse oral traditions of kinship and hierarchy rules that varied by family and chiefdom. Confused over how best to enforce a "native law" comprised of what they saw as "a maze of conflicting systems," colonial magistrates pressured the administration to create a single, unitary code that would apply across the whole region (Welsh 1971:159–60, 175). In the process, the code's drafters enshrined their own stereotypes about Zulu society, to the extent that the end product was less an honest depiction of actually-existing customary law than a reflection of colonists' vision of what African society *should* look like. Building on the fantasy of British administrators and early ethnologists—such as Lewis Henry Morgan (1870)—that "tribal" society was fundamentally monarchical, patriarchal, and authoritarian, the code cast diverse logics of privilege and hierarchy into a single system and attempted to cloak it with the authority of "tradition" (cf. Asad 1973; Wagner 1975; Ranger 1984, 1993; Vail 1989; Kuklick 1991).

The Natal Code of Native Law facilitated colonial control over Africans by vastly expanding the power of chiefs, entrenching the authority of male homestead heads over minors and women, and giving patriarchs unprecedented powers to enforce tribute, obedience, and respect. For example, the code granted the supreme chief the power to appoint and remove even hereditary chiefs (S.33, 34) and to coerce labor and tribute from peasants (S.35, 36). The supreme chief also enjoyed the power to punish "disobedience of his orders," "disregard for his authority," and any form of "disrespect" by arrest, fine, and imprisonment (S.2–5). Chiefs and headmen were granted the power to enforce "respect" even *within* their subjects' homesteads, ensuring "obedience to authority," "the duty of children to their parents," and "the obligations of inmates to their kraal heads" (S.18). Not only did the code grant powers to chiefs that far outstripped those of any precolonial arrangement, but it also removed checks on their authority by prohibiting desertion (S.24) and curbing the power of community councils.

Similarly, at the level of the family, the code massively bolstered the authority of the homestead head. It specified that each patriarch would own all household property, rendered all "inmates" (a telling reference to disciplinary incarceration) judicial minors, with the exception of married males (S.72), and stripped females of the right to inherit and bequeath property (S.143). The "kraal head" was given absolute authority over all members of his homestead, regardless of their age and sex. Indeed, the patriarch had the authority to control all family income (S.35), to arrest or inflict corporal punishment on any inmate "defying his authority" (S.40), and to disinherit disobedient sons (S.118), all while enjoying immunity from lawsuits by his subordinates (S.142). Like chiefs, homestead heads were permitted to rule by decree, free from constraints. The code also meticulously organized hierarchy within the homestead; it determined rules for the rank and status of wives, enforced tribute between junior and senior houses (C.XI), and determined patterns of inheritance and succession according to a system of male primogeniture (C.XII).

The magistrates who enforced the code leveraged it to police the personal lives of Africans. The code determined what types of marriage were permissible (S.57) and set rules for paternity and maternity, legitimate and illegitimate offspring, and the custody of children (S.30–32, 44). It also outlined a moral system that criminalized adultery, prohibited young men from "seducing" girls (S.162), and required men to pay "damages" to the fathers of women whom they impregnated outside of wedlock (S.137). Women were subject to particularly draconian measures under the code. "Native females" were deemed perpetual minors (S.27), daughters had to get formal consent from their fathers before marrying (S.59), and divorced or widowed women were placed under the authority of their natal guardians (S.78). The code also policed female sexuality by criminalizing "any native female who leads an immoral life," and debarring women from leaving their homesteads without the permission of the homestead head (S.163).[18]

At the very center of this system of indirect rule was the *umuzi*, the homestead. Homestead structure was central to the code; indeed, early versions even featured diagrams of the central cattle pattern (similar to fig. 2 above) illustrating the ranking of houses. With the rigidly hierarchical organization given it by the Natal Code, the homestead operated as the basic unit of what Mahmood Mamdani (1996) has so aptly termed "decentralized despotism."

The whole system of indirect rule hinged on a cynical cultural invention. Diverse precolonial arrangements of gender, authority, and hierarchy were gradually standardized and given teeth for the purpose of controlling Africans with maximal efficiency. The architect of this system, Theophilus Shepstone, sought to lend it legitimacy by drawing on collective memories of Shaka, who similarly revolutionized Zulu society in the 1820s by consolidating a centralized state and expanding it through military conquest

(Bjerk 2006).[19] Indeed, Shepstone explicitly cast his authority as secretary of native affairs in the mold of Shaka (Hamilton 1998). The rigid gender-hierarchical order that Shaka elaborated provided a fertile historical precedent for Shepstone's project. Of course, neither ruler invented anything out of whole cloth; rather, they manipulated already-existing cultural resources for their own ends.[20] Under Shepstone, the policy of indirect rule, the codification of customary law, the ossification of hierarchies and so on only worked because there was already something there to act upon. The success of indirect rule hinged on its ability to reference a set of institutionalized categories and practices that already had significant traction, even if only because of the work of an earlier despot.

In other words, colonial power operated by exaggerating the existing dimensions of earlier systems, and by standardizing certain existing forms (namely, that of the Zulu royal family, which Shepstone knew intimately) across the region.

Even so, indirect rule transformed the social milieux within which Natal Africans lived. Many of them were refugees from Shaka's violent expansionist campaigns—a period of upheaval known as the *mfecane*—and had not lived under any form of chiefly power for generations. The implementation of indirect rule in such cases meant, not the manipulation of existing hierarchies, but the artificial creation of hierarchies where none existed (Myers 2008:3). Furthermore, as a number of contemporary observers pointed out, the Natal Code did not accurately reflect precolonial African institutions, particularly concerning the position of women. One colonial administrator confessed that the code "stereotypes a concept of feminine inferiority unknown to the traditional society" (cited in Welsh 1971:166). The historian David Welsh buttresses this claim, stating that prior to the implementation of the code, African women could acquire and hold property, and that the code was "a serious abrogation of the rights that women had traditionally enjoyed" (1971:170). In other words, the code's restrictions on female majority and property ownership—among other inventions of indirect rule—were fabricated by colonial administrators to control Africans through a fantasy of patriarchal power.[21]

But the fact that these cultural forms were strategically manipulated by the state does not make them any less real to the people who lived within them. Indeed, after more than a century of subjection to the dictates of the Natal Code (which remains in place) and the tireless efforts of colonial administrators, missionaries, and anthropologists to reify Zuluness as an object of knowledge and control, rural Africans in

KwaZulu-Natal today defend these principles as fundamental to their cultural heritage—the very root of their autochthony. During my sojourns through the countryside and visits to migrants' hostels, I found that people use the term *umthetho,* which translates broadly as "traditional law," to identify the constellation of rules that ideally govern life in rural homesteads. This term is closely associated with the Natal Code: the principles to which it refers—the proper behavior of persons, the ranking of houses, the order of inheritance, and aspects of the homestead tribute system—are precisely those governed by the code. For many, *umthetho* embodies the most important markers of proper Zuluness itself; many invoke *umthetho* to distinguish Zulus from white people and other ethnic groups, and rural Zulus who respect the ancestors from urban Zulus who have abandoned them. In other words, the interventions of indirect rule played a crucial role in Zulu ethnogenesis.

The Natal Code was never able to overdetermine the social world of rural Zulus. For example, in the kinship system that I describe above, women exercise important powers in homesteads despite the code's attempts to reduce them to minors. But the code is nonetheless upheld as an ideal by some, and particularly by male migrants. As I illustrate in chapter 4, when male migrants invoke *umthetho,* they tend to emphasize the patriarchal dimensions of the code. When women speak of *umthetho,* however, they assert the values of difference and respect without calling for restrictions on female privileges—a vision of order that rejects the code's more draconian measures.

DIFFERENCE AND DEFERENCE

In colloquial use, *umthetho* refers to the rules of customary practice— everything from how to sacrifice a cow to how to organize a homestead. But the term is most frequently invoked to refer to the normative roles of men, women, wives, and children, and the standards of conduct that govern relationships across hierarchies. By far the most significant aspect of *umthetho* today is the system of taboo and avoidance known as *hlonipha,* which commonly translates as "respect"—a term that appears repeatedly in the Natal Code. *Hlonipha* refers to the deferential behavior that people adopt toward persons, spaces, and symbols of authority—it maintains and polices the social boundaries that carve up the homestead and distinguish persons, roles, and ranks.[22] For example, junior members of a homestead should walk with a slight stoop in the presence of an elder, eyes downcast, and when greeted should allow a few moments to pass before responding. *Hlonipha* also requires deference toward the personal possessions of an elder—such as their jacket or fighting stick—since such objects bear the substance of their owners.

Until they receive permission from the homestead's senior woman, *hlonipha* prohibits new brides from drinking milk from the homestead's cows and from touching the ash heap[23] by the gate—both of which are symbols of agnatic relatedness. *Hlonipha* conduct also debars premenopausal women from access to the cattle byre and requires subordinates to adopt an attitude of respect in the vicinity of ritual attractors such as the *umsamo*. *Hlonipha* prevents non-agnates from touching the central pillar of the great house, which bears the substance of the *umndeni*, and from partaking of *amasi* (sour milk), the exchange of which is one of the primary indicators of relatedness within the homestead. *Hlonipha* means abstention from sexual encounters in the great house, prohibits men from having intercourse with menstruating women, and requires pious decorum around gendered spaces, such as—for men—the uterine houses of the homestead, along with their kitchens. In addition, the seating arrangements inside round houses—discussed above—also reflect *hlonipha* rules.

Hlonipha conduct also includes a system of grammaticalized honorifics that comes into play in the context of asymmetrical relationships. Differential status-marking is incorporated into the grammatical rules of the language—not to mark one's own rank, but to mark the rank of others. These injunctions are particularly stringent for wives: *hlonipha* includes a taboo on the use of their husbands' names, on the use of key words that feature in the praise songs[24] of their husbands' families, and on any other word containing or sounding similar to the radicals found in them. Because this taboo affects such a large swath of everyday language, wives make creative use of obscure synonyms or invent neologisms—what Judith Irvine (2010) calls "lexical alternates"—to work around it. The use of such uncommon language operates as a marker of distinction; everyone can recognize a pious woman by the effort that she puts into avoiding taboo words.[25] While women use *hlonipha* speech to mark asymmetrical relationships in the context of the home and family, men use similar lexical indices to demonstrate respect for authority in the context of political speech,[26] which is used in the court and in the byre. Men are expected to *hlonipha* the names of the chief and the king, and use speech marked by euphemism and lowered affect.

Finally, *hlonipha* also regulates the gender division of labor. During the construction of a house, for instance, men erect the frame and women plaster it with mud. This reflects the anthropomorphic qualities of the house with reference to common notions of procreation: male semen produces the skeletal structure of the child, and female blood produces its flesh. Many other activities are subject to gendered divisions as well. While women give birth and act as midwives in rites associated with life, men are expected to handle rites associated with death—preparing the funeral ceremony, digging the grave, and interring the body. Following this logic, it is men who sacrifice animals, while women brew the beer for sacrificial ceremonies. In the realm of productive activity, cultivation (and beer) is considered the domain of women, while pastoralism (and meat) is considered the domain of men. Cooking is also a heavily gendered activity. While women build the hearth-fires and perform day-to-day cooking inside the kitchen, men take responsibility for cooking most of the meat yielded by sacrificial ceremonies, which they do outdoors in the center of the homestead yard. Only males (typically boys) may milk cows, but it is the work of women to transform milk into *amasi*. In a roughly analogous process, when men bring cash home from work they remit it to the senior woman of the homestead, who keeps it overnight at the *umsamo* of the great house before it can be used for ritual purposes, such as in the payment of bridewealth.

In other words, the yield of male labor—be it milk or wages—must go through women before it can be used to produce kinship. Maintaining the differences between males and females is not just about maintaining sexual differences, but about maintaining the symbolic oppositions that sustain them: right/left, bone/flesh, cattle/crops, semen/blood, death/life. If these oppositions collapse, then infertility follows.

MIGRANCY AND STRUCTURAL NOSTALGIA

It should come as no surprise that not all homesteads conform to the orthodox model with all the appropriate spatial distinctions. Partly, this is because people often lack the resources they need to achieve this goal, particularly as the rural subsistence base erodes and migrants' employment opportunities diminish (see Moodie 1994; Bank 1999). Impoverished households across the region can attest to this difficulty. But it is also due to the fact that social relations between ranked persons rarely go uncontested. Nonetheless, the orthodox model bears the status of a powerful moral ideal. If the sketch of domestic social life that I have rendered above appears to emphasize the structuralist dimensions of culture, that is because structure is precisely what occupies the moral and political imagination of the migrant workers that I grew to know. Like diasporas elsewhere around the world, rural migrants cultivate a deep nostalgia for a highly idealized version of home (see Clifford 1992; Radhakrishnan 1996). The figure of the ideal homestead—what we might call "homestead ideology"—serves to anchor the values that distinguish them from their counterparts in urban townships and provides the touchstone for their discontent with South African modernity. Not unlike the American Right with their longing for the Golden Age of the Family, rural migrants think of the home as a bastion of social and moral order in a world of chaos, decline, and decay. The homestead—envisioned as besieged by the liberal politics of the ANC—becomes a fetish around which migrants mobilize their political concerns; it becomes the material objectification of moral order.

These caricatures of the homestead are generated by the ritualized process of cyclical labor migration, which gives migrants sufficient distance from the messy reality of homestead life to render it in highly idealized form. Most of the time I spent in homesteads during my research coincided with migrants' return visits; indeed, I usually traveled back and forth with them specifically on occasions of ritual ceremony. In the absence of migrants, during nonritual time, I noticed that social life unfolds in a much messier way. Women and youth do not feel the need to observe spatial taboos with the same rigor, for example.[27] And disgruntled men who have never been able to secure work in town—the family "losers" (*izahluleki*)—appear to be less invested in maintaining the happy illusion of the idealized home than their more successful migrant counterparts. In other words, the ideals that migrants mobilize turn out to be rather precarious in everyday life, in part precisely because of the migrant labor system, which strings families across the landscape in a manner that lends itself to discord, misunderstandings, and extramarital affairs. Homesteads do not always operate as well-oiled unities; they are often shot through with tensions—jealous competition and witchcraft accusations mark everyday life, something that gets hidden behind nostalgic representations of home.

The migrancy system not only makes it possible for migrants to obscure these complexities behind an idealized vision of home, but structures a ritual of return that facilitates this ideal (McAllister 1985; Moodie 1994). When migrants return home, the homestead takes on a kind of festival atmosphere: people begin preparing for ritual sacrifices, weddings, funerary ceremonies, and various rites of passage, all of which require the cash that migrants remit. Indeed, the migrants' return becomes something of a ritual event itself, mobilizing and highlighting the family's most cherished values. During this time, people pay closer attention to their use of *hlonipha* language, they respect hierarchies and observe taboos with greater vigilance than usual, and they shunt aside many of their internal quarrels; the homestead (and its attendant registers of social and linguistic behavior) takes on the shape of its own caricatured ideal as people perform their representations of it. These moments of condensed ritual significance do not accurately reflect the way that life in the homestead normally is, but rather the way that people want it to be; they represent an episodic realization of ideals. And this performance is not without its effects: the heightened experience of ritual ceremony creates lasting dispositions in its participants, as people internalize the ideals that they performatively reaffirm.[28]

It is not uncommon for diasporic communities to organize the politics of nostalgia around domestic contexts fetishized for their highly structured nature. The Kabyle house has become one of the most famous examples of this in the anthropological literature. While Bourdieu described the Kabyle house as the bearer of timeless, authentic tradition and the locus of primordial cosmology, Goodman and Silverstein 2009 shows that this representation properly belongs in the genre of memory ethnography. Bourdieu's informants had been displaced from their historical communities by the FLN—the revolutionary party that assumed power in Algeria after independence—as part of its project to civilize "backward" rural peasants. They construed their sense of dislocation by conveying to him an idealized representation—based on their memories—of the structure of the "authentic" house, which became the signifier of their culture and identity in their efforts to lobby the state for recognition. Paul Silverstein (2009) refers to this fetishization of past cultural order as "structural nostalgia," a term that nicely captures the idealized representations of the homestead that I encountered so frequently among Zulu migrants.

DIFFERENTIATION AS FRUITION

But we should be cautious about settling with the claim that migrants' representations of homestead culture are *only* representations. The trend in anthropological thought since the mid-1980s bends in this direction, encouraging skepticism about whether "cultures" really exist by suggesting that they are artifacts of colonial power, identity politics, and various techniques of ethnographic inscription. I accept this critique, but I also hold—following Daniel Rosenblatt (2003:2–3)—that our ability to comprehend the political aspirations of the people whose lives we study depends on our ability to describe the meaningful worlds that they inhabit, the historically particular patterns of values, dispositions, and symbolic schemes that comprise their "culture" in the Boasian sense. The deconstructive impulse should not deter us from taking seriously the substantive content of different ways of being human.

For migrant Zulus, the social order that characterizes the ideal rural homestead is not only the central construct around which they organize their identity; it also carries real implications for the way that they interact with and interpret the world. It may be primarily migrant men who emphasize the importance of social differentiation and hierarchy in the domestic context, but these principles also inform a moral system that is very widely shared—by women, wives, and minors as much as by male elders—and organizes the way that people normally think about and explain evil and misfortune.

As I have already described, an enormous amount of social energy is poured into the elaboration of taboos and avoidance in the domestic context. Myer Fortes (1940) and the descent theorists, along with the structural-functionalist tradition led by Radcliffe-Brown (1952), saw such interdicts in other African societies as the expression of already-existing distinctions of statuses, roles, and responsibilities in an already-differentiated universe of persons and genders. But in the case of rural Zululand, I would argue that precisely the opposite is true: that the interdicts *produce* differences, rather than simply reflect them. As T. O. Beidelman (1966) has pointed out, *hlonipha* means much more than the English term "respect" captures; it also suggests "separation" and "differentiation." As rituals of indexicality, forms of *hlonipha* such as valorized partitions of social space and grammaticalized honorifics produce the hierarchical differences to which they refer. To use Michael Silverstein's (1992, 2003) terms, what appears as a presupposition of ritualized interpersonal exchange is actually an entailment of it.

For rural Zulus, the ritual production of social difference along these lines is the most basic form of human intervention in the world. According to my informants, the basal state of human relatedness is one of innate sameness, where all kin relations and all kinds of relatives are basically alike, and persons lack the distinctions of male and female, senior and junior. From this raw material, it is man's (literally) responsibility to create difference and thus generate the conditions for fertile social reproduction. To apply an insight from Roy Wagner's seminal article on "analogic kinship," the responsibility to differentiate through proper modes of taboo and avoidance bears the aura of a moral duty, for "if these distinctions are not drawn, or drawn improperly, or if the wrong or inappropriate ones are made, then the flow of similarity will appear as a kind of contagion, a moral degeneracy spreading from one kinsman to another" (1977:624). The logic of kinship here follows an *actional* model, as opposed to Radcliffe-Brown's classificatory model: the units of relatedness are ritually produced rather than presupposed.

Herein lies the irreducible premise of social action in rural Zululand: that the production of hierarchical difference generates the conditions for fruition and social reproduction. This principle becomes clear in the architecture of the homestead: the cattle byre, the hearth, and the *umsamo*—the ritually sacred spaces most thickly associated with the ancestors, sacrifice, and fertility—lie at the nexus of nesting scales of difference. This premise is borne out by its opposite: that egalitarian sameness results in sterility. Indeed, for rural Zulus, the violation of the hierarchical separations that these taboos enforce is thought to invite misfortunes and calamities (*amashwa*) conceptualized as a failure of re/productive processes. For example, if premenopausal women enter the cattle byre, if children disrespect their fathers, if mothers abort their fetuses, and if men brew beer and women milk cows, then droughts descend, fields dry up, miscarriages occur, and livestock fail to reproduce. It would be a mistake, therefore, to see the elaborate system of *hlonipha* as restrictive. On the contrary, the taboos are productive—in both the Foucaultian sense *and* literally—for they bring into being and maintain the fundamental conceptual differences, essential for fruition, that organize the social world.

Rural Zulus produce and maintain difference not only through the system of *hlonipha,* but also through ritual performances associated with life cycles, marriage, and death. These rituals are not—as Fortes and Radcliffe-Brown would have it—intended to produce solidarity and cement social relations among individuals and between groups. Rather, they aim to do the opposite—to *differentiate* between types of persons and produce *distinctions* between groups, and thereby to achieve a kind of integrated wholeness or unity.[29]

One can see this at work through the sacrifice of cattle and the distribution of meat in ceremonies that take place each weekend in any given village all across Zululand. During sacrifice, the homestead head uses the family's ritual spear to pierce the cow's spinal cord at the base of the skull, initiating a process that dismantles the cow—the embodiment of the *umndeni* and a symbol of the social whole[30]—and carefully recomposes it in the form of human kinship. After the slaughter, the cow is dismembered and distributed to the members of the *umndeni*: the head (gendered male) goes to the senior male agnates, the hind legs and the right ribcage (gendered female) go to the wives, the left ribcage and the left foreleg (female) go the daughters, and so on for the more than sixty named pieces that constitute the cow, each of which is gendered and "belongs" to the person that occupies the node in the social structure to which it analogically refers. This process is known as *ukuhlukanisa*—literally, "to make different"—as it produces qualitatively different types of persons within a system of hierarchical encompassment. The act of disaggregating the beast unmakes the undifferentiated social whole in order to disambiguate its parts, bringing into being certain relational possibilities and the parameters for reproduction. Without differences between categories of persons and the boundaries between them, society—and relationship—becomes unthinkable. All of this proceeds from the point of a man's spear, whose "piercing" (*ukuhlaba*) initiates the work of producing difference and fertility in a manner regarded as analogous to sexual penetration—the act of procreation itself.

I saw this logic at work in many of the rites that I attended while living in rural Zululand, specifically those related to marriage—the quintessential act of social reproduction. Before marriage, every girl has to undergo a nubility rite known as *umemulo*;[31] if she does not, it is said that she will be beleaguered by misfortunes and have difficulty attracting a husband. I had the privilege of accompanying my host, Walter Cele, to a number of *umemulo* rites while visiting his family in Entenjani. Following a period of isolation, the final phase of the *umemulo* ceremony takes place in a clearing in the bush away from the homestead; the maiden and her age-mates gather to dance on the downslope side of the clearing, facing her father and his male agnates, who sit upslope across from them. As the dancing progresses, the maiden takes her father's ritual spear, crosses the clearing that separates her age-mates from her agnates, and ceremoniously pierces the ground in front of him before returning to her side of the clearing. In response, her father removes the spear from the ground and crosses the clearing to return it to his daughter, withdraws paper banknotes from his pocket and fastens them to her hair. The maiden repeats the piercing for each of her male agnates, each time eliciting a gift of cash (fig. 6).

The *umemulo* ritual accomplishes the cultural work of transforming a daughter into a nubile woman. As the necessary precursor to marriage, it

FIGURE 6. A young woman dancing at an *umemulo* ceremony near Eshowe in 2008. Around her chest she wears *umhlwehlwe*, the fatty membrane that covered the bowels of the cow that was sacrificed for the ceremony. The *umhlwehlwe* symbolizes fertility and new birth; indeed, people often liken it to a caul, the membrane that covers some infants at parturition. Photo by author.

produces the possibility of exchange between two (male) agnatic units: wife-givers and wife-takers. Given their gendered sameness, agnatic units cannot reproduce with each other. *Umemulo* ritually extracts the daughter from her agnatic unit in preparation for her exchange for cattle in marriage. In other words, it differentiates the exchangeable female element from a male agnatic unit in order to create the possibility of fertile transaction with another male agnatic unit. Once again, the process of differentiation is represented as piercing. With the ritual spear, the maiden wields the power of differentiation, symbolically splitting the earth between herself and her father/agnates. This act of differentiation is followed by the symbolic bestowal of fertility as her father adorns her with money—an exchange homologous to the generalized transaction through which the ancestors bestow fruition on their descendants (at least, as we shall see in later chapters, those that observe the proper modes of social differentiation).

The wedding ceremony itself (*udwendwe*) enacts a similar process of differentiation and fertile recombination. During some weddings that I observed, the bride's family and the groom's family each slaughter a cow at their respective homesteads. The act of cutting is initiated by the bride, who makes the first medial incision down the underside of her father's sacrificial cow. The left/female "side" of the bride's cow is then exchanged for the left/female "side" of the groom's cow. This process symbolically differentiates two otherwise infertile unities (the agnatic clusters) in order to recombine them into a reproductive relationship that will yield legitimate children. Differentiation, once again, is essential to generating the conditions for fruition. Despite these ceremonies, however, even a married woman remains a liminal part of her natal agnatic unit for most of her life. She retains her father's name and is never fully incorporated into the *umndeni* of her affines until she has passed through menopause. The idea here—as I understand it—is that her fertility as a wife hinges on her differentiation from both her affines *and* her agnates. After she passes through menopause, and her fertility is no longer at stake, this difference ceases to matter, and she can be subsumed into her husband's family with full rights of access to sacred spaces in his homestead—even those that are normally reserved for males, such as the cattle byre.[32]

THE ETIOLOGY OF MISFORTUNE

These ideas about social differentiation and fruition play an important role in people's theories about what causes misfortune. The etiology of misfortune has long been a central theme in Africanist anthropology; many scholars have pointed out how people seek to understand the mystical causes—and ultimately the human agency—behind events that we might be inclined to dismiss as natural or accidental (e.g. Evans-Pritchard 1937; Hammond-Tooke 1970). Often this leads people to explain misfortunes as the result of witchcraft. This is often true in rural Zululand as well, but while living in the region I discovered that misfortunes are much more commonly explained as a consequence of the violation of kinship order and *hlonipha* rules. People say that such infractions displease their ancestors, and the ancestors display their anger by allowing misfortunes (*amashwa*)[33] to come upon them.

To understand how this works, we have to accept a basic metaphysical principle that people commonly uphold, namely, that the state of nature is characterized by chaos and misfortune. The good—cast in the idiom of "fertility" broadly conceived—must be *achieved* through the proper performance of ritual. When correct ritual protocol is observed and the social order is intact, the ancestors are pleased and protect their descendants from the "natural" chaos of the surrounding world; otherwise they "turn their backs" and punish their descendants by allowing them to be afflicted by painful misfortunes that will compel them to redress their wrongs. Instances of misfortune appear as glitches in productive and reproductive processes, manifesting as crop failure, drought, infertility, miscarriage, poverty, illness, joblessness, and even death. Misfortunes like these are generally believed to be diagnostic of violations of *umthetho,* such as breaches of respect or ritual oversights. Sometimes misfortunes are considered to be symptoms of witchcraft, but people construe vulnerability to witchcraft in the first place as punishment at the hands of ancestors angered by some violation of *umthetho.*

In Zululand, an entire industry of traditional healing and popular medicine operates within this framework. In 2009, my research assistant Jabulani Buthelezi and I collected narratives of misfortune from male migrants from rural Zululand staying in Mzimhlope hostel near Johannesburg. In each case we recorded the person's complaint followed by the etiology identified by the diviner (*isangoma*) that the person consulted. Of the seventy-nine case histories that we collected at the hostel, 81 percent featured misfortunes and afflictions that were caused—according to the diviners—by violations of normative homestead order and its rules of respect. For instance, most of the men who complained that they had lost their jobs or could not find work (the misfortune that migrants, unsurprisingly, cite most frequently) attributed their afflictions to moral violations related to kinship and gender. In some cases, patients learned that their fathers had not paid sufficient bridewealth to their mothers' families; in others, that their mothers or sisters-in-law had violated norms of respect by moving out of the homestead and pursuing extramarital relationships in town; in still others, patients had failed to perform the proper funerary ceremonies for their deceased relatives or neglected the nubility rites for their daughters; and among the most common causes was migrants' failures to link their productive pursuits in town back to their ancestors and their rural homesteads through remittances, the announcement of cash earnings at the homestead shrine, and the purchase of livestock.

In each case, the remedy prescribed by the diviner, who was almost always a woman, included an injunction to return home to rectify these oversights and reestablish the conditions for successful re/productive processes by, say, paying bridewealth debts, performing neglected rituals, and retrieving "lost" relatives.[34] Diviners act as family counselors, using clues provided by their patients to point to where their domestic orders—and the rituals that produce them—are out of line with "normative"[35] expectations of kinship and home. They operate as the protectors of families within a migrancy system that fragments kinship, deploying a therapeutic discourse in which the ancestors exert a sort of centripetal force, coaxing their descendants to return home.

These beliefs about healing illuminate conceptions of the person in rural Zulu society. Therapy seeks to cure the afflictions of individual persons with interventions directed at the social order. This is because, once again, the person is not conceived of as an individual as such. Unlike the liberal individual, who is presumed to be ontologically autonomous, discrete, and prior to society, the person here is considered to be emergent at the nexus of his or her social relationships. To borrow the words of Charles Piot, "we should see the person as composed of, or constituted by, relationships, rather than as situated in them. Persons do not 'have' relations; they 'are' relations" (1999:18). In short, the self is a relational construct, composed of and penetrated by external entities and constituted through the social order. Indeed, following the logic of encompassment and the anthropomorphic analogies between bodies and houses that I described above, the person can only be conceived as ontologically coextensive with kinship and homestead hierarchy. Given these analogues, any disruptions of relationships register in the bodies of individual persons and affect their physical well-being.[36] This is why people can unproblematically conclude that the neglect of a girl's nubility rites, for example, is the reason that her brother cannot find a job.

MORE THAN BELIEF

I pointed out in chapter 1 that most existing explanations of rural migrants' anti-liberal stance see them as driven by an interest in preserving their power as patriarchs and their control over the labor power of wives and other dependents. My observations suggest that perhaps a different model of interest is at play—one geared less toward an individual or class-based will to power and more toward the imperative to maintain the conditions for social reproduction and collective well-being. In the context of rural Zululand, persons are not the autonomous, contesting individuals that social scientific theory would have us believe them to be. Their interests can never be considered apart from the community of relationships in which they have their being, or from the people and houses that bear the effects of their actions. We have to understand that for many people who inhabit this cultural milieu, even the individual body is not experienced as clearly bounded—it is also continuous with the bodies of those who in liberal ideology would be considered "others" (cf. Bloch 1992:75).

Once again, none of this is to say that domestic life plays out according to a structuralist dream of rules and codes without difficulty or error. As suggested above, homesteads are shot through with tensions and divisions: people regularly quarrel over inheritance, land, seniority, paternity, and bridewealth. A quick look through the records of customary law cases is enough to illustrate how messy and contested family life can be.[37] The representation of the homestead that dominates the moral imagination of migrant workers is an ideal that comes from a dual process of invention: from the strategies of indirect rule through the Natal Code, and through the structural nostalgia generated by the migrant labor system. But the homestead, its hierarchies, and the moral order associated with it do not only operate at the level of representation. They are "more than belief," to borrow a phrase from Manuel Vásquez (2011); they also form a powerful social fact that, among other things, furnishes the logic for a theory of misfortune—and political action—that is widespread and resilient. In this sense, homestead culture is real. This is a crucial analytical point, not simply a relativist position. Without it we are liable to misinterpret the things that migrants say and do and find ourselves unable to explain what motivates their continued resistance to the principles of liberal democracy.

3

Urban Social Engineering and Revolutionary Consciousness

The township was the metaphorical home in whose living room the post-apartheid imaginary was largely conceived by a revolutionary movement that never really moved out of its urban base.

—Jacob Dlamini, *Native Nostalgia*

Popular resistance to colonial rule in South Africa had a varied geography. Much of it was mobilized in rural areas, as in the Bambatha Rebellion of 1906, the Sekhukhuneland Revolt of 1958, and the Pondo Revolt of the 1960s.[1] But the mass movement that finally brought the apartheid government to its knees in the 1980s and 1990s was based largely—indeed, almost exclusively—in the country's urban townships. What accounts for this particular geography of struggle? If IsiZulu-speaking Africans in Natal's rural areas were so resistant to the values of the National Democratic Revolution, why were their urban counterparts, who identified as part of the same ethnic group, so receptive to them? Unfortunately, the existing scholarship on the history of revolutionary consciousness in South Africa does not go very far toward helping us answer these questions. Scholars focus primarily on understanding where liberal and Marxist ideas came from in the first place. Some point to the influence of missionaries, unionists, and Garveyists during the twentieth century (e.g., Walshe 1971). Others point to the ready availability of Western discourses of universal human rights during and after World War II (e.g., Cooper 1996). While these accounts deal incisively with the role of global ideological flows in the making of the South African revolution, they tend to ignore a prior question. Ideas about liberal democracy, egalitarian rights, and class identity, we can hypothesize, will not take root just anywhere, as if human beings were universally predisposed to embracing them and recognizing their superiority over other ontologies; indeed, they are often vehemently resisted, as in the case of the Inkatha counterrevolution. What made it possible, then, for this particular ideological mode to gain mass traction in South Africa's townships? Why did these principles make sense in that context?

In this chapter I argue that the ideology of National Democratic Revolution managed to find traction in South African townships because of the specific forms of social organization that characterized township society. Focusing specifically on the province of Natal, I demonstrate that these forms were largely the product of violent exercises in social engineering through modernist urban planning deployed after the first decades of the twentieth century. As a tactic of control, this marked a decisive shift from earlier strategies used by colonial administrators, who initially sought to preclude urbanization in favor of governing Africans by proxy through patriarchal power in rural homesteads. When urbanization proceeded nonetheless in response to industrial demand for labor, colonial administrators worried that "detribalization" and the breakdown of the "traditional" African family would engender social indiscipline and political agitation. For them, the figure of the urban African upset categorical distinctions between traditional and modern and embodied the sort of dangerous anomaly that Mary Douglas (1966) has called "matter out of place." Administrators sought to reassert control over the urban African population by relocating it to planned, modernist townships, and by remaking the African family according to European expectations of domesticity. This was an extremely violent project, not unlike the villagization schemes of Maoist China or Julius Nyerere's Ujamaa campaign in Tanzania.

I trace this shift in colonial policy from indirect rule through rural homesteads in the nineteenth century to social engineering through urban townships in the twentieth century, highlighting the transformations of domestic social form that this entailed. I show that while township planners intended their communities to function as citadels of domestic docility (in the mold of America's Levittown), they ended up becoming hotbeds for political activism—precisely the outcome that the project was designed to forestall. The new social forms that characterized late twentieth century African urbanism engendered new types of subjectivity, fostered new kinds of political expectations, and facilitated the rise of the revolutionary movement led by the African National Congress. The logic of revolution, in short, was an accidental by-product of the colonial state's most draconian technologies of control.

This history of urban housing helps us understand the rise of the National Democratic Revolution in Natal. But it also helps us understand how rural migrants have come to imagine such a rigid opposition between township and homestead—an opposition that emphasizes the physical structure of the houses and the kinship structure of the families that inhabit them—despite the cultural exchanges that have long linked the two spaces.

DOMESTIC ORDER AND THE CIVILIZING MISSION

Change life! Change Society! These ideas lose completely their meaning without producing an appropriate space. New social relations demand a new space, and vice-versa.

—Henri Lefebvre, *The Production of Space*

People commonly believe that European colonialism in Africa was organized around a "civilizing mission" intended to make "traditional" Africans more like "modern" Europeans. But—as I demonstrated in the previous chapter—this does not exactly hold in the case of South Africa. For most of the colonial period, administrators regarded the idea of a civilizing mission with suspicion, fearing that "detribalization" would lead to social anomie, mass unrest, and the rise of a politically conscious class that would eventually undermine minority rule altogether. The Native Affairs Department sought to foreclose this possibility by propping up "tradition" through indirect rule in rural areas. The idea was to prevent urbanization by keeping Africans confined to native reserves, and to govern them according to a codified form of customary law through existing patriarchs and chiefs. Then, using an intricate network of influx controls, Africans were brought temporarily to the cities for work on fixed-term contracts, at the end of which they were expelled back to the reserves. The system was purposefully designed to prevent full proletarianization and forestall the rise of radical consciousness (Wolpe 1972).

European missionaries formed the one notable exception to this rule. For them, "tradition" was exactly the problem, and they sought ultimately to eradicate it in the process of transforming Africans into civilized Christians. Toward this end, they focused specifically on changing Africans' domestic structure and on remaking the rural African family in the mold of the bourgeois European model (Cock 1980; Gaitskell 1983; Hansen 1989; Hunt 1990; Hansen 1992, Burke 1996; Comaroff and Comaroff 1997). If colonial administrators treated the homestead as the locus of indirect rule, missionaries saw it as a signifier of heathen backwardness; it became the central site of their attempts to redeem Africans. From the early nineteenth century, missionaries promoted a form of familial life centered on the nuclear-family home in which wives were ideally to engage in unpaid labor and child-rearing while their husbands worked for wages.[2] This particular construction of domesticity first emerged in seventeenth-century Europe when the public, feudal household was replaced by the private, family home as industrial capitalism restructured society, separating productive from reproductive spaces, waged from unwaged work, male from female labor, and public from domestic zones (Carrier 1992; also see Rybczynski 1986; Davidoff and Hall 1987; Hall 1985; Morgan 1985; Hansen 1981; Darrow 1979; Oakly 1974). These societal characteristics gained the status of a moral order, which missionaries sought to recreate in Africa.

Models of European domesticity were not simply imported from the metropole to the colonies; they were in large part formed in the colonies themselves, as Europeans forged their civilized moral identities in contrast to the uncivilized others—the inhabitants of the "dark continent"—with whom they were engaged (Comaroff and Comaroff 1992). The trope of the savage was constructed with reference to prevailing patterns of African domestic life, so the homestead form and its attendant structure of social relationships became the focus of missionaries' moralizing attention. To the missionary eye, the homestead was a portrait of immorality, filth, and disorder, comprising a mix of persons not properly bounded from one another, lacking private property and enclosed plots of land, and enmeshed in dense kinship networks built on polygynous marriage. Perhaps most striking to the missionaries, African homesteads lacked the appropriate public/private distinctions and gendered divisions of labor that characterized middle-class British homes of the time. The missionaries' ideal notion of the Christian home thus crystallized their assumptions about social order and morality in the same way that the homestead structure embodied for its inhabitants the basic logic of society and the cosmos. The house became a major site of contest in the colonial encounter between Africa and Europe, generating what Comaroff and Comaroff have called "the dialectic of domesticity" (1992:273)—a moral battle waged over the structure of the home.

Because the colonial system of indirect rule that sought to keep Africans confined to rural areas was not watertight, it could not prevent the eventual emergence of an African population living in informal settlements on the outskirts of white cities in the early twentieth century, drawn by colonists' insatiable appetite for cheap labor. It was in response to this unauthorized urbanization that colonial administrators first began to adopt a moralizing approach to African domesticity similar in many ways to that of their missionary counterparts, although the object of their concern was the urban slum rather than the rural homestead. One reason for this is that African shacks and shanties presented the state with a serious problem of legibility, to use James Scott's (1998) term, which made them difficult to manage and control. In addition, however, and perhaps even more significantly, African slums appeared to Europeans as something of a social-evolutionary misfire. In South Africa, as across the colonial world, African urbanization was viewed as disorderly and dangerous, as much by colonizers as by the social scientists of the time. "Detribalized" Africans were considered liminal; as James Ferguson has put it, "urban natives . . . confused and confounded the orderly divisions between traditional and modern, native and Western, and rural and urban" (2007:73).

Reflecting on his visit to the region, Karl Polanyi represented "detribalized" South Africans in the most pathological terms. He wrote: "The Kaffir of South Africa, a noble savage, than whom none felt socially more secure in his native kraal, has been transformed into a human variety of half-domesticated animal dressed in the 'unrelated, the filthy, the unsightly rags that not the most degenerated white man would wear,' a nondescript being, without self-respect or standards, veritable human refuse" (cited in Ferguson 2007). Similarly, after visiting South Africa in the 1930s, Bronislaw Malinowski decried "detribalized" natives as "sociologically unsound" monstrosities who had lost the regulated order of "tribal" society but—given their lack of access to the necessary material resources—had failed to approximate the structure of "European" society (Malinowski 1945:159, cited in Ferguson 2007). In these accounts, the very existence of urban black South Africans seems to threaten the basic categories that underpinned both colonialism and social scientific theory, which drew structuralist distinctions between rural/tribal/African and urban/modern/European that mapped onto the Durkheimian bifurcation between mechanical and organic solidarity.

These concerns hinged on ideas about the family. The "tribal family" was imagined as a domain of extended kinship, clan solidarity, polygyny, and hierarchy, while the "modern family" was imagined as a domain of nuclear kinship, autonomous individuals, monogamy, and egalitarianism (albeit with its own version of husband-wife hierarchy built in)—precisely the evolutionary schema posited by early social scientists like Maine (1861), Morgan (1877), and Engels (1884) along the trajectory from savagery to civilization.

Given their out-of-category status, urban Africans were considered to be dangerous and threateningly powerful (cf. Douglas 1966). The colonial administration deployed professional urban planners to defuse this danger by ritually reordering the African social milieu through forced relocations into modernist townships laid out along rectilinear grids. They tended to approach the project from a welfare point of view, intent on creating hygienic communities that would facilitate peace, health, and happiness among urban Africans who would internalize the values of European domesticity. Drawing on evolutionary social-scientific theories popular at the time, planners determined that the simple nuclear family located in a detached single family home would best facilitate the development of Africans into happy, docile subjects. Toward this end, houses were allocated according to strict codes that dictated—and monitored—what types of people and what forms of families would be allowed to inhabit the new townships.

THE INFORMAL SETTLEMENT: THE BIRTH OF THE AFRICAN COUNTERPUBLIC

The migration of Africans into the Durban area began in the middle of the nineteenth century and intensified following the British destruction of the Zulu Kingdom in 1879—a military feat that was intended to force people away from their subsistence lifestyles and into the rapidly expanding labor market (Greaves 2005; Guy 1994). Many Africans who had immigrated to the city for work lived in "interstitial" spaces such as workplace storerooms or in their employers' backyards, while others constructed "makeshift" housing in small shack settlements. By 1900 as many as twenty thousand Africans lived in the broader Durban area, where their presence had become such a concern to white residents that the municipality began to monitor African access to the city for the first time (La Hausse 1997). Three years later, the city began to construct the first of a series of single-sex municipal hostels to house African workers near their places of employment (Maasdorp and Humphries 1975:11).[3]

But these housing projects were small-scale and piecemeal; the majority of migrants to the city continued to live scattered about in various informal settlements on the periphery, undocumented and illegible to the state. The influx of Africans increased after the crushing of the Bambatha Rebellion in 1906 and the further imposition of taxes on Natal Africans, so that by 1921 the African population in the Durban area numbered as many as forty-six thousand (Burrows 1959:24–25). Those unable to secure formal housing ended up overflowing into informal shack settlements, the largest and most famous of which became Cato Manor—known by its residents as Umkhumbane—which sprawled across the valley immediately west of Durban's commercial center. At its apex in the 1950s, over a hundred thousand Africans lived in Umkhumbane, and it had become one of the continent's best-known urban African settlements.

Communities like Umkhumbane that grew on the outskirts of Durban throughout the first few decades of the twentieth century constituted an indigenous African urbanism. Architectural records show that the state did not interfere in spatial organization or social structure—rather, spatial patterns and corresponding forms of sociality developed according to a vernacular geography, through everyday accretions that ignored modernist conventions of domaining residential, commercial, and civic zones in separate areas and allowed people to work, trade, and recreate through and among their homes.[4] Outside the purview of state power during their formative years, these communities provided a haven for thousands of men and women not legally entitled to live in Durban proper.[5] Dozens of self-employed artisans, mechanics, brewers, builders, and painters congregated in these precincts, where they could freely pursue independent livelihoods that the state precluded them from practicing elsewhere.[6]

These dense urban African communities differed quite dramatically from Natal's rural societies. In the informal settlements, outside the purview of the chiefs and the Natal Code of Native Law, hierarchies were not so rigorously policed. For one thing, the population was comprised largely of so-called stray individuals—including widows, runaways, and other independent women—who could not legally live in town but no longer had rural homesteads to which they could return. Many of these people (and a majority, after the 1930s) considered themselves dissociated from their rural families and regarded the city as their permanent home (Hellmann 1935). Given this fragmentation of kinship and owing to restrictions on space, households in urban areas began to depart from the normative structure of rural homesteads. Lacking both livestock and cash, many people in Umkhumbane could not afford to pay for bridewealth (*ilobolo*)—as many as half of all couples cohabited unmarried. In addition, architectural records indicate that residents of the informal settlements developed a new, more egalitarian organization of domestic space that, while often gesturing toward concentricity, partially subverted the gendered and generational oppositions that underwrote hierarchy in the homestead.[7] Furthermore, as Africans were prevented from owning land by the Natives' Land Act of 1913, informal settlements like Umkhumbane were characterized by a contract-based system in which Africans rented plots from Indian landowners whose authority they deeply resented—quite unlike in rural homesteads, where residents were ontologically encompassed by patriarchal authorities who allocated land in trust. In the informal settlements, people who occupied multiroom shacks were often renters unrelated to the head of the household. Household structure hinged less on agnatic kinship than on contractual relationships, creating the conditions for people to behave primarily as individuals—as the ontological equals of the people in authority over them.

The new egalitarian sociality that developed in Umkhumbane was reflected in its robust market economy, the most distinctive characteristic of which was the trade in traditional sorghum beer (*utshwala*).[8] While the state held a monopoly over the production and sale of beer in the city, the informal settlements sustained a flourishing trade geared toward workers who would frequent local "shebeens," or taverns, during weekends. In contrast to the rural areas, where it was consumed as a gift during ritual rites and only according to strict codes of segregation by gender and status, beer in the informal settlements became a true commodity, consumed in exchange for cash. Thus severed from its ritual moorings and the authority of agnatic elders, the beer-drink gradually became an inclusive, egalitarian public event. Umkhumbane in particular became known for its shebeens, which functioned as places of public sociality somewhat analogous to the coffee houses and salons of eighteenth and early nineteenth century Europe. Paralleling the developments that Jürgen Habermas (1998) has outlined in the latter context, the departure from homestead forms of hierarchy led to a tradition of critical egalitarian discussion akin to what Nancy Fraser (1990) identifies as the "subaltern counterpublic." As new discursive arenas where political matters could be freely debated, shebeens fostered a robust oppositional culture by democratizing the "domain of common concern" (La Hausse 1988, 1997). This emergent public sphere[9] replaced a system in which patriarchal authorities represented their subjects by encompassment with one where authority (the contractual authority of the state, landlords, and employers) was publicly monitored through critical discourse by the people. This new tradition of African democratic egalitarianism—first developed in the crucible of the informal settlements[10]—became a central plank in the platform of the early ANC (Kuper 1965; Walshe 1971).

The social changes that took place in Umkhumbane had significant implications for women, whose being was no longer strictly constituted within homestead-based systems of hierarchical encompassment, and who thus exercised increasing degrees of independence. The market in sorghum beer was structured by the persistence of a particular Zulu cultural rule, namely, that only women could brew beer. This meant that women controlled the beer trade and through it garnered incomes they could use at their own discretion. Owing to this new commercial autonomy—and given that women typically operated shebeens out of their homes—the rise of the so-called shebeen queen indicated the emergence of a public sphere that began to include women for the first time. Drawing on these new egalitarian possibilities, women were at the forefront of resistance against the Durban municipality when it tried to ban the beer trade through the 1928 Liquor Act. The popular mobilization that they galvanized, which reflected elements of feminist discourse (Bradford 1987), furnished the momentum behind political organizations such as the Industrial and Commercial Union and the Communist Party, provided the bedrock for the early ANC, and spawned a rich tradition of urban political activism that registered the informal settlements as hotbeds of terrorism in the minds of colonial authorities (see Walker 1991; Wells 1993).

In June 1959, thousands of Umkhumbane women, armed with pick handles and sticks, sabotaged Durban's municipal beer halls in protest against the city's alcohol monopoly, the police raids on the beer trade, and forced removal of unmarried women to rural homelands. Women saw the removals as an attempt to eradicate the egalitarian public sphere that allowed them to command their livelihoods. This resistance mounted to the point where, on the evening of January 23, 1960, a police party raiding for illicit liquor in Umkhumbane was ambushed by an angry crowd that killed nine state agents. The backlash sparked a wave of wider resistance and led two months later to an anti-pass law demonstration in Sharpeville. The police clamped down on the march, massacred fifty-seven African demonstrators, imposed a state of emergency, and banned all political organizations. The state then proceeded to raze Umkhumbane to the ground and initiated a nationwide program of forced removals in order to eliminate the social unrest and political activism that informal settlements fostered.

THE PLANNED TOWNSHIP: UTOPIAN MODERNISM AND SOCIAL CONTROL

[Modernist planning] works space on the principle of elementary location or partitioning. Each individual has his own place; and each place its individual. Avoid distributions in groups; break up collective dispositions; analyze confused, massive, or transient pluralities. Disciplinary space tends to be divided into as many sections as there are bodies or elements to be distributed. One must eliminate the effects of imprecise distributions, the uncontrolled disappearance of individuals, their diffuse circulation, their unusable and dangerous coagulation; it was a tactic of anti-desertion, anti-vagabondage, anti-concentration. Its aim was to establish presences and absences, to know where and how to locate individuals, to set up useful communications, to interrupt others, to be able at each moment to supervise the conduct of each individual, to asses it, to judge it, to calculate its qualities or merits. It was a procedure, therefore, aimed at knowing, mastering and using. Discipline organizes an analytical space.

—Michel Foucault, *Discipline and Punish*

As informal settlements grew during the first decades of the twentieth century, colonial administrators worried that urbanization was producing Africans who were unhinged from the control of rural chiefs and patriarchs and existed outside the strictures of indirect rule, no longer bound to their so-called tribal values.[11] For example, James Mathewson (1957), one of the apartheid state's most influential social engineers, believed that the deterioration of the patriarchal family and the decline of marriage rates demonstrated that urban Africans were falling away from "traditional" social forms. Mathewson's writings demonstrate that some white South Africans saw detribalization as a process of decay, as the decomposition of tribal social order into a chaotic tangle of random persons and unmarried women. This discourse about liminality and chaos was further reflected in representations of the slums themselves, which were regarded as makeshift and transient, in between the traditional African homestead and the modern European house.

As structuralist analysis would predict, these concerns about social disorder registered as anxieties about "danger" and "pollution" (cf. Douglas 1966) in the minds of Europeans. For instance, Robert Watson, the patron behind the well-known relocation scheme in Tongaat just north of Durban, wrote at great length about his perceptions of the people living in Natal's slums, who he regarded as "incurably filthy, diseased, and corrupt, a permanent menace to health and chronic disrupters of the peace" (1960:14). The crucial thing to highlight here is that policymakers perceived a direct correlation between domestic conditions and moral dispositions. For Watson, the slums themselves—as an architectural form—were "the source of all evil" and bred criminal behavior (1960:14). As another contemporary commentator put it: "disreputable homes have a direct and traceable effect in creating disreputable people . . . slum yards are breweries, selling foul liquor. They are dens of immorality, filled with loose women" (Phillips 1930:11). Administrators believed that "broken families" and kinship disorder would inevitably lead to anarchy, immorality, sexual deviance, disease, and—their greatest fear—violent political agitation, for violence was considered to be a product of spatial and social disorder (cf. Weber 1946).

An epidemic outbreak of the so-called Spanish Flu in informal settlements along the outskirts of Durban in 1918 provided the justification that authorities needed to take action. Administrators passed the Public Health Act that very year,[12] which allowed for intervention in urban African communities on the basis of public health concerns (Robinson 1992:292). This was followed by a spate of legislation intended to control the rural-urban migration of Africans. The Housing Act of 1920 and the Natives (Urban Areas) Act of 1923 provided for the establishment of African townships and required that Africans entering urban areas report immediately to registration officers to be assigned accommodation in either official hostels or a series of planned "native villages." Giving teeth to this project, the Slums Act that was passed in 1934 provided legal backing for the destruction of slums and the forced relocation of their African inhabitants.

Recognizing that urban Africans—who were needed as labor—could not be "retribalized," and fearing that social anomie would give rise to political unrest, the state undertook to forcibly relocate slum residents into segregated planned townships, where they could be "civilized" for the purposes of control. This was a reluctant colonialism—an unwilling embrace of the civilizing mission—and a considerably more expensive backup plan devised to deal with the leakages of indirect rule. It was the state's perception of urban Africans as "in-between" and "polluted" that propelled this new modernizing project. Like the missionaries before them, the architects of public housing sought to reorder the African social milieu, using forced relocations to restructure African families. Drawing on evolutionary social-scientific theories common at the time, planners believed that placing nuclear families in detached single-family homes would render Africans safe, docile, and productive. The idea, in short, was to domesticate urban Africans—particularly women, who had been at the core of the activist movement in Umkhumbane—by shaping them in the mold of mid-century European domesticity.[13]

The first planned townships were successfully constructed the same year that the Slums Act was passed, and housed many of the residents who had been forcibly displaced under this legislation. Baumannville, built in 1934, was followed by a much larger Lamontville, and then by an even larger Chesterville in 1945. But these were still relatively small-scale efforts, and could never keep pace with the rush of urbanization. During the Second World War, industrial employment boomed and Durban's African population leaped from 71,000 in 1936 to an astonishing 162,000 in 1951 (Maasdorp and Humphries 1975:9). Existing municipal housing could only accommodate a mere 11,000 of these, leaving a massive backlog that caused significant fear among white South Africans.

The National Party rose to power in 1948 with these concerns in mind, on a platform that promised to reassert control over urban Africans by focusing specifically on "native housing." Hendrik Verwoerd—minister of Native Affairs at the time—dedicated himself to ramping up slum clearances and developing new African housing projects.[14] The basic assumption behind this program was that the rational ordering of persons in rationally ordered domestic spaces would eliminate violence and engender docility. Not surprisingly, given its high profile, Umkhumbane became the target of the Natal government's first exercise in large-scale relocation and social engineering through black housing. In the 1950s, purportedly responding to increasing political upheaval and infectious epidemics in the slum, the state destroyed the informal settlement and relocated its residents to the massive, planned township of KwaMashu, north of Durban.[15] The project was completed in 1965, at which point around 83,000 people had been moved (Soni 1992:40).[16]

Township planners sought to reconcile two competing ideas: on the one hand, a fear that that "detribalization" of Africans would engender immense social dislocation and upheaval, and, on the other hand, a belief that "civilizing" Africans into an established set of European social norms would facilitate docility. Again, the driving theoretical framework held that residential environments had a direct influence on the mental and social disposition of their inhabitants, prefiguring Bourdieu's (1977) theory of practice. Indeed, most of the planners supported what at the time was the relatively progressive view that differences between racial groups were less "natural" than they were merely the product of environmental conditions. As P.H. Connel, one of South Africa's foremost urban planners, put it in his 1939 policy document: "We are dealing with a primitive and backwards people [whose] mental makeup is relatively easily changed, for better or worse, simply by altering their [lived] environment" (1939:50). In other words, planners believed that civilizing the built environment was the most effective way to civilize its inhabitants.

Connel's writings provide interesting insight into the philosophy of social engineering that was popular at the time. Assembling input from a team of psychologists and social scientists, Connel sought to resolve the tension between detribalization and civilization by housing Africans in blocks of flats, with a single nuclear family per unit. On the one hand, they thought the flats would help avoid too much individualism by maintaining the "communal" ethos that Africans were accustomed to in rural areas:

> Because of his natural communal tendencies it would be advisable to house the native in such a way as to enable him to live in close cooperation with his fellows . . . It is in the thrusting of the Native from a highly-organized life into the turmoil of self-sufficiency and independence (which is the keynote of city life) that we find one of the greatest psychological menaces. The [block flats] scheme . . . must stimulate a revival of that community spirit existing in the kraal, but destroyed or lost in the city. [Connel et al. 1939:82, 97]

On the other hand, however, the team hoped that the block flat system would break up the traditional patriarchal family and replace it with something more "modern, individualistic, liberal, and democratic." If the flat system *emerged* from a society bearing this structure, Connel reasoned, then certainly imposing the system on a different society could *engender* the same. In the flat system of the modern family, Connel claimed, "the individual has his own friends and activities, and is given a chance to develop his own individuality. There is not so much parental control and there is a greater amount of mutual regard and respect based on real merits" (1939:79–80).[17] Connel's overriding goal, then, was to protect urban Africans from abrupt detribalization while gradually encouraging them to internalize modern liberal values: "The social education of the Bantu should . . . aim at freeing the mass of natives from their reactionary conceptions, animisms, and witchcraft" (1939:67).[18]

A decade later, another influential planner, A. J. Cutten, worked hard to promote a quite different model of native housing, namely, a township made up of free-standing nuclear-family houses. Cutten thought that such houses would be more effective at engendering social stability than the block flats. While drawing on the spatial logic used by planners in nineteenth-century Britain, he—like Connel—sought to reproduce aspects of "native society" for the purposes of enhancing social control. He arranged the sections of the township around a central point where communal facilities would be located, such as schools, recreational facilities, and administrative buildings, to provide "an admirable basis not only for planning but also for guiding and controlling the lives of the individuals in the township." The idea was to facilitate surveillance by authorities but also to replicate the concentric structure of domestic space in rural areas. Each block would be centered around communal and social buildings: "radiating their influence around them, they become pivots on which the lives of the surrounding residents may be hinged, and by this means is reborn in the African the sense of social union that previously existed only in his native kraal" (1951:87). Drawing on a romantic conception of the Noble Savage, Cutten assumed that the values of tribal life were intrinsically stable and peaceful, and should be integrated with European mechanisms of panoptic administration as a bastion against urban unrest and immorality.

Adding to the work of planners like Connel and Cutten, D. M. Calderwood argued that the creation of stable township families was important for maintaining worker productivity and a steady labor supply. "Among Natives," he argued, "the lowest incidence of absenteeism is found in men who live with their wives and families in town, whereas the highest occurs in married men living away from their rural homes in migrant laborers' hostels" (1955:11). But even more important, Calderwood thought that proper township housing was critical for the creation of what he called "moral" persons and "responsible" citizens. He is worth quoting at length on this:

> Overcrowded slum areas cannot produce responsible persons; it is through good family living that responsible persons will grow. [Otherwise] the children will, as they grow older, run away to become vagrants, prostitutes, criminals or shebeen kings or queens through lack of employment or parental control. . . . The road to crime is being built upon a foundation of bad housing and broken family life. . . . If the children are given the chance of a full life now, then tomorrow they will accept their responsibilities and become contented and well-behaved inhabitants of the urban areas. . . . In respect of home ownership it must be immediately appreciated how desirable this is in fostering pride and responsibility in the inhabitants. [1955:12]

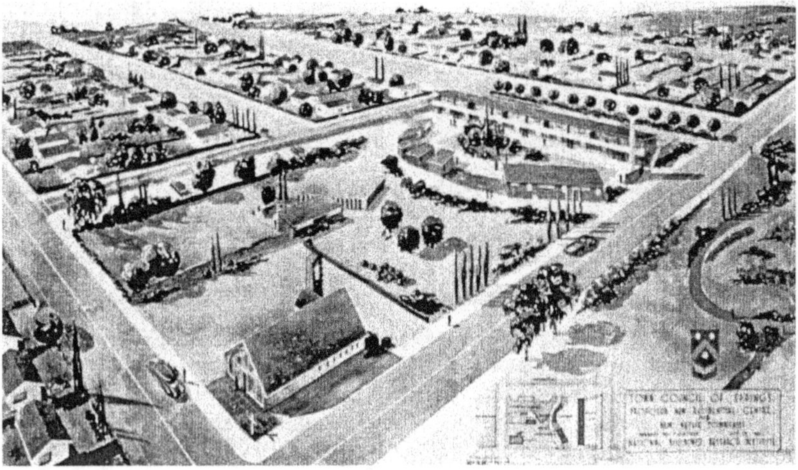

FIGURE 7. Artist's impression of KwaThema township (Calderwood 1953:94). In reality townships never came close to approximating this utopia.

Calderwood's emphasis on home ownership—like most influential planners before him—was supported by the National Housing Planning Commission circular of 1951, which argued: "home ownership is a stabilizing influence and one of the main bastions against Communism and other social ills" (1951:14). Still, the ownership ideal was not implemented in most areas until the 1980s, because it conflicted with the ideal of racial segregation.

As with many of the other social scientists and urban planners who helped design the townships, Connel, Cutten, and Calderwood were not nearly as draconian as the apartheid ideologues who employed them. Indeed, they considered themselves benevolent liberals who sought to foster welfare through decent public housing and wanted to bring Africans up to speed with European modernity. Pitting themselves against the hyper rationalism of apartheid bureaucracy and the alienating austerity of existing centralized planning efforts, they drew up models patterned after the "garden city" (see fig. 7) promoted by Ebenezer Howard in Britain and Le Corbusier in France (Evans 1997:127). Of course, the townships never actually turned out like this; in most of them one would have been lucky to find even a single tree.

There were, however, some apartheid administrators who appreciated this liberal discourse. Sighart Bourquin, director of the Department of Bantu Administration and the official in charge of the forced removals from Umkhumbane to KwaMashu, drew heavily on these ideas.[19] In line with his missionary background, he conceived of the relocations as an act of salvation, replacing the disease, disorder, and lawlessness of Umkhumbane with the beauty, cleanliness, rationality, and civic pride of KwaMashu. After the project was completed, he went around South Africa promoting its success with a slideshow. In his speeches he lamented the ills of the "sprawling shacklands of Cato Manor," where, to quote him at length:

> filth and litter accumulated and not only endangered the health of the people but blunted their senses and caused them to adopt an indifferent and casual attitude. Open drains spread sickness and disease [and] under these conditions children were born and reared, their only playground the sick soil between the shacks. Many died and those who survived had little to look forward to and were doomed to become loafers and tsotsis [thugs]. Here children in their most formative and impressionable years watched their parents turn from decent people to drunken wrecks.

He contrasted this scene of moral depravity with a utopian vision of KwaMashu:

> [The] city is well planned and well built and gives new hope and joy to thousands. . . . The Bantu becomes intensely house-proud and shows a keen sense for beauty in color and design. The proud house-owner will construct an ornamental gate, concrete pathways, steps and lay out a lovely garden. . . . With pick and shovel and assisted by his wife, [he] sets to work to clear the grass to pave his pathway, and to prepare a little garden so that he can hold his own with his neighbors. . . . Here he can live as a decent self-respecting man. Here he can offer his wife a secure home and bring up his children to become happy and useful members of the community. Here at last is a sound basis on which a happy and lasting future can be built.[20]

In this narrative of a journey from violent disorder to peaceful order, from depravity to salvation, Bourquin reveals that the KwaMashu project was not just about eliminating public health hazards and providing services to urban Africans, but about remaking urban African subjectivities and instilling a new, bourgeois morality centered on the values attached to the European nuclear family home. However, while some Umkhumbane residents may indeed have been pleased with the prospect of getting new houses, Bourquin's narrative elides the violent social reorganization that this process entailed. Not only were tens of thousands of people forcibly relocated to KwaMashu; they were also coercively rearranged into new family structures. People who could not fit into this mold were externalized to the reserves, so that KwaMashu would become a place occupied solely by families and persons conforming to a particular ideal. I shall develop this point further below, but first I want to discuss some of the architectural concerns that planners wrestled with.

"FIT AND PROPER PERSONS"

As I described above, Umkhumbane, like other informal settlements in South Africa, was marked by a spontaneous integration of domestic and commercial spaces such that its architecture inscribed little formal contrast between private building and public street. As the sites of a bustling beer trade, residential houses were not geographically distinguished from routes of circulation, but operated as crucial public nodes along those routes. In other words, the relationship between closed building and open space did not correspond to a rigid private-public code, but was in constant flux. It was this semiotic ambivalence between public and private that registered the settlement not only as "chaotic," "diseased," and "immoral" in the minds of Durban's authorities, but also as an incubator for political agitation.

The planned township was designed to redress this dangerous ambivalence and imprecise distribution of people by organizing a new kind of space. As Foucault (1979:143) has put it, modernist planning is a disciplinary project that seeks to "break up collective dispositions," order "transient pluralities," and prevent "diffuse circulation" by dividing space in such a way as to locate, measure, and supervise each individual. In South Africa, the detached, single nuclear family house was at the very center of this project. The goal was to obliterate public solidarities by relocating each individual into a nuclear family, binding them to a predictable set of interests, commitments, and responsibilities. In addition, as James Holston (1999) points out, the structured differentiation of public from private spaces forms an important component of modernism's doctrine of salvation. Townships like Kwa-Mashu were designed to neatly separate public from private life, and place the former under the strict control of the state to prevent it from facilitating political discontent.

This was done on three nesting scales. First, the new townships were erected a significant distance away from the city's central business district in an attempt to create a rigid opposition between the (European) commercial sector and the (Native) residential sector, which were connected by highway and rail.[21] This arrangement was designed to

FIGURE 8. Arial view of Meadowlands. This layout was typical of African townships developed after 1948.

exorcize any residue of the public street by transforming roads from spaces for pedestrian gatherings and marketplace exchange into purely functional conduits for moving workers between residential and industrial domains. The effect was to dismantle the urban marketplace that characterized informal settlements by reordering relations of commerce and residence, and by strictly separating capitalist production from domestic reproduction.

The second scale was within the township itself. Planners sought to eliminate the domestic-commercial reversals of the informal settlement in favor of an uncompromising clarity of function written into a spatial order designed for easy policing (see fig. 8). The scheme remade the family home as a distinctively domestic domain, precluding it from functioning as a locus of public interaction. Legislation prohibited production and trade outside of specially designated areas, severing the residential street from the place of exchange. Streets within the township were designed, not to connect houses to each other, but to connect houses to labor transport facilities and to enable police surveillance. Public life was confined to the church, the social center, and, later, the indoor shopping complex, which could be controlled and monitored on the state's terms.[22] Within the township, then, modernist intervention attempted to eliminate the possibility of robust counterpublics—such as that which thrived in Umkhumbane—by creating an isolated domestic life separate from a public life that could be thoroughly surveilled.

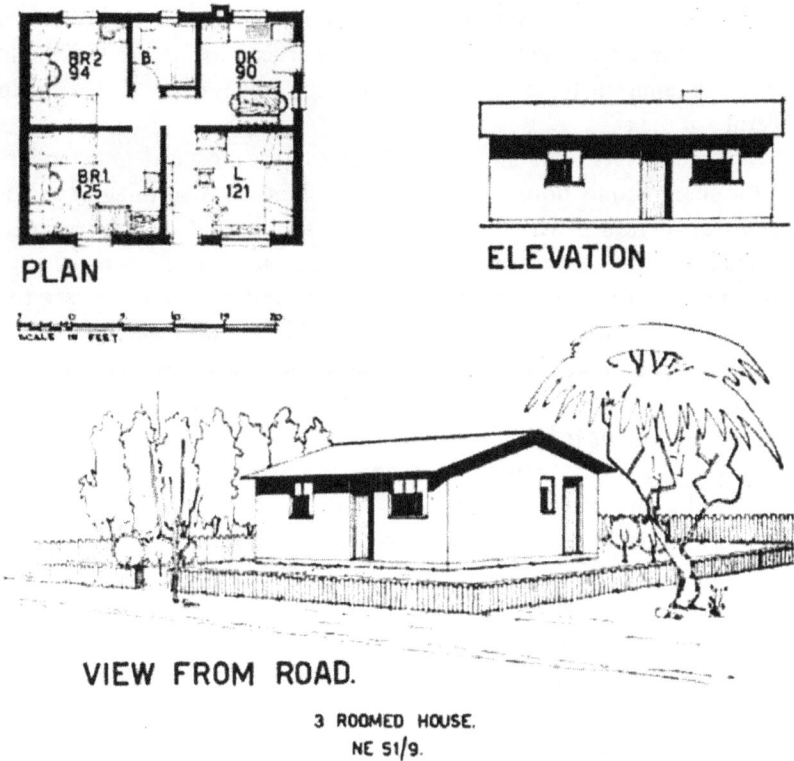

PLAN

ELEVATION

SCALE IN FEET

VIEW FROM ROAD.

3 ROOMED HOUSE.
NE 51/9.

FIGURE 9. House type NE 51/9, one of the most commonly used models in South African townships (Calderwood 1953:29).

The third scale was within the township house. Two architectural models ended up dominating township developments across South Africa: NE 51/6 and 51/9 (see fig. 9). The NE 51 (short for Non-European 1951) houses consisted of four rooms: a master bedroom, a children's bedroom, a kitchen, and a living room—all designed around the needs of the nuclear family. Ostensibly, the NE 51 model was selected by the National Housing and Planning Commission because it was "low cost," but in reality[23] detached single-family houses were dramatically more expensive in terms of land use and construction materials than row houses or duplexes. Mathewson, who penned the text that Bourquin used as a blueprint for KwaMashu, promoted the detached house because it embodied the conditions necessary for European standards of cleanliness, family structure, and division of labor (cf. Mathewson 1957:49). In other words, the NE 51 model was selected, not on the objective basis of cost and efficiency, but rather because the detached house fit the soteriology of European modernism as a sacred, divinely ordained domestic form thought to instill the values of good citizenship (Perin 1980:45).

The architect M. V. Pennington was one of the most ardent defenders of the single-family home. He devoted much ink to describing in painstaking detail how he thought these houses should operate. He regarded the family sitting room as essential for encouraging a sense of love and emotional attachment between parents and children. He saw the kitchen and verandah as spaces that would facilitate women's labor without cutting them off from family activities. He celebrated the master bedroom as the locus of companionate marriage, but insisted that the wife should have her own dressing space so as to guard her sense of dignity and chastity (Pennington 1978). These recommendations masqueraded as neutral assessments of housing needs, but I suggest that they are better understood as projections of Eurocentric assumptions about proper gender and family structure. Many people have Eurocentric assumptions, of course; but what made these particular assumptions so significant is that they were backed by the full power of the state, which reserved the privilege of forcing people to fit within these strictures.

The first houses in the KwaMashu development were handed over to residents in March of 1958 through a rigorous application process. Displaced residents of Umkhumbane were given first priority, but they had to meet a series of stringent criteria before they could claim their units. Bourquin and the township manager, a man by the name of R. G. Willson, had the final word when it came to the allocation of residential permits—near total power over social engineering. They made their decisions according to a set of rules established by the Natal administration known as Provincial Notice No. 383 of 1960, "Regulations for the Management and Control of Native Locations, Native Villages and Hostels."[24] This notorious and widely resented legislation decreed that black individuals could only claim the right to a house if they were male, fully employed, head of a family, and married to a woman.[25] In addition, the regulations declared that accommodation would only be allocated to "fit and proper persons," which gave the township manager the latitude to reject anyone who he felt failed to conform to European norms of personhood and family. Ironically, then, within the ostensibly "private" modern home, the state decided how the African family would be constituted.

These regulations sought to produce a new kind of family tailored to planners' vision of the ideal modern community. By dictating that a household head (a male, by default) could own no more than a single dwelling and in that dwelling could support no more than a single wife, Notice 383 effectively outlawed polygyny in urban areas. Furthermore, the proof-of-marriage condition rendered ineligible those couples united according to customary law, as acceptable proof of such unions was nearly impossible to procure. The ideal-typical township resident was therefore an employed, monogamous male head of a nuclear family in possession of a four-room, detached, single-family dwelling. Such individuals were permitted to have their dependents living with them, but only as many as could fit within the pre-fabricated confines of the dwelling without violating the personal space code of the Slums Act of 1934 (forty square feet per person),[26] and only so long as they were unmarried and—in the case of males—under the age of eighteen. Notice 383 prohibited household heads from allowing anyone who did not qualify as "family"—according to the definitional whim of the township manager—to live with them unless registered as temporary lodgers who qualified as "fit and proper persons" themselves. Only a single nuclear family was permitted to occupy any one residence, and homeowners were prohibited from building additional structures on their property for extended relatives or nonrelatives. Frequent police raids enforced compliance with these regulations, and violators were imprisoned or ejected from the urban areas outright.

According to Notice 383, alterations to housing units that compromised "the privacy of family life" in any way were expressly disallowed, and because the use of mud and thatch was forbidden, even acceptable alterations were prohibitively expensive. Residents were required to keep their units "clean," hygienic," and "free of vermin" at all times, and to be prepared for random inspection by the township manager for the purpose of preventing "contagion," presumed to spread so virulently among non-Europeans. Along these lines, residents were not allowed to take part in any activities which would "create a disturbance" or be "indecent or subversive to good morals," were precluded from keeping any livestock, and were prohibited from slaughtering animals except at specially designated places approved by the City Council. The regulations also enforced a new and very rigid division of spatial utility. It was illegal for residents to use their houses for anything other than "domestic" purposes; hawking within the township was prohibited and persons could ply their trades only in designated commercial precincts. The head of the household was required to be employed in the urban area. Individuals who found themselves unemployed without due permission, employed outside the urban area, or absent from their residential premises for over one month were liable to be deported.

UNEXPECTED FORMS OF FAMILY

The planners' scheme worked: families that had been forcibly relocated into townships showed a marked drop in multigenerationality and the simple-nuclear form became more normative.[27] This basic transformation in kinship structure was for the most part concluded by the late 1960s, after the completion of South Africa's biggest public housing projects for urban Africans.[28] What this history shows is that the "modernization" of the African family was not a natural process of development, as theorists like Maine, Goode, and Tierney have assumed, and as many ANC policymakers continue to believe. Instead of happening automatically, it required violence and coercion. This is an important point. Under normal processes of urbanization, new inhabitants of a planned settlement will innovate with space and kinship to create hybrid forms that depart from planners' expectations. But the apartheid state—like other authoritarian states—had the power to force compliance without regard for basic human rights.

Still, despite planners' best efforts, the type of social organization that emerged in the townships never perfectly matched the ideal of the male-headed nuclear family. First, inadequate wages drove women to seek employment outside the home to supplement family income, a trend that intensified after 1986, when influx controls were abolished. Second, the restriction of housing to married couples meant that many people sought quick unions simply for the purpose of acquiring a house and the right to live and work in urban areas, but most of these "house marriages" proved to be brittle and they frequently dissolved (Posel 2006). Third, a minor provision in Notice 383 allowed women to retain ownership of township houses after the death, desertion, or divorce of a household head in the absence of a viable male heir, which happened quite frequently. Finally, general poverty and the absence of livestock made it difficult for aspiring husbands to pay bridewealth to the families of their lovers—an exchange necessary to secure paternity according a Zulu cultural rule—and thus left many children to affiliate to families of their maternal grandfathers and live in the natal homes of their mothers.

The result was a rapid rise in female-headed families and households whose kinship narratives included moments of matrifocality and matrilineality, as if the women-centered core that lies hidden at the base of the kinship model I described in chapter 2 was left exposed. In townships today, houses are often owned and headed by unmarried women—sometimes as groups of sisters—and descent and inheritance are frequently traced through females. This trend is particularly evident in older sections of the townships (like KwaMashu's E Section) which initially conformed to the planners' nuclear family ideals but began to exhibit matrifocal tendencies after two or three generations.[29] Newer sections (like KwaMashu's J section) contain a high proportion of male-headed, simple nuclear families. According to residents, J section reflects what E section looked like when it was first occupied, and it will eventually conform to the matrifocal trend if its younger residents are not able to fund marriages. As one longtime resident put it to me: "This type of matrifocal family is very common. More common than the traditional (nuclear family) form. It is now the norm. Things have completely changed from those earlier years." Even when young men *are* able to fund a marriage, they often cannot afford to establish a neolocal residence—as the township planners intended—so they live with their wives in backyard shacks on the property of their natal homes, and their children grow up with the children of their sisters. If a young man is unable to get married, he will often remain in his natal home, which may fall under the de facto control of his sisters as they reproduce and establish matrifocal families of their own. Demographic data illustrate this well. Simkins (1986) shows a sharp rise between 1970 and 1980 in urban Africans' incidence of divorce, cohabitation, and premarital reproduction, while the marriage rate declined, precipitously in the case of females.

During apartheid, both liberal social scientists and conservative apartheid ideologues alike were concerned about the "demise of the African family"—the former in denunciation of the violent influx controls that tore African families apart, the latter for fear of social instability as a consequence of detribalization. In 1982, the Cabinet charged the South African Welfare Council with implementing a National Family Program that would attend to these issues. The policy document that they produced in 1989 stated that, "in view of the many signs of disorganization being shown in family life, for example the high divorce rate . . . and the high rate of extramarital births and cohabitation," there was "justifiable concern about the state of family life." It noted that "several factors have contributed to family disorganization, for example urbanization, industrialization, poverty and poor living conditions, altered family roles, negative changing values and norms, inadequate preparation for marriage, alcohol and drug abuse, community unrest, contract labor and employment."

But after enumerating these causes of family dislocation, the report concluded with an incoherent twist, stating that "Marriage and family life must be reinforced to stave off attacks from the outside" (NFP 1989), entirely ignoring the apartheid labor system in order to focus instead on the family as the object of state reform. In other words, the family—not "attacks from the outside"—became the focus of moralizing discourse.

In sum, the state's attempts at producing docile African nuclear families fell prey to the inconsistency between the racist ideologues of apartheid and the liberal urban planners that they hired. The planners envisioned utopian "garden cities" centered on the Fordist model of the industrial male breadwinner, but the racist state hobbled this vision by funding only the most perfunctory construction and keeping black wages artificially low—making it difficult for working men to support legitimate social reproduction. In other words, while the state wanted to produce docile, modern nuclear families, it refused to pick up the bill. The matrifocal family was an unintended consequence of incomplete social engineering, and is perhaps one of the reasons that women came to play such a central role in anticolonial resistance. In addition, this gap between the promises of modernity and the reality of racial exclusions generated a deep sense of betrayal, which resonated most intensely among frustrated young men who could not fulfill the expectations of masculinity that modernist planners laid out (cf. Hunter 2010). This generalized feeling of "abjection"—to use James Ferguson's (1999) term—fuelled the wave of workers' strikes in the 1970s and the service-delivery protests of the 1980s, culminating in a movement of mass discontent in the townships unlike anything that the planners could have foreseen.

THE REVOLUTIONARY BY-PRODUCTS OF SOCIAL ENGINEERING

As the above narrative demonstrates, the development of informal settlements such as Umkhumbane and the later forced removal of residents into planned townships like KwaMashu radically transformed the structure of kinship, gender, and personhood in the African family. Contrast these changes with the rural Zulu homestead. As I argued in chapter 2, the homestead embodies a basic articulation between hierarchical social organization and the layout of domestic space, and this order is shot through with taboos that structure conceptions of misfortune and causality. The forced relocations transformed this order in a number of ways. By reorganizing domestic space through the NE 51 house, planners subverted these normative structures of gender and hierarchy. They replaced them with new sets of hierarchies, of course—the more "modern" ones that define the nuclear family—but with a key difference. When planners eliminated key institutions like the cattle byre, the great house, the central hearth, and the ranked "houses" and "sides" of the polygynous family, they dismantled the spatial referents that define gender and hierarchy in homesteads, and eradicated the home's capacity to function as the material embodiment of that particular cosmological order. Building on changes that were already under way in the informal settlements, the NE 51 houses inscribed a new organizational logic based on the nuclear family. By obliterating the coordinates of encompassment, this process effectively individualized township residents; women and youth, for example, were no longer constituted as encompassed (spatially and ontologically) by male elders to the same extent—particularly as matrifocal families came to predominate.

The new spatial regime of the township also caused the taboo system to fall apart, for the layout of township houses made it impossible for people to observe the prohibitions on space and interpersonal interaction that structure social life in rural homesteads. In the absence of the great house, the *umsamo* (ancestral shrine) in most township houses gets relocated to the master bedroom, where the vital taboo on sexual relations in the vicinity of the shrine cannot be maintained—the most heinous among the innumerable violations made inevitable by the congested, inward-turned rooms of the urban house. Additionally, by illegalizing the ritual sacrifice of livestock on domestic property and prohibiting the construction of outbuildings like the great house, Notice 383 effectively excised the ancestor cult from the home and unhinged it from its moorings in kinship structure. Sacrifice was externalized to special "ritual zones" surveilled by public health officials, where it became impossible for practitioners to ensure the proper division and distribution of the sacrificial body that is so crucial to the maintenance of hierarchies—and thus health, fertility, and fortune—in the homestead. When restrictions on outbuilding construction were lifted in the 1980s,[30] many wealthier households erected small rondavels in their yards intended solely for prayer and offerings to the ancestors. Significantly, these structures are never referred to as *kwagogo* (literally, "home of the grandmother"—the term used in rural areas): the urban shrine is divorced from any particular location in the kinship structure of the household. As with the practice of sacrifice, the shrine has become like a church, a temple, an abstracted place of worship separated off into the modern domain of "religion" or "traditional beliefs" instead of intimately integrated into the fabric of the homestead.

As a result, in urban townships the ancestor cult and its attendant model of health and healing no longer necessitates attention to the arrangement of social relations in the household. In other words, the ancestors of township residents dispense blessings and cure misfortunes without compelling their descendants to perform legitimate kinship through the battery of ritual sacrifices, meat exchanges, and *hlonipha* observances that rural denizens—by contrast—know they must observe. Instead, township families often content themselves with the perfunctory offering of a piece of store-bought steak, a practice that rural people find absurd in that it ignores the very purpose of sacrifice, namely, the reconstruction of kinship through the deconstruction of the cow, the pieces of which correspond to the structure of society itself (see chapter 5). Proper kinship structure no longer holds primacy of place in establishing the conditions for social reproduction and good fortune.

These changes recall Marshall Sahlins's (1985) theory of "structural transformation": the idea that changes in one cultural category can generate changes in the relations *between* categories as well. He illustrates this by describing how the destruction of the Hawaiian taboo system altered relations between men, women, chiefs, and commoners in a sort of cascading domino effect; changing one element of the system altered all of the others. In the case of Natal, transformations of domestic space, kinship, gender, and hierarchy altered conceptions of misfortune and causality. The layout of township houses made it impossible for people to observe crucial taboos on space and interpersonal interaction. As a result, the taboo system fell apart, delinking kinship structure from ideas about the etiology of misfortune. In other words, re/productive misfortunes could no longer be attributed to violations of taboos related to gender and hierarchy. This transformation had significant implications for urban forms of political consciousness. While homestead-dwellers tend to consider poverty, illness, and unemployment to be the consequence of *hlonipha* violations, ritual oversights, or lesions in the family, township dwellers must look elsewhere for the sources of their misfortune.[31]

They find their clues written in the spatial structure of the township. The new townships structured rigid distinctions between public and private spaces. Reproducing developments associated with the industrial revolution in Europe, the state enforced an opposition between domestic/private/reproductive spaces and industrial/public/productive spaces as both an assumption of normative values and a method of governmentality (Foucault 1991). Ironically, in its attempt to fix the problem of public/private mixing in the slums, the apartheid state inscribed the concept of the "public" into the townships, thereby laying the groundwork for a proper public sphere that would resist the state and give rise to liberal democratic activism. In addition, by excising work from the home and repositioning it into a separate domain, apartheid's architects created the conditions for workers to become—in Marxist terms—a class in themselves. In rural homesteads, by contrast, all labor—both waged and unwaged—is tied to the reproductive pursuits of the family. Ideally, male migrant workers remit their wages into the gift economy, domesticating the chaotic fecundity of capital and harnessing it for the pursuit of homestead development and reproduction. In resisting full proletarianization, they ensure that their primary social identity remains that of homestead heads or sons, inextricably bound to the social order of the house (Moodie 1994). For township dwellers whose labor is reified and alienated from the family according to the terms of modernist architecture, the category "worker" becomes a class location. Occupying this new structural position, stabilized urban workers were ready targets for the political unions in the early 1980s, which sought to organize them into a class *for* themselves.

The structural transformations generated by the state's social engineering program opened the door for new forms of consciousness, rendering urban Africans amenable to ideas about individual rights, gender egalitarianism, and resistance to class exploitation in a way that their rural counterparts never were (cf. Mamdani 1996). In other words, the political consciousness of township dwellers developed along the lines of the socio-spatial structure of the township (cf. Lefebvre 1974). The township youth of the early 1980s were the first generation to have been born and raised in this new cultural context, which helps explain how they ended up at the forefront of a revolutionary movement that had a distinctly liberal, egalitarian, and class-oriented character (Chipkin 2004). As with rural Zulu homestead society, the manner in which the domestic realm was structured in the urban townships was implicated in and constitutive of how the public realm developed.

Ultimately, then, the apartheid state became the victim of its own strategy for social control, which initially sought to redress the intolerably "in-between" status of slum-dwelling Africans. The state's attempts to reorder this "polluted," "chaotic," and "dangerous" population through modernist social engineering was almost ritualistic; it recalls Douglas's (1966) discussion of how ritual is used to reintegrate and reorder chaotic elements to neutralize the danger they pose (see also Comaroff 1980). In a similar manner, social engineers sought to regain control over urban Africans by reordering their domestic milieu. Their basic assumption was that properly ordered nuclear families situated in a rationally planned environment would be intrinsically stable and docile. In their blind devotion to this cultural model, however, planners planted the seeds of the demise of the colonial project itself. Planners failed to foresee the political consequences of their scheme; they completely missed the fact that the fully proletarianized, egalitarian society they intended to produce would have new and powerful tools of resistance at its disposal. Instead of rendering Africans more easily controllable, the mass relocations produced new categories of personhood, entitlement and desire, and furnished the logic for new forms of resistance. In other words, the apartheid state's most draconian technologies of control—namely, the manipulation of African domesticity—ended up creating the conditions for the National Democratic Revolution.

There is one final point to make about this story. Pointing to the history of townships does more than explain the rise of a particular logic of revolution in urban Natal; it also explains how it is that people—and specifically rural migrants—have come to imagine such a rigid moral opposition between urban and rural, when in fact the relationship between the two is characterized by a long history of exchange and syncretism, not least because of the migrant labor system itself. There are real cultural differences that lead township dwellers and rural migrants to have discordant political visions, but their politics are also informed by the very fact of the difference itself. For migrants this difference gets reduced to a simplified distinction between two domestic structures: the township and the homestead. As we saw in the previous chapter, rural migrants place profound value on the homestead as a physical form—so it makes sense that their discontent with democracy refers to concerns related to domestic order. For them, the physical structure of the township house as crafted by urban planners embodies the inversion of the domestic order that they regard as so essential to processes of fruition and to their vision of meaningful democracy.

4

Neoliberalism as Misfortune

Aristocracy had made a chain of all the members of the community, from the peasant to the king: democracy breaks that chain, and severs every link of it. Thus not only does democracy make every man forget his ancestors, but it hides his descendants, and separates his contemporaries from him; it throws him back forever upon himself alone.

—Alexis de Tocqueville, *Democracy in America*

The two preceding chapters explored the operation of colonial power in rural and urban spaces, respectively, illustrating the bifurcated technologies that the state deployed to control and manage the African population. The dual nature of colonial governance in South Africa has long been the subject of academic commentary, most famously in Mahmood Mamdani's seminal text *Citizen and Subject* (1996). Mamdani argues that—like elsewhere in colonial Africa—the apartheid state employed two distinct modes of controlling Africans: indirect rule and direct rule. Indirect rule ("decentralized despotism") costumed colonial hegemony in the form of customary law and was employed to control rural Africans through institutions of patriarchal hierarchy. Direct rule ("centralized despotism"), by contrast, governed urban Africans according to the instruments of modern civic legislation, albeit in a manner riddled with racial exclusions. The result was that urban power spoke the language of civil society and rights, while rural power spoke the language of custom and tradition; the former was cast in the mold of race, while the latter was cast in the mold of tribe.

Mamdani argues that this historical bifurcation between modern law and customary law, between urban "citizens" and rural "subjects," informed the kinds of claims that Africans made against the colonial regime during the liberation struggle. As he puts it, "the form of [colonial] rule shaped the form of revolt against it" (1996:24), evoking the Foucaultian mantra that resistance is always an effect of power (see also

Abu-Lughod 1990). In other words, revolt mobilized in urban areas was predictably organized in terms of race and rights, while revolt mobilized in rural areas was predictably organized in terms of tribe and custom.

I accept Mamdani's argument that the two forms of colonial rule in South Africa shaped the two forms of revolt against it. But we can take the analysis one step further. The two preceding chapters have shown that colonial power exerted itself not only through the categories of modern and customary law, or through the constructs of race and tribe, but also through the manipulation of domestic space and family organization. At this level there was a single form of power (domestic manipulation) with two manifestations: township and homestead. The division between direct and indirect rule, then, produced, not only a division between categories of legal personhood (citizen and subject) or categories of solidary identity (race and tribe), but also a division between two forms of social organization and their concomitant moral orders. The division, in short, was cosmological.

This perspective helps us rethink the easy and very popular assumption that Zulu migrants' political aspirations are organized around ethnic or tribal identities. They are not, except perhaps in the most superficial way. The movement among migrants to resist the rise of the ANC may appear to take on the form of ethnic revolt given the rhetorical felicities of what Spivak (1987) calls "strategic essentialism" (see Donham 2011), but its internal logic bears an entirely different content. I argued in chapter 1 that in the middle of the 1980s, rural migrants began to resist the mainstream liberation movement because they objected to how it was run—that it incorporated liberal social principles, rejected generational hierarchies, and privileged the logic of secular political modernity. Today, as we shall see, this sense of discontent has coalesced into a much more general rejection of democracy. Operating within a particular cultural paradigm that holds social differentiation to be crucial to fruition and fortune, migrants reject the ANC's liberal project, which—because it equalized all persons as autonomous individuals—many of them regard as a harbinger of decline, decay, and the failure of social reproduction. In the following pages I seek to outline the contours of this widespread sense of moral panic.[1]

A HIJACKED REVOLUTION

To understand the present context of politics in South Africa, it is necessary to appreciate the gap that yawns between the expectations that people had of liberation in 1994 and the reality that most people inhabit today—a gap that can be explained largely as a consequence of the ANC's move toward neoliberal economic policy shortly after assuming power.

Official negotiations to end apartheid took place between 1990 and 1993, after the unbanning of the ANC and Mandela's release from prison.[2] Out of the public eye, however, discussions actually began much earlier than this. Oliver Tambo and ANC delegates met in London in 1985 and 1986 for discussions with key figures in South Africa's white business community. Later, between 1987 and 1990, ANC and National Party leaders met for a series of secret talks in Mells Park House in Somerset, England. The talks were arranged by British mining company Consolidated Gold Fields—the owner of the Somerset estate—which had significant assets in South Africa that it feared losing in the case of a revolution. One primary objective of the National Party at the time was to ensure that the transition would not undermine the interests of large corporations in South Africa. A second objective seems to have been to split the resistance between moderate elites—such as Thabo Mbeki and Oliver Tambo, who had spent many years in exile—and the UDF activists who were at the forefront of the struggle within South Africa itself. The latter were largely unrepresented in key transition negotiations.

At the time, the ANC's mandate was rooted in the Freedom Charter, the famous 1955 document that expressed South Africans' demands for the right to work, housing, freedom of movement, and—most radically—economic justice. "The national wealth of our country, the heritage of South Africans, shall be restored to the people," the Charter reads. "The mineral wealth beneath the soil, the Banks and monopoly industry shall be transferred to the ownership of the people as a whole, [and] all other industry and trade shall be controlled to assist the wellbeing of the people." As word leaked out about the preliminary talks between the ANC and the apartheid state, suspicions spread within the liberation movement that the ANC leadership was stepping back from some of these key demands. Mandela sought to quell these concerns with a widely reported 1990 statement that read: "The nationalization of the mines, banks and monopoly industries is the policy of the ANC, and a change or modification of our views in this regard is inconceivable."

Yet during the official negotiations of the early 1990s, the ANC made a number of major concessions to the National Party, not only backing down from nationalization, but also allowing the old apartheid bosses to continue to run the central bank and the treasury. To make matters worse, the final agreement made the central bank an independent entity, which effectively unhinged monetary policy from the democratic controls of the state in a manner consistent with the most radical recommendations of Milton Friedman and the so-called Chicago School. In other words, the transition agreement allowed the ANC to gain control of the state but denied them control over the economy, making their promises of economic reform impossible to realize. Furthermore, the redistribution of land, subsidies for infant industries, debt cancellation, provision of public housing and water, currency controls, a living wage—all of these developmentalist policies had been made impossible by a battery of agreements that the ANC made with the IMF and the World Bank during the transition period, particularly once South Africa signed the General Agreement on Tariffs and Trade (which became the WTO in 1995). The ANC gradually bargained away the country's economic sovereignty and granted South African capitalists immunity against the politics of the Freedom Charter in which the resistance movement had been rooted (see Bond 2000, 2006; Klein 2008).

Thabo Mbeki, Mandela's vice president and the person in charge of economic negotiations during the early 1990s, ardently supported the trickle-down logic of neoliberalism. For Mbeki—a self-proclaimed Thatcherite—the route to a prosperous new nation depended on global market integration and the pursuit of foreign direct investment by lowering trade barriers. Still, when the ANC assumed power in 1994, it implemented a policy initiative known as the Reconstruction and Development Program (RDP) that was widely regarded as progressive, if not fully socialist. The RDP was designed to promote equitable development and poverty reduction, mostly through the mass rollout of social services and infrastructural projects. This policy framework was abandoned a mere two years later, however, when Mbeki and then Finance Minister Trevor Manuel held clandestine meetings with World Bank advisors to draft a new economic plan known as GEAR (Growth, Employment, and Redistribution), which was implemented in 1996. Known by its detractors as the "1996 class project," GEAR pushed privatization, looser exchange controls, labor market flexibility, and further reductions to trade barriers.

This structural adjustment program succeeded in slowing inflation and reducing the nation's fiscal debt, but it proved to be disastrous for the majority of the population. Instead of creating jobs, GEAR more than doubled the unemployment rate, sending it from 13 percent in 1994 to a peak of 30.3 percent in 2001. More than four hundred thousand formal sector jobs were lost in the first three years of the program.[3]

Today unemployment stands at 25 percent, or as high as 38 percent including people who have given up searching for work.[4] According to the *Economist,* "half of South Africans under 24 looking for work have none. Of those who have jobs, a third earn less than $2 a day."[5] These figures are even worse for black South Africans as a group, most of whom are forced to rely for their livelihoods on the unstable informal economy (see Barchiesi 2011). Besides its dismal record on employment, South Africa also boasts a reputation for being one of the most unequal countries in the world. Not only has aggregate income inequality worsened since the end of apartheid,[6] income inequality between racial groups has worsened as well (Leibbrandt et al. 2012). Today, black households earn only 16 percent as much as white households earn,[7] and 61.9 percent of all black South Africans live below the poverty line—a figure that rises to 79.1 percent in the rural areas of the former homelands.[8]

The ANC government has papered over the worst of these problems by unrolling an extensive program of social grants, which now supply a vital lifeline to some fifteen million people. This departure from strict neoliberal dogma provides an important stop-gap solution to the failure of trickle-down economics,[9] but the contradictions of South African capitalism remain painfully apparent. The country's mineral wealth, including some of the richest seams of gold, platinum, and coal in the world, remain in the hands of corporations such as British-based Anglo American. And the finance sector, which under GEAR has ballooned to 21 percent of the country's GDP, remains mostly monopolized by a few predominantly white-owned conglomerates. For the South Africans who expected the ANC to deliver on the Freedom Charter and fulfill its promise of "a better life for all" after liberation in 1994, all of this contributes to a widespread sense of disappointment. For many it also prompts a feeling of serious betrayal by the party they had trusted to carry the hopes of the revolution.

Among the rural migrants I grew to know, the consequences of neoliberalization have been experienced as what Mark Hunter (2010) has so aptly identified as a "crisis of social reproduction." One of the most obvious manifestations of this is that marriage rates have been declining precipitously, down to less than half of 1960 levels, so that today only three out of ten South African adults are married. While this trend can be attributed partially to the influx of women into the workforce and their growing independence from men after the abolition of gender-specific pass laws in 1986, it is due mostly to a widespread deficit of the financial resources that young people need to get married and establish independent households. With unemployment rates as high as they are, most young men find it impossible to raise the resources they need to pay *ilobolo*—the lynchpin of legitimate social reproduction and homestead development in rural areas, and long one of the primary objectives of male migrant labor.[10]

Of course, the fact that neoliberalism undermines the conditions for social reproduction is not a novel argument. What is interesting here is the culturally particular way in which this plays out in rural KwaZulu-Natal. I found that the theory of misfortune that I described in chapter 2 gets evoked by migrants not only to interpret afflictions on the domestic scale, but now also to interpret the state of the nation more broadly. It is not uncommon across the Zululand countryside and in the hostel districts around Durban to hear embittered lamentations of increasing poverty, unemployment, and HIV transmission as symptoms of mass *amashwa* (misfortune). This deployment of local, "indigenous" categories to think about extra-local, extraneous historical events recalls Marshall Sahlins's (1985) theory of the "structure of the conjuncture." Sahlins's analysis of the Hawaiians' understanding of Captain Cook as the god Lono has become the quintessential example of how, to quote Joel Robbins on the same topic, "traditional cultures transform themselves by reproducing their basic shape even as the categories that make them up stretch themselves to take in new elements" (2004:8). This process allows people to interpret new information, experiences, and historical events in terms of old, familiar categories.

In rural Zululand, the cultural category of *amashwa* has been extended to apply to misfortunes on a national scale, and broadened to encompass the nation as a community. As we shall see, the expansion of this category has come along with a curious and somewhat disturbing entailment: it allows people to interpret the old apartheid regime in new ways, as a time when *umthetho* was upheld by the state and *amashwa* were kept in check.

THE TROUBLE WITH TOWNSHIPS

Things fall apart; the centre cannot hold;

Mere anarchy is loosed upon the world . . .

—William Butler Yeats, "The Second Coming"

While the etiology of homestead-level misfortunes gets traced back to very specific violations of *umthetho,* national-level misfortunes are thought to be caused by a much more general and widespread departure from "customs" (*amasiko*). To many rural migrants, the ANC and the urban townships with which they are associated cause mass misfortune because they so consistently violate—and legislate against—the basic principles of moral order that are necessary for maintaining the conditions for social reproduction. Migrants see township residents as disassociated from their families and neglectful of the proper order of gender and hierarchy. Speaking of Umkhumbane, the informal settlement discussed in chapter 3, one migrant worker I interviewed claimed: "People there forgot everything they were doing in the homesteads. They just stayed together haphazardly, without structure. They were only considering immediate relationships, between individuals . . . now those who were born in the townships have lost their families, and have lost their culture."

This fear of the diffusion of individuals into a disorganized morass of undifferentiated humanity gets repeated in discussions about physical domestic spaces in townships. Another migrant man with whom I spoke pointed out that:

> In the homestead you are using only one entrance, for respect. If you don't fence and you just use any entrance, you're not following what you're supposed to be doing. In the township you are just walking anywhere [i.e., violating spatial taboos]. This is not respect, not proper code of conduct, and it causes a lot of problems [*amashwa*].

To Zulu migrants, the two- and four-room "matchbox" houses that define urban townships lack all of the meaningful spatial markers that constitute the social order of the homestead. They have no center, no periphery, no ranked sides, no apex, no byres, no hearths, and no shrines. As one middle-aged migrant man lamented:

> The *amadlozi* [ancestors] do not enter the townships. This is because the wife stays in the same room as the husband and the children, all together, all in the same *indlu* [uterine house], violating taboos. A child may have a boyfriend, and they will have a baby and the father and the mother and the baby will stay together in the same *indlu*. That is the problem. The *amadlozi*, they don't like that. Where is the *indlunkulu* [great house]? It is not there! And in the townships there is no *umsamo* [shrine], there is no *sibaya* [cattle byre], there is no right side and left side . . . not there.

The claim here is that the physical structure of the township house militates against the kinship structure of the rural family.

While the layout of homesteads creates distinctions of generation, gender, and seniority, township houses, by contrast, appear to migrants to have a democratizing effect on the family, eradicating proper differences in personhood associated with proper differences in space. If homestead space produces proper persons, then township space produces cultureless mutants. As one migrant from Hlabisa put it: "The way the townships are made is destroying the culture of the Zulus." Many assert that the worst aspect of township housing is that it fails to inscribe distinctions between male/female and senior/junior spaces. As a result, another migrant told me, "people do not know what to do, what not to do, which rooms they can and cannot enter, or what spaces they cannot traverse, like spaces reserved for the elders and the men." This structural deficit is often blamed by migrants for the rising rates of rape, sexual abuse, child molestation, and domestic violence in urban areas. But equally problematic in their view are the cosmological consequences of these structural malformations. The same man who offered the above analysis of township architecture linked the collapse of the homestead's structural categories directly to misfortune, saying:

> The *amadlozi* do not like these things. That's why so many people are poor now. The problem is that the *amasiko* [customs] are no longer being followed. You can find a person who has been arrested for crimes, that person was not contacting the ancestors. You find that you get stabbed and killed, or hit by a car in the road. Any problem. *Amashwa*. The *amashwa* are increasing these days. You see people are dying every day. Because people don't have *umthetho* and *hlonipha* [respect/taboo/separation]. Both men and women.

Migrants also express concern that township dwellers have broken relationships with their ancestors. For one, regulations in urban areas require that corpses be buried in designated cemeteries rather than on household premises, as is the custom in rural areas. Migrants like to point out that, as a result, the ancestors of township residents get "mixed up" in cemeteries and can no longer "work" to ensure the fortune of their descendants' households; instead, they wander around in a sort of limbo, a liminal state of cosmological confusion, rootless, aimless, and homeless. The ancestors are further disarticulated from households because the spatial constraints of township houses and yards (the lack of byres, for example) make it difficult to perform sacrificial ritual; indeed, migrants perceive township residents as incompetent when it comes to ritual performance. As Bhungu Gwala, the IFP councilor of KwaMashu's A Section at the time, lamented during an interview with me: "The nation no longer knows how to slaughter for the ancestors." The neglect of crucial life-stage rituals in townships leaves ancestors unable to "recognize" and protect the persons meant to be constituted by those rituals: as migrants commonly assert, "How can the ancestors help someone who they do not know?" In the words of one migrant shop steward:

> You can't stop *amashwa* because the township people do not believe in their *amadlozi*. Some of the churches say you are not supposed to kill any goats or cows [for life-stage ritual]. When you are not doing that, that's when the problem starts. They think we just kill the goats so that people can eat meat. That's the way that people are losing culture.

While migrants tend to imagine townships as the opposite of home-steads, in reality the contrast is not so stark—particularly given that construction codes have been relaxed since the end of apartheid, leaving people free to modify their dwellings as they wish. For instance, one of my acquaintances—a conservative man originally from rural Zululand who moved his family to Lamontville township to be closer to his work—designed a house that would accommodate his ancestors. He installed a purpose-built room in the center, a sort of apse, to serve as the *umsamo* where he burns incense for the ancestors and hangs sacrifi-cial meat. Other migrants buy ready-made houses in townships but treat them as extensions of their rural homesteads rather than stand-alone homes—satellite units situated within the broader schema of homestead hierarchy. Such syncretism is common, but it gets erased in migrants' discourse as they construct a reified image of the township as a foil for their own moral ideals.

PERCEPTIONS OF ANC POLICY

Many migrants consider township culture to be both the incubator for and expression of the ANC's liberal policies, such as the legalization of abortion[11] and homosexuality,[12] the extension of equal rights to women and children, the child-support grant, and the emphasis on female home-ownership, all of which they find offensive. In rural KwaZulu-Natal, 89 percent of people reject the ANC's abortion law (Harrison et al. 2000).[13] Most believe that abortion signifies not only murder (and thus brings about *umnyama,* or "pollution"), but a rejection of the fertility granted by the ancestors. Moreover, in the context of marriage, abortion is thought to obliterate the distinctive role of the wife. According to one Inkatha official, "The problem with abortion is that it allows wives to go anywhere they want to go. They can get pregnant and take it [the fetus] out. The government wants to make man and wife the same now!" This perspective articulates with a general disapproval of the ANC's gender egalitarianism, which migrants—most of whom are male—regard as collapsing the distinctions between men and women. This concern usually gets cast in the register of "disrespect"—a fear that township dwellers no longer adhere to the dictates of *hlonipha* that govern interactions between genders. In the words of a Durban hostel-dweller I spoke to,

> Yes, in the townships respect is very low. In the homestead the wife respects the husband. For a start, if the wife is cooking you food, she can't just leave it there on the table. She has to give it to you kneeling. It's very important! Otherwise it's a lack of respect. When you lack respect, the ancestors will complain and you will get *amashwa*, and there will be a crisis.

Current disaffection with the ANC among Zulu migrants relates strongly to housing policy. Under the Reconstruction and Development Program (RDP), the postapartheid government promised to provide millions of low-cost housing units in place of slums. To accomplish this, they tore a page out of the apartheid housing playbook: removing people from unplanned slum areas, segmenting extended families into their nuclear components, and placing them in the ordered grids of identical two- and four-room houses. But with an egalitarian bent: the ANC's goal has been to ensure that the majority of new home-owners are women. This scheme is an abomination to rural norms that generally disallow women from establishing their own neolocal households. It appears to disarticulate the uterine house from the homestead that should properly encompass it. To make matters worse, the ANC is giving houses to *single mothers,* which—as rural Zulus see it—not only sanctions premarital pregnancy but entirely inverts the norm whereby single mothers are supposed to stay with their natal homesteads and affiliate their children to their mother's uterine house. Finally, that the homes are being given away for free violates the very premise of masculinity for rural men, who see the slow, laborious process of "building the homestead" to be central to the performance of respectable manhood,[14] and who believe that independent homes should only be developed *after* a couple has had children and the father of the husband's natal homestead has died (cf. Ngwane 2001). This is why migrants tend to believe that township men fail to live up to the standards of proper masculinity. According to one Umlazi hostel resident:

> Those in the township, those who were born without bridewealth being paid, do not have *ubudoda* [manliness]. They don't know the rules of the

ancestors. They have lost *umthetho*. [But] I have *ubudoda*. I grew up and worked and got money and . . . got married [with bridewealth]. . . . You become a man if you have a wife and children and a home and you teach your children how to behave [*hlonipha*]. That is *ubudoda*. . . . The ones in the township, they have killed *ubudoda*. They no longer respect their parents.

The ANC's Child Support Grant scheme (colloquially known as *imali yeqolo*, literally, "money of the back" for single mothers) is regarded by many migrants as a significant part of the problem, as it is thought to incentivize premarital reproduction. While township residents use the term "money of the back" to indicate state support for women whose backs are burdened by the chores of child-rearing in a context of precarious employment, migrants see "money of the back" as state support for a sexually promiscuous lifestyle indexed by the sensual thrust of the lower back during intercourse. In this vein, migrants regard the townships as rife with sexual immorality and identify this as a primary cause of national misfortune. "If a woman behaves badly and sleeps around," one hostel-dweller insisted, "she will bring *amashwa* on herself and *amashwa* will enter the home, enter the family. Sometimes lightning [a sign of chaotic, destructive anti-fertility] will come inside, and everything becomes bad at home. Money will go away, cattle will die." The decline in the marriage rate in townships also becomes a focus of concern for rural migrants, as men and women reproduce without ever legitimizing the paternity of their offspring through bridewealth exchange. "*Amashwa* is increasing because so many children are being born 'illegally' [without bridewealth]," one migrant insisted. "That's why we see crime increasing. Because the ancestors from each side claim the child; the ancestors fight, so the child's mind is divided and it runs mad. It doesn't know where to go."

The ANC's support for children's rights is thought to exacerbate this problem. According to one Inkatha official:

> The ANC says that children are the same as their parents and have the right to do what they please. The government does not understand that we have stages of growth [rites of passage and age-grade hierarchies] for our children. Now they can go to the police station and tell them that you are abusing them if you insist that they obey you. Your child will not respect you as it is growing up and will become a gangster, because the Constitution makes things level. What do you mean that the government can orchestrate things inside my house? And with my children? This is the reason that now we are being killed by HIV/AIDS: because there is no discipline, no respect, children and women can do what they want.

This perspective links the dissolution of family structure to national disaster on the level of the HIV pandemic. This apparently absurd correlation makes sense in the context of rural conceptions of illness, which hold that violations of respect lead the ancestors to remove their protection and leave their descendants vulnerable to witchcraft in a manner widely considered to be analogous to inducing immunodeficiency. The analogy is further served by the "wasting" symptoms of AIDS, given that slow wasting—which symbolically reverses the process of growth and fruition—is considered a classic symptom of bewitchment. Claims by public health professionals that the virus is passed by sexual promiscuity dovetail neatly with perceptions that violations of respect (such as extramarital pregnancy) are punished by the ancestors with exposure to witchcraft and the wasting that ensues (cf. Nyamanga et al. 2006; Ashforth 2002).[15]

The notion of "respect" mobilized in these sentiments signifies something much more than simply deference to authority. It serves as shorthand for the entire complex of *hlonipha* rules and taboos, and calls to mind the socio-spatial structure of the ideal rural homestead that rigorously distinguishes between types of persons by the roles they perform and the spaces they can traverse. But it is important to keep in mind that the domestic ideals evoked in these statements are precisely that— ideals—mobilized by migrants and their political representatives who have a stake in portraying their rural homes in a certain light.

Many Zulu migrants like to negatively contrast the present ANC government with the apartheid regime that preceded it. As one Inkatha member put it, "Apartheid was very good because it made each of the groups follow their own culture and stay in their own place, the Indians, the Zulus . . . it did not try to make them lose their culture or change their culture like now." They regard the ANC, by contrast, as trying to homogenize South Africa's various cultural groups under the same Constitution: "We each have different ways of doing, but the ANC wants us to live by one way of life. . . . The government is overpowering our culture . . . We cannot have the government telling us to hate our family customs." I pointed out in Chapter 1 that Inkatha enjoyed a deeply complicit relationship with the National Party in opposition to the ANC before 1994. But statements like the one above reveal that the relationship was not just an alliance of convenience against a common enemy, but bore the marks of an ironic ideological convergence. Many migrants insist that segregation was good in that it allowed them to maintain their culture, and thus the conditions for social health and good fortune. In the words of one discontent: "These days the ANC lets Zulus and Indians and Whites go to the same schools, so there is a mixing of cultures and a changing of values. We have to go back to segregation! The Boer government was very bad to us, but at least they didn't enter our homesteads to change things . . . at least there was respect!"

Statements like this—while disturbing—recognize a kernel truth about the nature of colonial governance: that the policy of indirect rule operated in rural areas in two ways—by maintaining culture and promoting "tribal" identities, and by ossifying and giving teeth to patriarchal power and the domestic hierarchical relations connoted by the term "respect." Migrants worry that the ANC, slowly abandoning these aspects of indirect rule, is not only contributing to the "mixing" and breakdown of cultures, but bypassing the authority of homestead heads to directly govern interpersonal relationships in the family with liberal legislation:

> Politics is not right to enter inside the homestead. The *amakhosi* [chiefs] do not enter the homesteads. The *amakhosi* know that there is a family that manages the homestead. . . . The ANC is trying to take the position of the ancestors; but that is the role of the parents, not the government, no! South Africa is full of problems like crime and poverty for this reason . . . this is the reason that we are now being killed by AIDS.

I recorded these statements from migrants in 2008 and early 2009, just before Jacob Zuma claimed the presidency. Anti-ANC sentiment among migrants has softened somewhat since then, for they see Zuma—who plays the role of Zulu traditionalist with aplomb—as upholding their own rural values. In chapter 6 I discuss how some migrants have even switched party allegiance and voted for the ANC in the 2011 local elections, significantly eroding Inkatha's control over rural districts.

RIGHTS VERSUS RITES IN THE POLITICS OF GENDER

To illustrate contemporary debates about liberal rights, let me turn to a recent incident of violence in Umlazi, a township just south of Durban. Umlazi includes a hostel district known as T Section, situated on its southeastern periphery. Built along with the township in the early 1960s, the hostel initially housed only men from rural areas who had managed to find employment as migrant workers in the Durban area, earning it the name *empohlweni*—the place of bachelors. Most T Section residents never became part of the urban population proper: they continued to think of their rural homes as their primary residence, to which they would send remittances and return upon retirement. In the 1980s, the residents of T Section found themselves locked in outright warfare with neighboring sections of the township and "Uganda," the informal settlement nearby, which were hotbeds of UDF activism. The animosity that began during that decade persists today, so that township residents—especially youth—assiduously avoid walking through T Section for fear of assault. Township dwellers see T Section residents as "Zulu nationalists," "reactionary," and "backward," a bunch of uneducated rural bumpkins blinded by "traditional" culture and illiberal assumptions about gender and authority.

T Section continues to live up to the conservative reputation it has earned for itself in township discourse. In 2007, residents assailed a young woman by the name of Zandile Mpanza, stripped her clothes off, burned them, and then incinerated her home. Her crime? Wearing trousers—something that women resident in T Section are not allowed to do according to an unwritten rule. To make matters worse, some T Section leaders resolved thereafter to apply the same treatment in the future to anyone found violating what they saw as a basic principle of *hlonipha*.[16] The Mpanza incident provoked a great deal of controversy in the media, which followed the case as it unfolded in the national courts.[17] In discussing the case, township residents insist that the behavior of the assailants rubbed against the very grain of democracy. They point out that women in the New South Africa have rights, and are thus free to dress and behave however they like. In asserting this, they invoke the IsiZulu term *amalungelo* to capture the English notion of "rights."

On the other side of the trenches, however, T Section residents denounce Mpanza for violating what they believe to be normative gender roles. Interestingly, to capture their understanding of role distinctions T Section residents *also* invoke the term *amalungelo*. What accounts for this remarkable slippage in terminology? What explains the term's apparent double meaning? In mainstream discourse—and certainly in the media—*amalungelo* directly corresponds to the English term "rights," and typically denotes the new freedoms that individuals (specifically women and children) have enjoyed since the demise of the apartheid government. Even those who contest the meaning of the term, as T Section residents do, recognize this mainstream denotation, but they associate it with all manner of "modern" evils. As one longtime T Section resident put it, disdainfully:

Amalungelo goes with democracy. Democracy is going badly. If I want to go out at night [for extramarital sexual encounters] I am free, because I like it, it is a democratic country. If [a woman] wants to sell her body, it is up to her, you mustn't interfere with her. That's what democracy says. If your son wants to be a homosexual, he is free to do that, because it's a democracy. Democracy says do what you want, says there is no *umthetho. Amalungelo* is the culture of white people.

This same resident then offered an alternative reading of the term *amalungelo,* saying, "We [residents of T Section] want a different kind of *amalungelo,* the good *amalungelo,* the *amalungelo* of respect. We respect, and we want others to respect. Because we belong to our ancestors, we don't like whores, we don't want gay men." He draws a distinction, therefore, between "bad *amalungelo,*" which he associates with the liberal sort, and "good *amalungelo,*" which he associates with homestead order. When asked about the distinction, hostel dwellers claim that the term *amalungelo* bore a different meaning before it became associated with democratic rights:

Before, the meaning [of *amalungelo*] was that a woman could not conduct herself in a carefree manner. She had to conduct herself well, because she is a mother. And she must respect! As a man you would tell your wife that you were having a ceremony on a certain date, and she would know that she had to make beer. It is her duty . . . it falls within her domain. It is her *ilungelo.*

"The *amalungelo* of men," according to another hostel dweller, "[used to mean that] our women would normally stay at home [in rural areas], we would support them, give them money, give them food, we would do everything for our women. Those are *amalungelo.*"

In these statements, the term connotes duty, role, or responsibility, reflecting the gendered division of labor and authority in the homestead. Tellingly, the root of the word, *-lunga,* signifies a constellation of concepts that includes "to be correct," "of good behavior," "membership of a body," "anatomical joint," and "order" (Doke et al. 1990). In this sense, *amalungelo* are simply the pieces of *umthetho,* the bits of order that constitute normative social structure. In alluding to bodies and joints, the term evokes the pieces of a cow's body, which represents the material embodiment of homestead social order and the privileges particular to specific persons or classes of people (see chapter 5). In rural Zulu discourse, then, *amalungelo* (as "roles") *differentiates* persons, whereas in mainstream discourse *amalungelo* (as "rights") *equalizes* them. While the ANC holds that *amalungelo* represents productive individual freedom, their detractors see it as inviting destructive social chaos.

Female migrants also invoke the importance of hierarchical differentiation as a counterpoint to their distaste for democracy, albeit with a slightly different spin than men. According to one woman, the trouble with the "modern structure" of democracy is that by equalizing men and women—by conflating them into the same category of juridical-moral personhood—it undermines the unique prerogatives that women can otherwise claim based on their positions within the "traditional structure," as they call it. When asked to compare the position of women in the townships against the position of women in the homesteads, one female shop steward who had lived in both spaces offered the following assessment:

> In theory the townships are more gender progressive. But in the homestead it is 50/50.[18] . . . During sacrificial ceremonies, there is a structure: there are places for the men to sit and the women to sit, for the boys to sit and for the girls to sit. And the left side of the hut is for women and the right side is for men. A man cannot come to the woman's place; he could be attacked. And there are certain things that the men do, and certain things that the women do. They are separate, and their [ceremonies] are separate. And when the meat is distributed, it will be half for men, half for women, equally . . . with those special parts for men, and the special parts for the women. If there are ten containers of beer, five must go to the men, and five must go to the women. There is equal distribution of what we have. There is also a certain caucus of the home; if you do not call the females, there will be no caucus.

She negatively contrasts this arrangement with the townships:

> Townships are influenced by the modernized, by other people outside. In the urban areas, men can take any decision without considering what the women want. And go to shebeens [taverns]: the majority there are men. Go to the companies: the majority of the people employed are men. I don't see the structure where the females are participating in townships. There are no female structures in the townships. So, theoretically, urban areas are seen to be more radical, but practically, to me, women in the rural areas are respected.

In the minds of township liberals, the fact that rural homesteads involve spatial taboos that prevent women and children from entering certain areas constitutes a clear violation of democracy. But migrant women reflecting on homestead life see this division of space as precisely the substance of democracy. Many assert that women who live in townships are more vulnerable to abuse by their husbands than women in rural areas, for they can lay no claim to specific privileges or protected domains, because all people have exactly the same rights.[19] They link this deficit to the apparent lack of order in township domestic space, where the differences between men and women are not inscribed in the architecture of the household. Furthermore, women often note that homestead architecture itself actually assigns prominence to women over men, as they operate as the formal heads of uterine houses and homestead "sides" (see White 2010). Indeed, an elder woman can end up with tremendous power not only over her side of the homestead, but—after the death of her husband—over the homestead itself, even becoming the primary conduit of ancestral power. When migrant women invoke rural *hlonipha* then, they seem to emphasize the structure of difference itself. Migrant men, for their part, tend to emphasize the *hierarchical* nature of that difference, which they imagine as a rigid form of male domination—despite the fact that gendered power in homesteads is in reality quite dynamic.

Mainstream discourse all across South Africa represents the rights-oriented policies of the ANC under the rubric of "democracy." Yet many Zulu migrants read this form of democracy as culturally retrograde: it undoes the ritual work of differentiating persons, dismantles the hierarchical structure of kinship, and returns the world to a primordial state of chaotic, sterile sameness. In hierarchical societies like rural Zululand, persons at different social locations are not thought to be ontologically equivalent types of beings. But according to the logic of liberal democracy, as Alexis de Tocqueville has pointed out, each individual is thought to be fundamentally equal to all other individuals. By equalizing all persons across boundaries of gender, generation, and genealogy, democracy dissolves the re/productive differences essential to social life and threatens the foundations of fertility, health, and development, opening the door to all manner of misfortune. Democracy, in short, appears to bring about a kind of social death.

DOMESTICATION IN SYMBOLS

The data above illustrate the contours of what amounts to collective moral panic. To many rural migrants, postcolonial South Africa represents a topsy-turvy world of chaos, disorder, and immorality that threatens to collapse in a cataclysm of crime, disease, and poverty. The primary image is one of evolutionary regression, of culture giving way to amoral, animalistic impulses. As one IFP councilor put it, with a mix of sorrow and disgust:

You see, today South Africa does not know where it is going. It is like a round circle, it is going without direction, and everything is upside down. . . . The ANC, they behave too differently from us; they live in a way that is like the way of animals. They do not follow what is natural [*imvelo*] . . . they want to destroy it.

Analysts of urban-rural tensions in KwaZulu-Natal have noted that township residents denigrate their hostel-dwelling migrant neighbors as *inyamazane* (animals) as part of a broader prejudice that regards rural "country bumpkins" as backward and uncivilized (Segal 1992; Chipkin 2004; Mamdani 1996). But this prejudice also works the other way around, in similar but not identical terms. While township residents regard rural migrants as evolutionarily behind on a teleological trajectory that runs from traditional to modern—a liberal-Marxist discourse that privileges the autonomous individual with enlightened class consciousness—rural migrants regard township residents as evolutionarily regressive, undoing culture and slipping backward toward a state of nature and animalistic social disorder.[20] The image of regression and social decomposition resonates with widely held understandings about processual kinship. For rural Zulus, the process of building up a homestead through marriage, bridewealth transactions, reproduction, and life-stage rituals stands in for a broader process of creating kinship from individuals, culture from nature, cooked from raw, domestic from wild.

The crucial metaphor here is *domestication,* which, as we shall see in the following chapter, plays out most clearly in the process of ritual sacrifice. The symbolic binaries at work here can be represented like this:

nature	culture
raw	processed
individuals	kinship

Building on this concept cluster, proper social persons who demonstrate respectful decorum along lines of gender and hierarchy and observe spatial taboos stand in contrast to animals, which lack all forms of social decency. In a homologous manner, society itself—epitomized in the form of proper domestic structure—is distinguished from and pitted against wild, outside nature. Conceptually, this distinction appears most clearly at the boundary between homestead yard and surrounding bush, which becomes the object of treatment by healers solicited to protect households from the dangers of the outside, usually cast in the idiom of witchcraft. To the binaries above we could add:

animals	persons
bush	homestead
outside	inside

A further set of conceptual homologues operates in the realm of money and exchange. The process of labor migration integrates peasant and capitalist modes of production, and brings "commodity logic" into conflict with "gift logic" (Gregory 1982). According to gift logic, the health and reproduction of the body politic depends on the distribution of beer, meat, cattle, milk, and wives. When wage-earning migrants fail to redistribute their earnings through these channels, they can be accused of causing misfortunes or even of using witchcraft. The accumulation of money is therefore negatively valued within the gift economy: the commodity system's maximizing individual is the gift system's witch. As I shall demonstrate in chapter 5, in order to heal and restore the social relations damaged by workers' engagement with capitalism, certain healing rituals counterpoise an initial "heating" phase with a later "cooling" phase—also used in Zionist rites (Kiernan 1978, 1988). In some communities, money earned by migrants (thought of as "hot", unpredictable, and socially destructive) must be symbolically treated with ash (thought of as "cool", stable, and associated with fertility) to tame and domesticate the capricious fertility of capital, transforming it into a socially constructive force. Cash is often contrasted with livestock: while the former is "slippery" and "dangerous", the latter is cool and productive.

hot	cool
capricious	stable
commodity	gift
cash	livestock
destructive	productive

Notions of fertility and social reproduction are closely linked to these symbols of domestication. The act of conception and fetal development is understood as the mixing of "cool" semen with "hot" blood: male emissions "curdle" and give form to female menses. In broader idioms of fertility, rain (cool) is contrasted with lightning (hot). While rain "fertilizes" the land and brings forth crops, lightning—typically sent by witches—is regarded as a cosmically destructive force that obliterates families and homesteads:

blood	semen
lightning	rain

Each of these binaries evokes notions of processual fertility, or social reproduction as a process of *making*. These creative forces are always under threat of being reversed—a threat epitomized in the figure of the witch (*umthakathi*), the paragon of evil and social destruction. The witch is an anti-social creature that straddles the boundaries between inside and outside, society and nature. Witches go about naked (instead of clothed) during the night (instead of day), eat raw meat (instead of cooked), hold meetings in the bush (instead of the cattle byre) and associate with familiars of ambiguous taxonomy, such as baboons and bush babies, that trouble the distinction between human and animal. Not only do witches induce infertility in the people they affect, but they are known even to kill their own kin in the pursuit of cash and self-enrichment—the quintessential anti-social act. For example, witches are thought to have access to a mystical snake, known as *mamlambo,* which generates endless amounts of wealth as long as its owner continues to satisfy its craving for the flesh of his or her kin. In addition, witches are thought to have the power to "steal" the ancestors of others, unhinging them from their descendants' homesteads in order to make them "work" for their own enrichment. In effect, witchcraft represents the very antithesis of fruition and legitimate social reproduction. Witches cause sterility and social death, they disrupt generative processes by making women sterile and men impotent; they signify the very unmaking of society.

Representations of the ANC as evolutionarily regressive draw on these concept clusters. The party's policies are thought to destroy kinship, promote individual accumulation, undermine norms of respect, and promote chaotic, "animalistic" behavior among people incapable of distinguishing one person, status, or space from another. For rural migrants, the policies of the ANC are "foreign," "white," "Western," "global," supposedly derivative of ideas that ANC leaders picked up while in exile during apartheid and "imported" to South Africa.[21] When Zulu migrants cast the ANC as outsiders, they fit them squarely into the inside/outside framework within which witches are conceptualized. In Zululand, the most powerful witches are said to come from foreign places such as Swaziland and Mozambique, for the foreign registers as simultaneously powerful and dangerous. Like a witch, the ANC is also considered both powerful and dangerous. Many rural migrants I spoke to accused township residents and ANC members, not only of promoting policies that "break up families," but of "being like animals" in their sexual lives, "just having sex haphazardly, with anybody," "even copulating in public like dogs." They regarded township dwellers as "raw," uncultured beings who live in domestic structures that lack the spatial distinctions so critical to homestead life. Because of their egalitarian polices and the politics of individual rights—which are thought to promote sterile sameness—the ANC appear as active agents of anti-fertility. It is not surprising, then, that the postapartheid government is sometimes associated directly with witchcraft (Ashforth 2005; Niehaus et al. 2001).

HOUSES AND VIOLENCE

These observations help us understand the animosity that many migrants harbor toward the ANC today. Yet they may also help make sense of the forms of violence that migrants deployed in their vigilante war against the ANC and UDF during the 1980s and 1990s. The tactic that they most commonly used was to systematically burn township houses.[22] Richard Lyster, a leading lawyer for the Truth and Reconciliation Commission who investigated incidents of violence during the period, pointed out to me that "house-burning was almost without exception a tactic employed by Inkatha against the ANC. Very rarely was it the other way around. Countless houses were burned down; often with families still in them." Lyster recalled standing on a hill looking down over Mpumalanga township while Zulu *izimpi*—bands of warriors brandishing traditional weapons and regalia—looted and burned the settlement's houses one at a time, with the protection of police vehicles. We know that many rural migrants regard township houses as embodying the structural inversion of proper social order and standing for all that is wrong with democracy and individualism. While it would need more evidence to prove, it is likely that these same sentiments drove vigilantes to focus their violence on township houses during the 1980s and 1990s.

The fact that vigilantes *burned* these houses is significant. Before the political violence of the 1980s, arson was an uncommon occurrence and was usually only ever used to punish suspected witches. Witches are said to destroy the homesteads (both kinship relations and physical buildings) of their victims through ancestor-theft or by causing sterility, blocking the channels of social reproduction. But they are also known to use lightning,[23] which they send as a "blazing bird from the heavens"[24] to incinerate the homestead's great house. By striking the great house—which symbolizes the unity of the *umndeni*—witchcraft lightning destroys the material locus of social reproduction and the touchstone of moral order, and effectively unmakes all of the meticulous ritual work that goes into producing proper kinship. Suspected witches are punished with their own medicine: their houses are burned, turning them into icons of their moral flaw in a sort of homeopathic correction.[25] Reducing witches and their homes to ashes also accomplishes the symbolic work of transforming them from "hot," uncontrolled, chaotic fecundity to "cool" ash. People from rural Zululand interviewed by the anthropologist Axel-Ivar Bergland justified the long-standing custom of burning witches' homes as necessary to "cleanse the land of evil" (1976:304). Similarly, Hammond-Tooke (1977) shows that, in Zulu mythology, house-burning is deployed as punishment for incest and other crimes that violate the parameters of social reproduction.

In rural Zululand, the figure of the witch exists in what Giorgio Agamben (1995) has called "a state of exception." In ancient Greece, people who violated certain serious laws or taboos assumed the status of *homo sacer,* which meant simultaneously "sacred" and "vile" (also both "powerful" and "dangerous") in a manner redolent of the ambivalent nature of tabooed things (Hubert and Mauss 1964; Douglas 1966). *Homo sacer* exists outside of the law and outside of culture, straddling domains like a hybrid of human and animal, divided between the wilderness and civilization. In this state of legal exception, they may be killed by anyone without their murder counting as homicide, but— according to Agamben—they may not be sacrificed. This logic might help us understand why many rural Zulu communities feel within their rights to kill suspected witches. It is commonly said that witches must be killed by burning because they "cannot be cut up." Since Zulu sacrifice is considered to be the quintessential act of "cutting up," this suggests that witches—like *homo sacer*—cannot be sacrificed. The immolation of the witch signals that the witch is *not* being sacrificed; it operates not to ritually place the witch back within proper categories (which is what sacrifice is intended to accomplish), but to eliminate the witch from the system altogether, to purge the system of the dangerous contradictions—the matter-out-of-place—that the witch embodies.[26]

As I pointed out above, some migrants regard liberal township dwellers as analogous in some ways to the figure of the witch, for they violate so many of the taboos considered sacred in rural Zulu society. Indeed, migrants frequently represent township dwellers as being outside the law (*umthetho*), like the figure of *homo sacer*. Having apparently abandoned human culture, township dwellers appear as "cultureless animals," living in a state of what Agamben would call "bare life" (as opposed to living according to the proper mode of a particular human culture). As the anthropologist J. P. Kiernan (1990) has pointed out, for migrants, the township itself exists in a state of exception, riddled with mystical dangers due to its ubiquitous infractions of taboos. Using Agamben, we might say that this is what made it not only thinkable for migrants to orchestrate mass violence against township dwellers, but gave it the aura of legitimacy, for it was violence in the service of culture—the same general logic that makes the violence of the modern state seem legitimate.

Given these resonances, it is possible that Inkatha vigilantes burned down township houses in the 1980s and 1990s as a way of dramatizing their conviction that urban sociality—which the mass democratic movement was setting up as normative—destroys the conditions for human flourishing. If so, then arson was more than simply instrumental. It was a bid to heal the land by eliminating the agents of anti-fertility. It was a purgative strategy redolent of the witch-hunts that have become increasingly common across the subcontinent (Auslander 1993; Niehaus et al. 2001; Smith 2008). It was a call for the restoration of the social good freighted with normative conceptions of cosmological order. This is not unheard of. In his study of the Rwandan genocide, Christopher Taylor (1999) notes that violence perpetrated by Hutus against Tutsis unfolded according to themes that referred to popular ideas about illness and healing. Tutsis were regarded as blockages to the flow of good fortune within a specific cosmology. Acts of violence against them were not discharged indiscriminately, but were carried out according to a symbolically meaningful logic.

Nor is this kind of violence unprecedented in Zululand's history. Following the rinderpest plague that decimated herds and crops in the late 1890s, a prophesy swept through Zululand in 1905 that blamed the disaster on patriarchs who were collaborating with colonial administrators and had conceded to new bridewealth rules, the introduction of more lenient divorce legislation, and colonial appropriation of ancestral land, all of which was thought to compromise their ability to ensure the fertility of their chiefdoms. The prophesy claimed that lightning would strike these collaborators and incinerate their homes, for—given their role in hobbling social reproduction—they deserved the punishment due to witches. Galvanized by this prophesy, youths instigated a campaign to purify the land by attacking compliant patriarchs who had failed to fulfill their obligations to their communities, in what became known as the Bambatha Rebellion (Carton 2000: 63, 94). This reaction was in keeping with a long-standing motif in the indigenous politics of southern Africa: when chiefs disobey the ancestors, they are considered unfit to rule and their subjects may revolt against them, assuming the role of restorers of the land and upholders of ancestral values (see Lan 1984).[27]

The rationalizations that former vigilantes give for their attempts to sabotage the ANC in the run-up to 1994 seem to follow this motif. Given the ANC's apparent disavowal of the ancestors, the upending of gender roles and social hierarchies, and the obliteration of domestic order, they regarded the ANC as bent on destroying the conditions for legitimate social reproduction and therefore saw them as unfit to rule. Indeed, the rise of the ANC and liberal democracy was attended by its own modern-day rinderpest—a plague of HIV, rising poverty, and plummeting employment that followed on the heels of neoliberal structural adjustment—a series of misfortunes that suggested a serious case of ancestral wrath. This occasioned not only a rebellion against the ANC as the rising rulers of the nation, but a campaign of purgation that had rebels burning the houses of ANC stalwarts in townships. Today, conservative migrants continue to perceive the ANC in the mold of an illegitimate chief—one that has failed to keep the land whole and maintain the basic conditions for well-being.

In chapter 1, I examined some of the existing theories about Natal's transitional violence, pointing out that most analysts have read the conflict as driven by ethnic nationalism, by warlords, or by males eager to defend patriarchy in order to retain control over the surplus labor of women. All rely on a form of methodological individualism that leads analysts to regard the violence as merely instrumental. But it seems to me that we cannot take the violence itself for granted, for that is where the most important clues appear; the particular form of violence illuminates the perpetrators' conception of the social ills at hand. The fact that the violence was focused on township houses and the fact that it involved arson and immolation suggest that it performed a certain cultural work, that it was meant to act upon the social world beyond its immediate object. The particular form of the violence was not incidental or external to its purpose; the form was the purpose itself. To draw on J. L. Austin's (1962) notion of speech acts, vigilante violence against the ANC was perlocutionary, intended to convey a broader message about moral order, the social good, and the consequences of their violation.

The various incarnations of the instrumentalist approach—transactionalism, behavioralism, and rational choice theory—assume that humans everywhere maximize utility in line with rational calculations of cost and benefit. This approach suffuses most of the literature on conflict in the field of political science and informs the growing school of terrorism studies that sees terrorists as actors with predictable interests and economic motives, but it tends to miss a fundamental point: that the interests of actors vary across time and space, and can only be intelligible with an ethnographic understanding of the schemas of value and meaning within which decisions are made and actions take place (Gledhill 1994). Without knowledge of the mythology, ontology, and beliefs about ritual and healing that supply the animating force behind moments of violent conflict, rational choice theory cannot always fully explain political behavior—particularly that of subaltern insurgents against the modern state (cf. Kapferer 1988).

DEBATING DEMOCRACY

The perception among rural migrants today that liberal democracy is bringing about a kind of social death is partly a historical accident. Political liberation in South Africa has always been a double package: along with new individual liberties came economic liberalization. Indeed, the latter was smuggled in under the umbrella of the former, and found its legitimacy within the same rhetoric of "freedom." David Harvey (2005) posits that individual freedom is the justification that lies at the core of the neoliberal project, the mystification—or false consciousness—that produces mass consent for a program of systemic exploitation and uneven development. In other words, social liberalism and economic liberalism become two sides of the same coin. In South Africa, this double package was brought in by the ANC under the sign of "democracy," in precise accordance with the Washington Consensus model.

Given the effects of neoliberal economic policy, it seemed to many rural Zulu migrants that democracy was causing misfortune on a national scale just as theories of *amashwa* would have predicted in the wake of a widespread obliteration of hierarchies, dismantling of kinship, and departure from the ancestors. The reason they were so negatively affected by the neoliberal turn was because colonialism had stripped them of the land they needed for sustainable subsistence and integrated them into the industrial capitalist system, leaving rural homesteads totally dependent on wages from labor migration. So when deindustrialization hit South Africa and migrants lost their jobs, rural homesteads were left with very limited options for livelihood. Had this not been the case—had colonial capitalists left the rural periphery well enough alone—social reproductive processes in homesteads would have been left largely insulated from the effects of deindustrialization.

I often wonder how things might have turned out differently if after assuming power the ANC had implemented their liberal social reforms while establishing a just and equitable economic system that actualized the values of the Freedom Charter. What would migrants have to say about democracy—or, more specifically, liberal social policies—if it had not been attended by the misfortunes of neoliberal decay? I suspect they would not be reacting against it.

This is not the only reason that they object to democracy, of course. The other is that the ANC forces a certain set of values on them. And on this point rural migrants have developed quite a coherent critique. We can see how this plays out in the context of the labor movement. In chapter 1, I described how the rise of political unionism in the middle of the 1980s caused a rift between rural and urban workers who had previously coexisted without much difficulty. While COSATU sought to connect workers to the National Democratic Revolution, a number of so-called workerist unions refused to align with the ANC and UDF-led struggle and thus came to serve as a sort of refuge for workers—particularly rural migrants—who rejected NDR politics. One of these unions, called National Union, became very popular in the mid-1980s and claimed some 25,000 members at its peak.[28]

Today the idea of democracy has become a pivotal point of contestation between the two unions. COSATU claims to have a highly democratic system of representation. They back this claim by pointing to their structures of representation that nest local, regional, and national bodies in a clear system of accountability. Its leaders—from the national executives to the local shop stewards—are elected on a regular basis according to the one-person-one-vote principle, and candidates are judged (at least in theory) based on standardized performance assessments. COSATU requires its leaders to be accountable to shop stewards, requires shop stewards to be accountable to members, and purports to maintain strict transparency in all of its proceedings. Finally,

COSATU's constitution was collectively ratified and is readily available in the form of an accessible and attractive pamphlet, which organizers regularly consult. In sum, COSATU unions attempt to conform to the ideals of the democratic public sphere: every member enjoys equal voice and equal representation, leadership is contractual instead of ascribed based on status, and decisions are made without regard to the claims of kinship or clan loyalties (again, at least in theory).

COSATU organizers regard National Union, by contrast, as mired in nepotistic hierarchy with an authority structure that stifles critical thought. National Union does not hold regular elections of either shop stewards or executive leadership. Indeed, once elected (or appointed, as is often the case), most of its shop stewards serve until retirement, at which point the leadership nominates replacements. Apart from the momentary flux instigated by an internal split in 1985, the leadership of National Union has remained remarkably constant since its inception—for more than thirty years. Loyalty to particular leaders—sometimes along kinship lines, and often with reference to the lineage of the Zulu royal family, to which both National Union's founder (Selby Nsibande) and president (Zeblon Mbatha) belong—is highly prized, and often cited by workers as the reason for which they support the union. National Union's constitution is unimportant to both its leaders and members; the document itself was lost long ago, and nothing serves in its place to regulate policy and procedure. National Union members often disparage COSATU's tradition of open, inclusive debate, complaining that its young members "have no respect for their elders," that they "can say anything they wish without discipline," and that they "think that the old people know nothing."[29]

In a strange twist, however, National Union members insist that their union is more democratic than COSATU. This puzzling paradox flags an ongoing debate over the very nature of democracy itself. Members of National Union have particular expectations of the process of representation, conceiving it in terms of a given hierarchical order—not unlike the way representation works within the homestead. In other words, when National Union members use the term "democracy" with positive valence, they freight it with their own ideas about how representation should operate. While migrants from rural Zululand model democracy in terms of hierarchical encompassment, COSATU and the ANC model democracy in terms of transparency and accountability, striving for an egalitarian social field wherein each autonomous individual "naturally" represents his or her own interests.

The important point to grasp here is that these opposing variants are not simply models for *doing;* they are models for *being.* When COSATU's leaders emphasize equal franchise and the rule of constitutional law, they are not simply asserting guidelines for organizational procedure; they are insisting on a certain type of subject, consistent with that assumed in the modernizing narrative of National Democratic Revolution: a subject that is enlightened, rational, individual, and free from the restrictions of traditional norms and cultural beliefs. This ontological entailment is masked in the neutral rhetoric of democracy that COSATU deploys, which directs attention to the state of the public domain rather than to the state of the individual's soul, which is the real object of reform.

This dual purpose of democracy is precisely what the members of National Union realize and insist on illuminating. When they object to COSATU's democratic practices, they are not objecting to its institutional arrangements as such, but to the form of *personhood* that the organization enforces. As COSATU continues to gain power in workplaces across KwaZulu-Natal, National Union's members fear that the ever-expanding franchise will foist its brand of liberalism on the whole workforce through "closed-shop" agreements that require workers to join its unions. National Union's leader, Stefanos Nhleko—a trained *isangoma* (diviner)—is fond of criticizing what he sees as COSATU's malicious agenda of cultural homogenization:

> COSATU is trying to put everyone into one pot by force. God created us to be different, but COSATU and the ANC are trying to forcibly legislate a certain morality. That is not right. We cannot have a blanket morality for everyone. . . . They shouldn't import these foreign ideas to us, ideas they got while they were outside the country! . . . They have rubbished the idea of the rainbow nation.

Nhleko picks up on the fact that the notion of multiculturalism so central to the construct of the "rainbow nation" is something of a ruse; that, in reality, cultural diversity will only be tolerated so long as it conforms to the basic contours of a singular national subjectivity. Indeed, some cause for Nhleko's concern about homogenization is born out in one of COSATU's best-known mottos, which reads: "One Party, One Union, One Government, One Country." Along with their vision for unified nationalism ("One Country"), COSATU's leaders imagine a particular type of national subject, one consistent with the township sociality and liberal consciousness that gave birth to the revolution in the 1980s.

National Union members refuse to be tricked by the conceptual slippage between "democracy" and the liberal subject-making project that it entails. From the perspective of rural migrants, democracy does not liberate. It destroys. It disembeds persons from their encompassing social relationships and dismantles the hierarchies that supply the conditions for good fortune and social reproduction. The idea of democracy—as it is used in the mainstream sense—summons the specter of a fragmented, immoral social order. For them, not only does COSATU "have no culture," it actively "destroys" it. True democracy, they claim, would allow them to retain their commitment to illiberal values without being ejected from the public sphere. The National Democratic Revolution, as they see it, is actually not very democratic at all.

5

Death in an Age of Wild Ghosts

Every group . . . will entrust to bodily automatisms the values
and categories which they are most anxious to conserve.
They will know how well the past can be kept in mind by a
habitual memory sedimented in the body.

—Paul Connerton, *How Societies Remember*

Many rural migrants view the past two decades of South Africa's history according to a narrative of decay. They see the project of liberal democracy as a moral hazard, a disease that infects their families and threatens their already-precarious well-being. In the run-up to the democratic transition in 1994, many reacted to this project with violence. But today, while the conditions for violence endure, people respond primarily by ritual means. They invest a considerable amount of money and energy into restoring their homesteads as privileged domains of moral life, shoring up the fragile institutions of respect, taboo, and hierarchy that they believe to be under siege. Just as the township house became the symbolic center of counterrevolutionary violence, so the homestead—as a touchstone of nostalgic ideals about social holism—has become the symbolic center of their efforts to reconstitute a threatened moral order.

Paradoxically, this process of reaffirming life emerges most clearly in the context of rites pertaining to death. This aligns with Richard Huntington and Peter Metcalf's observation that mortuary ritual "throws into relief the most important cultural values by which people live their lives and evaluate their experiences" (1979:2). This chapter explores ritual death ways as they are typically celebrated by people across the Zululand countryside today. Given that KwaZulu-Natal has among the highest incidences of HIV in the world (39.5 percent of women attending prenatal clinics)[1] and an average life expectancy of only 51.5 years,[2] mortuary rites are a continuous concern and constitute the most exacting household expenses toward which migrants must funnel their meager wages. As with other life-cycle rituals, the rites of death must be performed with careful precision, for any breach of protocol could offend the ancestors and send the homestead spiraling into the chaos of serial misfortunes. But the inverse holds true as well: in a context of endemic poverty and joblessness, rural migrants often believe that their families' misfortunes are due, not to the predations of neoliberal capitalism, as we might expect, but to past breaches of ritual protocol. They attempt to redress these breaches by interfering in the afterlife to restore the social relations of the dead. Usually this entails reincorporating the wild ghosts of "lost" ancestors, liminal spirits that wander restlessly across the postapartheid landscape and pose grave danger to their progeny.

While these rites ostensibly aim to reincorporate the dead, they also achieve an equally important—if less explicitly acknowledged—outcome, namely, reordering the relations of the living. The practices of sacrifice and the ceremonial distribution of meat allow migrant workers to reconstitute the social order of the homestead and rebalance its structure of gender and authority. By leveraging the symbolic dimensions of bovine anatomy, these ceremonies restore persons to their proper roles and reassert the principles of social hierarchy. This ritual work reestablishes a familiar moral terrain that helps mitigate the abjection that has become the defining characteristic of rural life in neoliberal South Africa. It locates a habitable place in a morally ordered landscape, a hoped-for community enunciated in liturgies of grief and dramaturgies of mourning.

Even more important, funereal orthopraxy assembles an oppositional practice of time, a practice that runs against the official narrative of development and modernization. The people in the rural communities I studied hold that the future—progress, prosperity, development, and so on—must be built, not on rejecting the past, but by returning to it, looping back through time to reorder the dead. Many scholars have dismissed these subaltern narratives as the superstitions of an uneducated people, but they raise important questions that should not be ignored—questions about what it means to live in the aftermath of colonization and how to constitute community under a neoliberal state. In this chapter I read the quotidian death ways of rural Zululand as reflective of people's struggles to articulate calls for justice and express longings for reconciliation, and as collective ethical responses to the predations of the past. I take my cue here from Eric Mueggler (2001) and

Veena Das (1997), whose work pays close attention to what people accomplish through processes of mourning. In the context of the Kwa-Zulu-Natal countryside, how do people inhabit worlds fissured by post-colonial capitalism? How do they represent and interpret their pain? On what resources do people draw as they struggle to heal their wounds, and what images of restoration do they marshal? Finally, how can we make sense of the connections between mortuary ritual and the violence that still simmers across the province?

SPECTRAL FISSURES OF THE PAST

Shortly after I settled down in Durban for an early stint of fieldwork in 2007, I met a young man from a village in the Zululand hills whom I shall call Bhekimuzi, which means "guardian of the homestead,"—for his story relates to his domestic responsibilities. At the time, Bhekimuzi—a lanky, pensive young man in his mid-twenties—was in the midst of the drawn-out process of preparing for his marriage to Lindiwe, a young woman from his home village. Having completed his schooling and reached the age at which any respectable young man should set out to make a living for his family, Bhekimuzi was on the hunt for a job. Actually, he had already been promised one. The first in his family to have attended university, he had received a bursary for his tertiary studies from the state—a scholarship that came packaged with guaranteed employment in the Department of Social Welfare. But a year after graduation, while Bhekimuzi's peers had already received their appointments, the state had failed to open his position. To make matters worse, things with his girlfriend were not going smoothly: Lindiwe's father had grown skeptical of Bhekimuzi's ability to provide for his daughter, and her mother had taken to fighting for control over the bridewealth payments. Bhekimuzi, for his part, had started to slip into a mild depression, wondering whether the many years of structured gift-giving and careful negotiation between the two families were going to come to naught, leaving him wifeless as well as jobless—a portrait of emasculation.

With his prospects for establishing a homestead and securing a productive domestic future slipping away, Bhekimuzi sought out diviners to help him determine the genesis of his misfortunes. Through his consultations with these mediums and a series of late-night conversations with his aging grandmother, he concluded that his misfortunes derived from a careless mistake made by his father—Mandla—some twenty-five years prior. Bhekimuzi had always known that he had been conceived out of wedlock. Mandla had impregnated a casual girlfriend during one of his stints as a migrant worker in Johannesburg at around the time he married his present wife. When Bhekimuzi was born, his biological mother let Mandla take him to the home he had begun to establish with his wife, with the expectation that the wife would raise the child as her own. What Bhekimuzi had not been told, however, was that Mandla had never delivered *inhlawulo* to his biological mother—the fine, usually one cow, customarily due to the family of the mother of an "illegitimate" child before its father can claim paternity. In fact, Mandla, impecunious at the time, had failed even to perform the sacrifice that would have "brought" him from his mother's family's home to that of his father, a ritual intended to alert a child's ancestors to its whereabouts. This double oversight meant that Bhekimuzi was effectively "lost," that his existence had no ritual legitimacy, that he had fallen off the register of the living so vigilantly kept by the dead. Torn between his maternal and paternal families, stolen from the home of the former and unknown in the home of the latter, Bhekimuzi had no ancestors to protect him and ensure his success. This tear in the ritual fabric of his kinship manifested in his inability to secure a wife and a job—the preconditions for successful domestic reproduction.

With the support of his grandmother—Mandla's mother—Bhekimuzi confronted Mandla with his concerns, and asked him to pay *inhlawulo* to the family of his one-time lover. But Mandla, an aging patriarch beleaguered by the financial demands of his many dependents and peeved by his son's impertinence, refused to rectify his ritual malpractice. Disappointed but resolute, Bhekimuzi decided to take matters into his own hands. Marshalling all the cash he could gather, he made plans to purchase a cow and a goat, find the family of his biological mother, and—acting in the place of his father *as if* he were a responsible young suitor—deliver the cow as *inhlawulo* to his deceased maternal grandfather, ritually remediating mistakes committed by his parents before he was even born. He would then slaughter the goat in order to announce to his maternal ancestors that he would be "moving" to his father's homestead, thereby retroactively securing their blessing for him to receive the recognition and protection of his paternal ancestors.

Given that most families lack the financial means to execute all of the ceremonies that they technically should, it is not uncommon across the Zululand countryside for life cycles to be out of sync with their ritual representations. In Bhekimuzi's case, the diviners flagged the fact that, in retrospect, his life was a contradiction, that he existed in a world in which his existence was not yet socially possible. In such situations a series of misfortunes usually illuminates a ritual omission in the past. The only solution is for the living to return to the past to act as if they were the agents of its present, carefully filling in gaps that would only be recognized in its future. This is why one can find postmenopausal grandmothers performing sacrifices meant to announce their nubility, or young men paying bridewealth to their mothers on behalf of their deceased fathers. The ever-present possibility of finding errors in the past is one of the reasons why people devote such extraordinary attention to the details of ritual protocol (White 2001:464) and helps explain why rural Zulus tend to obsess over *umthetho,* as described in chapter 2.

THE DOMESTICATION OF WILD GHOSTS

Death lives with us every day. Indeed our ways of dying are our ways
of living. Or should I say our ways of living are our ways of dying?
—Zakes Mda, *Ways of Dying*

Pointing to how past ritual omissions have left people lost and disconnected from their ancestors is a common way of explaining misfortune. But another, equally common explanation is that the ancestors themselves have become lost. I encountered many such stories while living in rural Zululand, but one from a family in a village near Eshowe stands out in particular. The Shabalala family had long been preparing for a sacrificial ceremony in honor of their deceased patriarch, Zweli. Custom dictates that each of a deceased patriarch's sons, in order of geniture, must buy and sacrifice an ox to ensure the patriarch's full integration into the communion of ancestors in a ceremony known as *umkhuphulo,* "the lifting up."[3] It was the turn of Kwanele, the diffident youngest son of Zweli's fourth and last wife. He had just saved enough money from his new janitorial job in Johannesburg to buy an ox— which cost R4,000 (about $360 at the time)—with which to discharge this duty. But as Kwanele was en route to the homestead, the ox died suddenly along the way. Because the beast had not been sick or injured, everyone suspected that its death was punishment by the ancestors for some mistake.

Concerned about this shocking onslaught of misfortune, the agnates arranged to visit a particularly famous diviner—renowned as the most powerful in Zululand—in order to learn what had gone wrong. After an expensive, all-day journey, we returned home with some disturbing new knowledge about Zweli. He had died while living in Johannesburg, where he worked at Soweto's sprawling Baragwanath Hospital. After learning of his death, his brothers had travelled to the city to collect his body from the morgue, returning it for burial in the center of his rural homestead. But now, two generations later, the diviner revealed not only that Zweli had died a violent death—that he had been stabbed— but that his spirit (*idlozi*) had been accidentally "lost" along the journey home, unhinged from its corpse, and was now wandering as a wild ghost somewhere between the city and the countryside. Misfortunes would continue to beset the homestead until the spirit was "fetched" and brought back home.[4]

To recover the *idlozi*, Kwanele and his agnates had to travel to the Johannesburg morgue where Zweli's brothers had originally picked up his body. I did not accompany them on this journey, but was able to piece together the story after the fact. Gathering solemnly before the drawer in which the body had been stored, they waved the branch of a certain small thorn tree[5] to incantations intended to inform the *idlozi* who they were and what they were doing. Kwanele, meanwhile, held out the inner stomach (*incekwa*) of the goat they had sacrificed at the homestead the previous day in order to announce their journey to the ancestors. The branch and the stomach are used to "attach" to the wild ghost so that it can be lured back to the homestead. In all of this the agnates repeated the exact actions that had been performed by Zweli's brothers decades before, but were careful this time not to offend the slightest detail of protocol and thus risk losing the spirit all over again.

During the trip home, in a hired minivan that had been smeared with *umswane*—the mulch taken from the stomach of the sacrificial goat, which is used to draw the spirit along—the men observed strict silence. Kwanele broke the silence only to inform the *idlozi* when they changed roads, when they crossed rivers, when they transected district boundaries, when they stopped for food and fuel, and when they disembarked from the minivan to finally ascend the hills surrounding their homestead on foot, rehearsing the well-worn homeward journey like a liturgical prayer. The poetry of travel while escorting the dead operates as healing practice itself, stitching the two poles of the migratory existence together into a seamless whole, bridging the pain-ridden bifurcations of space and time that separate rural from urban. To use Erik Mueggler's elegant language: "Moving with deliberate rhythms through spatial and temporal geographies, the walk poetry of exorcisms unravels [domestic] congestions, restoring smooth relations in lived places, allowing difficult memories to recede into past time" (2001:249; see also Gilbert 1991).

During the journey, the men focused intensively on the *idlozi,* almost willing it along, knowing that any lapse of concentration into idle chatter or disrespectful laughter could mean its re-disappearance altogether—a devastating eventuality of which they would not be aware until additional misfortunes struck the homestead, perhaps years in the future. This tenuous hold on the liminal spirit offers poignant commentary on the experience of migrancy itself, reflecting the constant anxieties that families have about "losing" their relatives to the cities, along with the support that they promise for their often-desperate rural homesteads. Just as the domestication of wild ghosts is necessary in order to make the ancestor "work" for the homestead, so migrant workers are enjoined to "work" for the homestead by remitting their wages and returning with livestock for use in ritual and exchange. The spectral image of the wild ghost reflects the image of the morally abhorrent *isibhunguki* (absconder), the migrant worker who abandons all responsibility for his rural home and never returns, thus severing the crucial link between industrial wages and rural subsistence upon which rural social reproduction remains predicated.[6] According to one of my acquaintances, the *isibhunguki* "is regarded as someone very bad and selfish," someone who "completely disconnects from his family and runs [away] with his money."[7]

These anxieties about the geographical fragmentation of families reflect how rural Zulus imagine postcolonial space, as still bearing the residue of racialized fissures between rural and urban, but without the pass laws that once helped prevent migrants from being folded into the cities forever. Today, families endeavor constantly to draw migrants back toward the center, rescuing them from the anonymity and infectious individualism of urban spaces. The morally freighted discourse about witchcraft adds another dimension to this critical commentary. Witches are thought to "steal" the ancestors of others, appropriating the vital force of the dead in order to protect and enrich themselves, while leaving their victims' families unprotected.[8] Drawing on this idiom, many migrants see urban employers as parasitic, witch-like figures that appropriate the life forces of laborers, engorging themselves by sucking the vital energies of rural men away from their already-impoverished homesteads.

Upon arriving home, the agnates took the branch—with the wild ghost attached—to the great house, where they announced their arrival to the ancestors, imploring them to receive the spirit of their dead kinsman. They then prepared for a sacrificial cleansing ceremony known as *ukugeza*. Because Zweli had died violently, his spirit was considered "dirty" and unfit to enter the homestead. To bury a violated body in the homestead is to render the rest of the family susceptible to the same fate, vulnerable to death by stabbing for generations to come. With this in mind, the cleansing ceremony takes place outside the homestead, where the dirty body cannot infect the family. If the body is present, the blood of the deceased is mixed with the bile[9] and *umswane* (digested mulch) of a sacrificial goat—substances that, given their association with digestion, are capable of "domesticating" the wild ghost, making it fit to enter the home. If the body is already buried, as in the case of Zweli, the bile and mulch are mixed with water and sprinkled over the grave. This ceremony highlights the powerful analogies between the homestead and the bodies of its individual residents. The injunction to cleanse and domesticate the wild ghost (outside) mirrors the imperative to maintain the purity and integrity of the homestead (inside). If the body of the deceased is violated, then the homestead cannot be whole, its boundaries become vulnerable to transgression by dangerous outside forces. Like life cycles and ritual time, homesteads and their constituent bodies must be kept in step with each other; any gap between the state of the homestead and the state of the body promises to invite pain and ruin.

REMAKING THE HOMESTEAD

I was not present when Kwanele eventually performed the *umkhuphulo* ceremony he had originally intended to do before the mayhem set in. But I attended many similar ceremonies, which are designed to "lift up" a deceased family member into the community of ancestors. One of these took place in the homestead of Bhekimuzi and his father Mandla—the family I introduced at the beginning of this chapter. I recount this ceremony in detail in the pages that follow, since it forms an important part of the ritual activity that people across rural Zululand engage in so as to shore up the conditions for fruition and good fortune in their homesteads.

Like all ceremonies entailing cattle sacrifice, *umkhuphulo* rituals unfold over a period of four days. On the first day—a Thursday in early August—the agnates slaughtered a white goat to "report" the impending ceremony to the ancestors. This initial stage was a private affair, conducted with very little pomp; outsiders knew not to attend, for the meat was to be consumed solely by the members of the homestead. Hanging the goat's inner stomach (*incekwa*) at the shrine of the great house, the agnates gathered to explain to the ancestors the purpose of the event and the outcomes that the family desired, namely, to integrate the spirit of Mandla's father, Phumlani, into the community of ancestors that protect the homestead. But, as we shall see, the ceremony does not accomplish these ends by magical means. Rather, its efficacy lies in the motivated minutiae of the performance, the nuance of its mundane details.

By the second day—the day of the slaughter—all of the diasporic members of the *umndeni* had arrived, and neighbors had come by to help with the heavy labor of handling the meat. As per custom, the beast selected for sacrifice had been purchased with the wages of the family's migrant members. When I asked him about this, Mandla told me that sacrificial beasts should be purchased with cash from wages rather than culled from the homestead's existing herds, the idea being to link the workplace to the homestead and ensure that otherwise capricious, "slippery" cash is tied to kinship-making and contributes to the homestead's reproduction. In this respect, sacrificial ritual reflects the awareness that all productive pursuits—especially wage labor—must refer back to the homestead and ancestors as the source of fruition, counteracting the centrifugal individualism of selfish pursuits in the capitalist economy.

As Phumlani's seniormost living son, Mandla assumed the role of ritual priest for the family and directed the proceedings. Clad in the blue, two-piece cotton coveralls that he wore at his workplace, Mandla entered the byre where the cow was tied and used the homestead's heirloom spear to sever its spine at the base of the neck. The cow collapsed in a peal of loud bellows, to which women—standing outside at the top of the byre—ululated excitedly in response. The most sacred act of the ritual, *ukuhlaba,* "the piercing," metonymically symbolizes the sacrificial process in its entirety. Having squatted silently near the entrance of the byre until this point, Mandla's agnates moved into action. They inverted the body of the beast and positioned it firmly between two logs, coordinating its head up toward the great house and its hindquarters down toward the gate, so that its "junior" and "senior" sides corresponded isometrically with the "junior" and "senior" sides of the homestead, reiterating the intimate correspondence between the dwelling and the body of the cow. Splayed out in this supine position the beast reflects the left/right, high/low, inside/outside, center/periphery, male/female, junior/senior dimensions of the human body, the house, and the homestead.

FIGURE 10. Mandla, surrounded by his agnates, skinning the sacrificial cow. August 2007. Photo by author.

With the cow in position, the second phase of the rite commenced: the elaborate processes of *ukuhlinza,* "the skinning," and *ukuhlahlela,* "the cutting up." At this point a wrinkled elder assumed the role of ritual specialist and dictated—in a gently pedagogical tone—procedures to the young men who had descended with knives upon the carcass. He instructed them in the conventions of indigenous anatomical classification, teaching them how and in what order to cut out certain pieces of meat, how to distribute the cuts, and how to prepare them for consumption. Each cut of meat bears three explicit characteristics: (a) a *gender,* marking it male or female; (b) a *status,* reserving it for possession by a particular category of person; and (c) a *recipe,* designating it for either roasting or boiling. In the process of teaching this matrix of classifications—which encompasses around sixty named cuts of meat— the elder effectively conscientized the young men to appreciate the associations between anatomical structure and social order.[10]

The procedure for disassembling the carcass followed a protocol referred to—unsurprisingly—as *umthetho,* the same word that is used for the rules of kinship. Any violation of the rules might undermine the efficacy of the ritual, incite the wrath of the ancestors and threaten the health of the homestead. Mandla described the process of skinning and cutting as one of "peeling away the layers" of the beast, working inward toward the most important elements of the cow. Initiating the skinning process, Mandla made the first cut down its underside from throat to anus—a metonym for the whole process—and handed over to the younger agnates who slit the hide down the limbs before peeling it off and arranging it like a tarp beneath the carcass. Then they began the disaggregation of the body. They carefully extricated the outermost layer of muscle—the sacred *insonyama*—from around the outside of the abdominal cavity and hung it on the fence at the head of the byre. The senior-side *insonyama,* coded male, belongs specifically to the ancestors, the chief, and the homestead head. Just as this thin, outer-layer muscle encompasses the body of the sacrificial beast, these male principals metaphorically encompass the kinship group and the territorial district. According to the same logic of encompassment, the junior-side *insonyama* belongs to the senior wife of the homestead.

The forelegs of the beast were removed next, beginning with the limb corresponding with the senior side of the homestead. The "senior side" foreleg—coded male—was then subdivided into three parts, from higher/inner to lower/outer: the scapula for the elders, the humerus for the young men, and the ulna/radius for the little boys, so the limb becomes homologous with the age-grade hierarchy of authority and geniture. The "junior side" foreleg, by contrast, is coded female, and formally designated for the daughters of the homestead. Unlike its senior counterpart, the junior foreleg is not subdivided, reflecting not only the less elaborate hierarchy among daughters as compared to sons, but also the less elaborate hierarchy on the junior side of the homestead as compared to the senior side. The distinction between the senior and junior forelegs somaticizes everyday distinctions between the two sides of the homestead—patterned *explicitly* according to a hierarchical logic and *implicitly* according to a gendered logic.[11]

Next, the agnates cut off the hind legs, beginning, again, with the senior side. The hind legs both bear a female coding and belong to the agnates' wives,[12] with the two tibias reserved specifically for the wife of the senior son of the homestead. Unlike the senior-side foreleg, the hind legs bear no internal hierarchical distinctions. The different prescriptions for the four legs of the beast mirror the relative significance of the portion of the homestead to which they correspond—again, as if the supine beast represented a map of the homestead itself, with hierarchical and gendered elaboration increasing from bottom to top and from left to right.

Then the agnates shifted their attention to the abdominal cavity and the internal organs that it contains. They split the rib cage medially down both sides with an axe, and then removed the chest in one piece like the lid of an enormous pot—an analogy they use themselves, for the chest, coded strongly female, belongs to the agnates' wives and signals their role in cooking/domestication. Following its removal, the agnates pulled out the internal organs through the back of the carcass onto the floor of the byre. The rumen—the first and largest segment of the stomach and considered the quintessential meat of the agnates' wives—was cut open and the *umswane* (mulch) scooped out into a pile on the ground. The second stomach and the intestines also belong to the agnates' wives and were similarly slit and purged of their partially digested contents. The task of handling the digestive tract usually belongs to women, marking the only time at which they participate in the sacrificial process.

With the digestive organs removed, Mandla cut out the gallbladder (*inyongo*), being careful not to spill its contents. By far the most ritually significant part of the beast, the gallbladder can only be handled by the homestead head or other senior agnates. Before conveying the gall in a jar to its place at the central hearth of the great house, Mandla sprinkled some of it onto the pile of *umswane* removed from the stomachs, symbolically "cleansing" the family, which the *umswane* represents. Meanwhile, the other agnates extracted the remaining internal organs, all of which bear a male coding: the heart, lungs, and spleen—which belong to the boys—and the liver, which belongs to the homestead head and his chief as a symbol of the "blood" through which rural Zulus read the principles of patrilineal and patriarchal authority, courage, and strength.

The gallbladder carries its curious import for two reasons. First, because it contains the enzymes necessary for effective digestion; and second, because it has only one opening, like a cul-de-sac in an otherwise continuous tube through which digestive matter flows, meaning that it contains the concentrated essence or spirit (*ithunzi*) of the beast. For these reasons, the gallbladder signifies the principle of homestead domesticity cast in the idiom of digestion, and represents the sacrificial beast in token form. It is said that when the ancestors see the gallbladder at the hearth, they know that a beast has been sacrificed for them. The association between digestion and domesticity also helps explain the significance of the inner stomach. While the rumen processes the cud into a rough mulch, the inner stomach digests it into a fine gruel. Like the gallbladder, the inner stomach represents not only the digestive principle but also the essence of the beast, which is why it is hung at the shrine as the "favorite" meat of the ancestors. The female gendering of the two stomachs and the fact that they belong to the agnates' wives implies that the digestive principle itself bears a distinctively female/ motherly character, as it invokes notions of passage from *wild nature* (raw) to *domestic homestead* (cooked)—the defining characteristic of cultured humanity in Zulu idiom. The chest is gendered female by association, since it encompasses and protects the processes of cooking and culturing, like a pot.

After excising the internal organs from the carcass, the agnates separated the sides of the rib cage[13] from the spine with an axe. The senior side, coded female, was given to the agnates' wives, while the junior side was given to their sisters' daughters. As they removed the sides, Mandla instructed them to leave two or three ribs on each side of the spine intact, jutting out like "branches" and thus creating the image that patriarchs employ to describe their genealogy: a series of eldest sons (vertebrae) that descend from the clan hero (the head), with junior sons (ribs) branching off.

The agnates then separated the clavicles from the top of the spine and the pelvis from the bottom. People consider these particularly sacred portions of the cow. Like the *umswane,* they can only be handled by the closest and most trusted members of the *umndeni* in order to prevent them from falling into the hands of witches (because these pieces symbolize the *umndeni* itself—by representing the two ends of the spine that bracket the cow—witches can use them in concoctions that can destroy the homestead). The agnates then cut the spine into pieces that they place in the pile of *umswane* on the ground. Bearing the twin associations of cooking and cleansing, the *umswane* serves as a key metaphor for domestic socialization. At funerals, family members who have had contact with the corpse wash their hands in water mixed with *umswane* before entering the homestead in order to keep pollution out. During some ritual ceremonies, the celebrants cut into the stomach of the cow and place a coin into the *umswane,* which acts to symbolically root wealth into the very center of the properly structured body politic, covering it—cleansing it, socializing it—with a substance that represents the domestic principle.[14] Placing the segments of the spine into the pile of *umswane* thus creates an evocative image of the patrilineal-political principle "cooking" in (and being domesticated by) the hot, still-steaming surrounds of the digestive-domestic principle.

With all other pieces removed, only the head remained on the blood-soaked hide. The head is gendered powerfully male and symbolizes the great house, the head of the homestead, and, by extension, the general principle of patriarchy.[15] More than any other cut, the meat of the head functions as the principal item of exchange out to the other men of the chiefdom. By contrast, the quintessential female meat—the stomach—stays inside the homestead to be eaten only by its residents. Metaphorically, then, the meat of the head extends *outward* while the meat of the stomach centers *inwards,* reinforcing the symbolic dichotomy between the head as the principle of male hierarchy and political extension, and the stomach as the principle of female reproduction and domestic centeredness. Similarly, all male cuts extend beyond homestead kinship to people throughout the community who occupy the generalized category that each cut represents, while female cuts are limited solely to persons related to the homestead.[16]

As they removed each piece from the carcass, the agnates carried it up to the great house, placing it at the back and toward the right side of the hut. In doing so, they traced the sacrosanct path of male *hlonipha,* moving down through the lower gate of the byre and up through the right side of the homestead along the inner yard, mapping the key coordinates of authority and inscribing the proper contours of the ideal family. I noticed that this same pattern of movement was followed during ceremonies even when the celebrants' homesteads looked nothing like the orthodox model (many resource-poor homesteads are poorly maintained and often even lack a real cattle byre). In such cases, the pathway of *hlonipha* is almost entirely imaginary—yet the celebrants tread it nonetheless, as if recuperating the inscriptions of an older social older from beneath the worn parchment of the real (cf. White 2001).

But it is not only the physical movements of the agnates that reinscribe the family. The laborious process of dismantling the sacrificial cow does so even more powerfully, moving inward from sides/periphery toward the center, reducing the body to its most symbolically significant elements epitomized in the evocative image of the head left attached to a naked spine. The act of disaggregating the beast and distributing its pieces is known as *ukuhlukanisa* (lit., "differentiation"), for it produces the differences that rural Zulus take to be so crucial to social being. This formulaic process unmakes the cow in order to remake the homestead, breaking apart the undifferentiated whole in order to disambiguate its

#	Anatomical Part	Translation	Gender	Status	Preparation
1.	*ibilo*	dewlap	none	ancestors	boiled
2.	*insonyama* (senior)	(see description in text)	M	homestead head	roasted
3.	*insonyama* (junior)	(see description in text)	F	agnates' wives	boiled
4.	*umkhono* (senior)	foreleg[a]	M	men	roasted
5.	—*isipanga*[b]	scapula	M	old men	roasted
6.	—*elifupi*	humerus	M	young men	roasted
7.	—*ugalo*	ulna/radius	M	young boys	roasted
8.	*umkhono* (junior)	foreleg	F	daughters	curried
9.	*imilenze*	hindlegs	F	agnates' wives	boiled
10.	—*ugalo* (senior)	radius	F	senior wife of eldest son	boiled
11.	—*ugalo* (junior)	radius	F	assistant to senior wife of eldest son	boiled
12.	—*amavenge*	radius meat	F	agnates' wives	boiled
13.	*ibele*	udder	F	daughters	roasted
14.	*isikababa senkomo*	penis/testicles	none	none	discarded
15.	*isifuba*	chest	F	agnates' wives	boiled
16.	—*ungeklane*	sternum fat	F	agnates' wives	boiled
17.	*imikhele*	pieces of side meat	M	headman, men	roasted
18.	*amantshonthso*	"stolen" bits of meat	M	agnates	roasted
19.	*inyongo*	gallbladder	none	ancestors	none
20.	*umhlwehlwe*	peritoneum[c]	F	daughter at menarche	n/a
21.	*usu*	first stomach	F	agnates' wives	boiled
22.	*itwane*	second stomach	F	agnates' wives	boiled
23.	*inanzi/incekwa*	third stomach	F	senior wife	boiled
24.	*umswane*	cud	F	females	none
25.	*amathumbu*	intestines	F		
26.	—*omhlope*	"white" (large) intestine	M	headman, men	roasted
27.	—*omnyama*	"black" (small) intestine	F	agnates' wives	boiled
28.	*ithunjana*	appendix	none	none	roasted
29.	*isibindi*	liver	none	men, young men, agnates' wives	roasted
30.	*inhliziyo*	heart	M	young boys	roasted
31.	*imiphaphu*	lungs	M	young boys	roasted
32.	*izinso* (senior)	kidney	M	men	boiled

#	Anatomical Part	Translation	Gender	Status	Preparation
33.	*izinso* (junior)	kidney	M	young men	boiled
34.	*indlala engasensweni*	adrenal gland	M	males	boiled
35.	*ubende*	spleen	M	young boys	roasted
36.	*inyaka/amanyikwe*	pancreas	none	none	none
37.	*amasende*	testicles	M	young boys	boiled
38.	*umbukhu*	meat along spine	M	homestead head	roasted
39.	*umhlubulo* (senior)	rib cage side	F	agnates' wives	boiled
40.	*umhlubulo* (junior)	rib cage side	F	daughters	boiled
41.	*izimpukane,* or *imidikizo*	thin muscle beneath skin	M	homestead head	burned
42.	*umkokhodla*	spine	none	*umndeni*	boiled
43.	*amanqina*	hooves/feet	M	young boys	boiled
44.	*isingqe*	pelvis	none	*umndeni*	boiled
45.	—*ubambo*	meat on pelvis	F	agnates' wives	boiled
46.	*umbanqwana*	sternum	M	elder men	roasted
47.	*indlala yegilo*	thyroid gland	M	males	boiled
48.	*inhloko,* or *ikhanda*	head	M	men	boiled
49.	—*isicanti/isehlula umpisi*	clavicle	M	homestead head, men	boiled
50.	—*izunguzungu*	top ribs	M	homestead head, men	boiled
51.	—*ulimi/umthombo*	tongue	M	men, young men	boiled
52.	—*ilunda*	nape	none	children of daughters	boiled
53.	—*idhevu*	upper portion of face	M	young boys	boiled
54.	——*imihlati*	jaws, cheeks	M	young boys	roasted
55.	——*ubuso,* or *isikoko*	face	M	young boys	boiled
56.	——*umpemulo*	nose	M	young boys	boiled
57.	——*izindlebe*	ears	M	young boys	boiled
58.	——*amehlo*	eyes	M	young boys	boiled
59.	—*izimpondo*	horns	none	ancestors	none

[a] Where the meat in question comes attached to bones—as with the legs, for example—it is the bones that technically "belong" to certain persons/statuses/roles rather than the meat itself.

[b] Dashes indicate that the piece in question is a sub-piece of the above. For example, 5, 6, and 7 are all sub-pieces of 4.

[c] A fatty membrane covering the bowels. IsiZulu speakers often say this is similar to a caul, the membrane that sometimes covers a newborn, which may explain why it is used to cloak celebrants in rites of passage.

parts through careful separation and distribution. During this process the sacrificial beast serves as a textbook of normative social order, a mnemonic of morality that reminds the community about the roles, statuses, and rights of properly social persons. Through the exercise of unmaking the sacrificial beast and distributing its parts, the homestead—and by extension, society itself—gets remade in its image.

COOKING THE FAMILY

The meat was left in the great house overnight so that it could be "smelled" and "licked" by the ancestors—a process that is said to turn the meat "red." The following day, preparations for the feast began in earnest. The meat was cooked over a makeshift outdoor hearth in the center of the homestead on a fire kindled with coals from the hearth of the senior wife's hut. Young men also built a fire in the byre, where they prepared many of their designated cuts themselves. As the table above illustrates, most male cuts must be roasted and most female cuts boiled. The gendered division of labor holds that the roasting is done by males *outside,* and the boiling done by females *inside.* The boiling takes place in cast-iron pots, which bear a female valence and are frequently associated with both wombs and houses. The operative distinction here opposes "meat cooked with fire" (fire = red, hot, capricious, dangerous) and "meat cooked with water" (water = white, cool, stable, healing). Cooking with water is thought to mark a more "cultured" way of preparing food than cooking with fire, since it mediates the raw heat of a fire through the medium of water (cf. Hammond-Tooke 1977; Lévi-Strauss 1969).

This gendered symbolism inverts the usual coding of females and males, where femaleness typically invokes the "heat" of unpredictable female fertility and maleness the "coolness" of the stable, structuring order that men bring to female reproductive potential through bridewealth. This inversion helps foreground the *domesticating* functions of the sacrificial ceremony, which brings migrant males from the workplace (a masculine space rife with the capricious fertility of "hot" money) to the homestead (a feminine space[17] and the material embodiment of socio-structural order). The act of returning home with wages dramatizes the imperative to *socialize* money by integrating it into the gift economy of the homestead. The purchase of cattle for sacrifice somaticizes this process of domesticating money into a force for legitimate social reproduction. During the feast, roasted meat (fire/hot) is served and eaten first, as a starter, to be followed by a main portion constituted by boiled meat (water/cool). This sequence mirrors the sequence of many healing rites that move from fire/heat/chaos to water/cool/structure.

The most conspicuous exception to this general pattern has the cow's head—the most masculine portion of the beast—assigned to the boiling pot, while all other male meat gets roasted. The boiling of the head is the most important aspect of the cooking process, and takes place as part of a side event known as "the crushing of the skull." In an additional inversion of gender roles, males attend to the boiling of the head in cast-iron pots in the center of the homestead. Working upon the association between iron pot and hut/womb, the symbolism of this event reflects the key concepts of the great house, which is an *androgynous* house that represents both the homestead head and his mother—the two primary figures of power and authority. The boiling of the head reflects this crucial androgyny, inasmuch as the head—which represents masculine political authority—gets *encompassed by* the cast-iron pot, which symbolizes the principle of domesticity. This complex symbol both reflects and reproduces the notion that male authority in the homestead hinges on the sanction of one or more female principles: *always* his mother—his most immediate link to ancestral presence—and often also his bridewealth-linked sister, who is said to have "built" his homestead by bringing in cattle from her own marriage to finance his.

As the members of the homestead, their relatives, and their guests partook of Mandla's feast, they found their places in a rigid spatial order. The elder men gathered in and around the great house, while the young men gathered in the byre. The boys, meanwhile, took their cuts of meat—the lungs and the heart—*outside* the homestead, after which they were called by an elder into the byre to finish off the ears and lips on the head, symbolically beginning to assume the prerogatives of the higher age-set. As with the other ceremonies I attended, Mandla and his family placed a premium on maintaining generational and gender separateness during the feast, seeing this respect for spatial boundaries as critical to proper *hlonipha* behavior. Migrant workers who lament the disintegration of kinship, respect, and gender roles in the urban townships often refer for evidence to the seating arrangements prescribed during ceremonial feasts, noting that when township-dwellers gather for ceremonies, they are all "mixed up" and lack all understanding of "structure."

The distribution of the female portions of the sacrificial ox happened through a process known as *isithebe*—a word also used to refer to the

Eucharist—whereby the female relatives receive portions of meat to take to their houses for their husbands and children.[18] There are two parts to this process. The first happens in the senior wife's kitchen and includes only the mothers of the homestead head and their sons' wives. The senior wife typically assumes responsibility for cutting and dividing the meat equally among the women.[19] The two legs, the chest, and the digestive organs—all of which are boiled—were divided with meticulous attention to equality, regardless of the status, seniority, or size of each woman's family. By contrast, the senior side of the rib cage was roasted by a young boy (for roasting should only be done by males) and was eaten casually by the women as a snack. The portion of meat received by each "house" then enters into a complex process of tribute[20] whereby the junior wives of each side of the homestead offer portions of their meat to their seniors, and the senior wife of the junior side of the homestead offers portions of her allotment to the senior wife of the senior side. In this manner, women use the body of the ox to rehearse the lines and nodes of authority that define the homestead. Thereafter, the married sisters and daughters of the agnatic cluster began the second *isithebe* in one of the homestead's vacant huts. They divided the udder, the junior side *insonyama*, the junior side of the rib cage, and a portion of the digestive organs among themselves, to be packed up and taken back to their marital homesteads.

During the process of feasting, the sacrificial cow—which is identified with the individual whose wild ghost is in question (in this case, Phumlani)—literally gets absorbed into the family. The wild ghost is thus rendered back into its moral form: dissolved into the fabric of society and effectively "returned" to the homestead.

THE EFFICACY OF SACRIFICE

I noted above that the process of disaggregating the body of the beast symbolically restores an imagined normative social order in an attempt to redress imbalances that have led to affliction. But the idiom of restoration here is misleading, for there is never an identifiable moment in the past when a given homestead actually aligned with the ideal that ritual practitioners attempt to recover. The ritual acts *as if* it is restorative, but it is actually constitutive; or, to use Michael Silverstein's (1992, 2003) terms, while kinship order appears as a presupposition of the ritual, it is actually its entailment. That is the mode of its efficacy. The ritual cannot actually be about restoration, because the homestead is not composed of people who exist in a certain a priori order, as if born into predetermined pigeonholes; the ritual actually *produces* that order. Much of this happens during the mundane process of preparing for the ritual, when decisions are made about who will visit the diviners, who will fetch the livestock, who will slaughter the animals, who will do the cooking, and who will be invited to attend and receive certain pieces of meat. These negotiations produce the statuses, roles, and relationships that appear as fait accompli once the ritual begins and the pieces of meat are distributed. In other words, the preparations for the ritual produce the social order to which the ritual refers.

The process of distributing the meat operates in a similar way, by differentiating persons and constituting kinship. For example, it is not just that men are men and *therefore* they eat the head, but that men are men *because* they eat the head. The process of consuming the meat of the head makes a person a man, disambiguating him from the morass of humanity and marking him as a particular kind of person imbued with the meanings that the head carries. This is an actional model of kinship: kinship relations are not static, classificatory, or given in the natural order of things; they are created, and in this case created in part through the distribution and consumption of sacrificial meat.

For rural Zulus, both dimensions of the ritual appear to recenter kinship and restructure the home: the capture of the wild ghost restores the domestic orientation of the ancestors, while the distribution of meat reestablishes the socio-spatial parameters of the ideal homestead, even where it exists only in the imagination. Both recall the structure of Arnold van Gennep's (1909) *rites de passage*. The wild ghost, having been separated from its family at death and suspended in a state of dangerous liminality, must be ritually reincorporated into the society of ancestors. In the same manner, the family, suspended in a liminal state of dangerous misfortune (Douglas 1966), must reorient its coordinates in accordance with a normative vision of gender and hierarchy to resume full re/productive order. Therapy, as Jean Comaroff (1980) notes, is about reintegrating the symbolic categories of a structurally configured social universe.

On the face of it, the themes of reintegration and reincorporation of kin—both living and dead—that weave through these rites seem to affirm the conclusions of Durkheim (1915) and Radcliffe-Brown (1964), who saw funerary ritual as producing social solidarity and reproducing social structure. But ritual practitioners in rural Zululand have a different theory. For them, the value of the rites lie not in forging social solidarity, but in producing the hierarchical social *differences* essential to normative reproductivity. The sacramental moment of piercing captures this schema well: the homestead head, in his ritual role as mediator between the ancestors and their descendants, uses the sacred spear from his mother's house to pierce the beast, symbolizing the generative differentiation of the whole into its constitutive parts: a phallic thrust that ignites an explosion of social fecundity.[21] As one common origin myth has it, humanity itself was belched forth from the bowels of a cow.

If democracy threatens the nation with an infectious, barren sameness, then the rituals of death offer a powerful antidote: a dream of differentiated, generative community deployed to counteract the nightmare of decline and sterility that characterizes neoliberal South Africa. The rituals of death provide a symbolic statement about home and family that reinvigorates people's commitment to recuperating the moral order of an idealized past and recovering the favor of their forbears. Ritual, as Durkheim (1915) observed, has the power to create these collective commitments by regimenting bodily movements and stirring up emotional effervescence.

These outcomes are crucial for migrant workers desperate to redress the dislocations that their homesteads suffer in a society fissured by a century and a half of colonialism, apartheid, and neoliberal capitalism. These political-economic systems have pried men from their wives, wives from their children, and families from their land and ancestors by forcibly drawing them into the urban wage economy. Now, to make matters worse, the social transformations of the liberal dispensation appear to blur the lines between male and female, parent and child, chief and subject. Migrant workers from rural Zululand express deep anxieties about this state of affairs and yearn to reestablish the conditions for successful social reproduction by reordering kinship—in the ritual imaginary if not in lived reality. They pursue this end by pressing cash wages into the local gift economy in the form of expensive sacrificial livestock.

In so doing, migrants forge strong associations between *labor* in the capitalist market and *work* in the ritual world. In their excellent discussion of cattle economies among the Tswana in South Africa, Comaroff and Comaroff (1990) demonstrate a distinction between two conceptions of "work": *tiro*, which connotes the production of inalienable persons and relations; and *bereka*, which refers to the alienated wage labor required by market capitalism. Migrants from rural Zululand posit no such distinction. Both wage labor and ritual sacrifice are called *umsebenzi* (directly translated as "work")—a homology that makes sense given the imperative to transform wages into livestock. Insofar as its yields are properly remitted, wage labor *is* ritual sacrifice, and sacrifice *is* labor. In this manner, migrants resist the alienation that usually attends the capitalist mode of production. The dress code observed by homestead heads and their fellow migrants during ritual ceremonies confirms this: they wear the standard-issue blue cotton coveralls that they wear at work in the towns—long-standing symbols of wage labor—illustrating the connections between their labor in the cities and the work of domestic ritual.

The fact that migrants spend so much of their disposable incomes on sacrificial ceremonies suggests that they devote their lives to laboring in the cities for precisely this purpose: for the ritual reaffirmation of a normative social order. Workers and their families imagine the migrancy route between rural and urban as connecting the monetary wealth of the wage-labor system with the ritual life of the rural homestead, fostering an *expansion* of the latter (cf. Moodie 1994). This recalls Christopher Gregory's (1982) point that even people who find commodity-logic to be socially destructive can harness the profits of the capitalist economy to effloresce the gift systems that are so crucial to their lifeways. Capitalism's subalterns, notwithstanding their forced proletarianization, engage with the wage economy, not to become more like Westerners, but to become more like themselves—to enrich their own ideas of what humankind is all about (Sahlins 1992).

But mortuary ritual does more than just reconstitute the homestead. It also assembles an oppositional strategy of time—to use Michel de Certeau's (1992) terms—that subverts the official ANC narrative of modernization. The postapartheid state relies on a vision of time that portrays the ANC as leading the country's rural population from the darkness of an ethnically fractious, primitive past toward the bright future of national development. Rural superstitions and social relations, in this narrative, are part of the colonial legacy that must be purged along the road of history. In contrast, the narrative that rural Zulus construct through mortuary ritual proclaims that any launch to grasp the abundance promised by modernity and development must begin by reestablishing the order of the past, cleansing its wounds, and suturing its fissures to lay a firm foundation for the fortunes of the future. If the revolutionaries who led the struggle in the 1980s and 1990s rejected the construct of "culture" on which colonial domination was premised, the priests of ritual orthopraxy insist on rejuvenating it.

This alternative narrative supplies a critique of the ANC's neoliberal modernity, which, instead of remediating the injustices of the apartheid past, has actually accentuated them, further entrenching the dislocations of agricultural degradation, urbanization, labor migrancy, landlessness, homelessness, and unemployment. If the apartheid labor system stretched the rural family between the homestead and the city, the social and economic policies of the ANC have—in the minds of many migrants—obliterated it altogether, spinning out the wild ghosts of the dead to haunt the living forever. This is not the liberation they bargained for. In the face of the failed promises of freedom and modernity, in the abjection that marks the aftermath of deindustrialization (Ferguson 1999), the intimate practices of ritual death ways articulate a poetic call for justice and offer an alternative vision for the state of the nation.

REBOUNDING VIOLENCE

But why violence? How are we to make sense of the fact that the moral concerns of rural migrants and their alternative visions for society were so easily mobilized—by Inkatha's opportunistic leaders—into a campaign of violent political sabotage during the 1980s and 1990s? One explanation that scholars have offered is that the violence has to do with ideals of martial masculinity (e.g., Morrell 1996; Waetjen 2004), suggesting that Zulu men have found value in embracing the warrior idiom of Shaka and the glory days of the Zulu kingdom (notwithstanding the fact that these representations derive largely from Western stereotypes; see Isaacs 1836; Hamilton 1998; Wylie 2008). This explanation is intriguing but ultimately indeterminate: it gives us a theory for why rural Zulu men might valorize violence, but cannot explain why they act violently in some situations rather than others, and nor can it explain the particular form that violence takes. The same might be said of my account thus far. In chapter 4, I suggested that rural migrants' attempts to sabotage the ANC may have had to do with two interrelated agendas: to reorder a society and cosmos that had succumbed to chaos, on the one hand, and to purge the land of witch-like agents of anti-fertility, on the other. But this does not explain why migrants embraced violence as a legitimate tool of redress. Part of the answer may lie in the details of sacrificial ritual.

Most of the dozens of sacrificial ceremonies that I attended in Zululand between 2007 and 2011 included two discrete moments of ritualized violence. The first—known as *iphaphu* ("the lung event")—involved only the young boys of the district and would unfold as a side spectacle. The boys would take their designated meats—the heart and lungs—around to the back of the homestead where they would roast them over a small fire. There they would prepare a cut of meat known as *ubedu,* usually by stuffing a small length of the trachea with the tip of the heart and the fat that covers the upper portion of the lungs, and tying it off with sinew at both ends like a sausage. Young men in the higher age-grades would then incite their juniors to challenge one another to stick fights,[22] in which each contestant attempts to strike his opponent on the head while defending his own. The fighting carries on until a champion emerges and earns the right to eat the *ubedu.* Until he gets overthrown at a later ceremony, the champion remains at the top of his age-grade hierarchy, and others respect him as "the one who eats *ubedu.*"[23]

Having won the *ubedu* and the seniority that it entails, the champion also controls the heart and lungs. After eating his fill of the meat, he distributes it out in pieces to his subordinates, assuming the role of patron in the guild of chief or homestead head. Not surprisingly, the analogy between *ubedu* and age-grade political authority is made possible through the logic of encompassment: just as the *ubedu* symbolically encompasses the lungs and the heart (as the "apex" of those organs), so the champion encompasses his peers. Often boys will express their deference to a champion simply because "he has eaten *ubedu,*" implying that the process of eating the cut imbues the champion with the status that it bears. The supremacy of the champion, then, hinges on and refers to the body of the sacrificial beast. The performance of *iphaphu* demonstrates that (political) hierarchy and authority are reckoned in terms of the social structure inscribed in the cow's body. As the violence of stick-fighting refers to that socio-somatic structure, it forges a strong association between martial authority and the maintenance of normative categories of status and role.

The second spectacle of ritualized violence occupies a more central place in the ceremonial agenda. As the feast concludes, the agnates file into the cattle byre and the lead celebrant begins a prayer to the ancestors—spoken in a solemn register intended to replicate the "deep" language of tradition—describing the ceremony that has just been performed and reiterating what the family wants it to accomplish. Afterward, the agnates begin *ukugiya.* They kneel in the soil of the byre and one by one rise to demonstrate their martial prowess in dance. With fighting sticks in hand, each performer slashes and stabs wildly through the air as though challenging an imaginary enemy while chanting his praise poetry[24] in call-and-response format to the men assembled before him, inviting a flurry of ululations from the female spectators. Often as many as a dozen men will take turns performing such dances. *Ukugiya* always forms the conclusion of ritual sacrifice, and is often the most anticipated moment of the ceremony.

During *ukugiya* performances, no identifiable enemy is at hand; the violence is directed against an imagined, external other. But sometimes—at the conclusion of the sacrifices at wedding ceremonies—*ukugiya* is replaced by mock battles against *actual* others. This is known as *umgangela:* a massive stick fight between teams organized by district. The opposing sides line up in a semicircle and perform *ukugiya* dances in order to provoke each other to battle. While *umgangela* is always referred to as a "game," it often results in severe casualties (see Clegg 1981).

Why are sacrificial rites followed by expressions of ritual violence? The theory of sacrifice that Maurice Bloch outlines in *Prey into Hunter* (1992) provides some potential clues. The purpose of the ritual sacrifice I have described above is to move the community from a state of moral chaos to one that more closely approximates the ideal social order. This takes place in two stages. During the first stage, the patient (in this case, Phumlani's family) is symbolically killed by the ancestors through the sacrifice of the cow, which is possible because cows are so intimately associated with humans and can act as substitutes.[25] The idea that the ancestors seek to "kill" their descendants is borne out by the fact that the ancestors got their attention and requested the sacrifice in the beginning by afflicting some of them—on top of their misfortunes—with a "stabbing" or "piercing" pain in the ribs redolent of the stabbing of a cow during sacrifice.[26] The killing is a necessary step in the transformation of the patients from one state to another, within an idiom of death and rebirth.

In the second stage of the ceremony—the feast—the patients recuperate their lost native vitality by plundering new vitality from an external source. In Zululand, this takes the form of consuming the meat of the animal that was sacrificed in the first stage. The sacrifice itself (the destruction of chaotic vitality) is not sufficient to cure the patients of their misfortunes. The feast (the consumption of ordered vitality, represented by the structured parts of the cow's body) effects the cure and makes the ritual successful; the family becomes what it eats. Zulu sacrifice is unique—and departs from Bloch's model—in that the native vitality and the external vitality coexist in the body of the same sacrificial cow. The cow is native in the sense that it inhabits the cattle byre at the center of the homestead and comes to symbolize the family itself. But it is also external in the sense that it has been purchased as a commodity with migrants' wages.

Bloch understands the two stages of sacrifice as a process of "rebounding violence": the violence directed toward the patients in the first stage rebounds as violence that the patients direct externally in the second stage. He notes that sacrificial feasting tends to take on a military idiom as it proceeds, and is often followed by mock battles or expansionist military campaigns (1992:50), just as we see in Zululand. To explain this, Bloch suggests that "rebounding" violence directed outward against other human communities is a logical entailment of the rebounding violence of the feast; both serve as means for plundering and controlling the vitality of some external source. This happens because the logic of sacrifice and feasting "easily furnishes an idiom of expansionist violence . . . an idiom which, under certain circumstances, becomes a legitimation for actual violence" (6). The performance of *ukugiya* or *umgangela* draws on the logic of sacrifice and foregrounds the possibility of directing the same vitality-plundering violence against other humans for the sake of regenerating the moral community of the homestead. This slippage is possible because of the close symbolic association between cattle and people. Performed as the grand conclusion of sacrificial ritual, *ukugiya* allows the warrior idiom to emerge as central to the protection of domestic order. Violence crowns the reconstitution of moral society.

Media and scholarly accounts of Inkatha-led political violence in the townships focused obsessively on the warrior-like image that the aggressors purveyed. Newspapers depicted fearsome men bristling with traditional shields, spears, and fighting-sticks (or garbage-can lids and broomsticks in their stead) while marching down township roads to military incantations. These scenes inspired the discourse about Zulu tribalism that dominated popular interpretations of the conflict, and the media cast the violence as an epic struggle between ethnic traditionalism and cosmopolitan modernity. But perhaps these accounts misread the imagery. Given the ritual logic I have identified above, perhaps the use of traditional weapons referred not to ethnic chauvinism but to the practice of *ukugiya* and, through this, to the practice of sacrifice that gives material form to normative conceptions of moral order. In other words, it is possible that we can read migrants' violence toward the townships as not only purgative—as I claim in chapter 4—but also as gesturing toward the rituals that reconstitute domestic hierarchy and reproduce the life-giving differences that democracy seems to threaten.

RITUAL AND POLITICAL IDENTITY

If sacrifice furnishes a logic of political violence, it also provides a metaphor for speaking about political identity. While sitting with gatherings of men at sacrificial feasts in the Zululand countryside, I participated in a number of debates about national politics. Most men I encountered tended to be highly critical of the ANC government. When I would ask why they so disliked the ANC, some would respond: "because it is the party of the Xhosas." When I followed through by asking why they so disliked Xhosas, they would explain that they believed Xhosas have *amasiko* (culture, customs) and *umthetho* (traditional law) that are incompatible with those cherished by rural Zulus. Often my interlocutors would illustrate this assertion by pointing to the body of the sacrificial cow. As one man in Entenjani put it to me:

> According to the culture and law of the Zulus, men eat the head and the women eat the chest of the beast, as we are doing now. But according to the culture and law of the Xhosas, it is the *women* who eat the head and the *men* who eat the chest. In all of South Africa, it is only among the Zulus that the men eat the head.

While this particular claim about the gendered inversions of Xhosa sacrificial protocol is false, there are a number of points at which Xhosa norms do follow a different pattern. For example, the left and right sides of the second stomach, the forelegs, and the sides of the ribcage are shared between men and women, respectively, in a manner that bolsters common stereotypes that Xhosas tend to be more gender egalitarian than Zulus. But regardless, the more important point to take from the above quotation is that rural Zulu men tend to cast "Xhosa culture" as the inversion of their most sacrosanct values with reference to the structure of sacrifice. The image of the head-chest inversion illustrates serious anxieties about gender and hierarchical disorder, suggesting that Xhosas—and, by extension, the ANC—confuse norms of gender and authority. Former ANC presidents Mandela and Mbeki, who claim Xhosa heritage, are frequently derided by rural Zulus as effeminate and amoral, along with the liberal dispensation that they helped to inaugurate in South Africa.

The actual differences between "Zulu" and "Xhosa" customs are immaterial, of course. And the ANC is not really composed solely of

Xhosas: it has been led by self-identifying Zulus for most of its history,[27] and in KwaZulu-Natal the vast majority of self-identifying Zulus in urban areas call themselves members. People know this fact—especially now that Jacob Zuma has assumed the presidency of the ANC government—even if many believe that Xhosas have tended to exercise disproportionate power in the organization. But for rural Zulus the contrast is nonetheless good to think, for—as in the discussion above—it removes politics from the ether of abstraction and somaticizes it in the body of the sacrificial beast, where it can be debated more concretely. The response "I dislike the ANC because it is the party of the Xhosas" works by substituting "Xhosa" (a cultural entity) for "ANC" (a political entity), which allows people to locate their distaste for the ANC in its promotion of distorted social values of gender and hierarchy, shifting the conflict from the level of abstract political ideology to something more tangible: ritual practice.

This not only explains rural Zulus' attitudes toward the ANC, but also reveals something important about their understandings of Zuluness itself. As one of my interlocutors put it: "To be a Zulu is to respect *umthetho:* the laws and the structures of Zulus." Illustrating his point with reference to the sacrificial cow, he continued: "To be a Zulu is to know what *ubedu* is, and to know that during the ritual ceremony the wives, the men, and the boys each must sit in certain places. To be Zulu is to follow the rules of *hlonipha* [respect, taboo]. We are the only nation that has *hlonipha.*" For rural migrants, Zuluness is not about genetics (as the apartheid segregationists wanted to claim) and not about identity (as the ethnic-nationalism narrative would have it) but about *practice;* a form of practice that both reflects and creates a particular hierarchical order of statuses and roles essential to the social good as they conceive it.

TACTICS OF MEDIATION

The constant replication of ritual sacrifice rehearses the values (both symbolic and moral) by which rural Zulus—and particularly migrants—define themselves against the liberal modernity of the ANC. These collective representations are phenomenological—not abstract, cerebral concepts, but part of the immediate, practical equipment of everyday life with which people are routinely engaged: the spaces of the homestead and the pieces of the cow. Yet this assiduous attention to ritual protocol is not unselfconscious. It is an obsession driven by the anxiety that the ancestors will not be able to understand "modern" language or practice that departs from traditional norms.

The ritual observances I have described above require the use of special linguistic resources that depart from everyday ways of speaking in an attempt to approximate the language used by the ancestors (cf. Du Bois 1986). This linguistic trick is crucial to the success of these rituals, for their efficacy hinges on their ability to collapse time, drawing the past into the present in order to remake the present on the foundations of a remade past. In other words, to use Michael Silverstein's (1981) terms, the form of ritual speech serves as a figure for what the ritual purports to achieve. We can see this most clearly in the "fetching" ritual, which is accompanied by a poetic prayer that traces the journey homeward as it unfolds across a memorable and unalterable natural landscape, river by river, mountain by mountain. This metapragmatic narrative refers to the very actions it is undertaking in an attempt to mediate the gap between the ancestors and their descendants, who need to be brought from their disparate spatiotemporal locations to inhabit a single space and time (cf. Silverstein 1976).

And herein lies the difference that rural Zulus perceive between themselves and the urban ANC: one acquaintance of mine in Entenjani insisted that while rural Zulu families preoccupy themselves with "returning the dead," people who support the ANC "leave them to wander," spectral icons of the fractious families of liberal modernity. If we understand the ancestors to embody a temporal construct—namely, the family values of the past—then ritual attempts at communicating with the dead contribute to the broader agenda of linking the present to the past; a past that, once haunted by the ghosts of apartheid segregation, has been reimagined as a time of stable moral order. In this sense, constructions of the idealized past are mobilized as blueprints for imagined futures. It is this nostalgia—often denounced as "counterrevolutionary" by the ANC—to which I turn in the following chapter.

6

Colonial Nostalgias and the Reinvention of Culture

To our revolutionaries-turned-rulers, these nostalgic feelings might be nothing more than the musings of reactionaries and even apologists for apartheid. Far more difficult, I think, would be to take seriously these sentiments as one possible way through which we can understand the past and contemporary South Africa.

—Jacob Dlamini, *Native Nostalgia*

Thus far I have represented urban township residents as devotedly modern, firmly rooted in the liberal tradition that guided the ANC through much of the twentieth century. But this is not exactly accurate. Returning once again to the Durban-area townships that I discussed at length in chapter 3, this chapter examines a set of interesting and unexpected cultural developments since the democratic transition in 1994. Beleaguered by a neoliberal economy that has rendered social reproduction increasingly precarious, township residents express a curious longing to return to the "traditions" of their ancestors—the very traditions that they once considered backward and associated with the counterrevolutionary proclivities of the rural migrants with whom they have long been in battle. But the vision of tradition that propels their nostalgia does not necessarily match the hierarchical cultural world that rural Zulus inhabit or the values to which they subscribe. Instead, it draws on the constructs of family and gender that the apartheid state inscribed into the townships during the postwar era of the 1950s and 1960s, during a time of greater economic stability. Facing increasingly uncertain futures in the wake of neoliberal structural adjustment, South Africans seem to be curiously nostalgic for certain aspects of apartheid social order.

Over the course of the past decade or so, a few anthropologists have begun to notice and reflect on what Richard Werbner has called "a boom in colonial nostalgia" (1998:1) among their interlocutors in the postcolonial world. Expressions of longing for an idealized colonial past can be embarrassing for a Western ethnographer to encounter; it is tempting to dismiss them as trivial, unthinking sentiments or counter them with a more accurate rendition of the colonial past as characterized by violence and racial exclusion. But colonial nostalgia deserves a more empathetic treatment, if only for the sake of explaining its ubiquity. In his excellent study of postcolonial Zanzibar, William Bissell argues that nostalgia should be understood as shaped by specific cultural concerns and urges us to ask, "What social and political desires are postcolonial Africans giving voice to when they speak well of the colonial past?" (2008:217). He shows that nostalgic rhetoric draws on the past as a rich, imaginative resource that provides tools for critical commentary for people whose postcolonial fortunes have been less than splendid. In Bissell's words, "popular nostalgias reconstruct the past as a means of establishing a point of critique in the present, calling to judgment the failures of the state and the mysteries of the market. If we just dismiss them as deluded or reactionary, we run the risk of ignoring the way in which they create a space of possibility for a politics that cannot be conducted in other forms or by other means" (239).

But why the explosion of colonial nostalgia now, at this particular historical moment? Fred Davis (1979) and Svetlana Boym (2001) suggest that the condition commonly emerges in contexts of transition and discontinuity, fueled most notably by revolution and other large-scale social upheavals. It is no surprise, then, that poignant lamentations about the passing of colonial rule in Africa reflect the profound sense of crisis that has attended the recent reorganization of global capitalism and the extension of neoliberal market orthodoxy across the continent, which has rendered everyday livelihoods increasingly precarious (Barchiesi 2011; Comaroff and Comaroff 2000; Ferguson 1999). As James Ferguson (2006) demonstrates in his study of neoliberalism in Africa, the wave of independence in the 1950s and 1960s and the postcolonial industrial revolution generated immense expectations for the continent's "takeoff" to modernity and its debut into the new global society. But instead of launching African countries into the ranks of the First World, the 1980s inaugurated a two-decades long trajectory of steep decline, which saw per capita incomes fall, GNPs shrink, life expectancies erode, and the number of people living in basic poverty nearly double.[1] Not only have globalization and market liberalization failed to usher in the prosperity that their proponents promised, it has actually made things a good deal worse: economies have undergone suffocating structural adjustments and states have been forced (by dint of their debt obligations to the IMF and World Bank) to cut spending and abandon social services that their citizens desperately need. As Ferguson puts it, "For much of Africa, the new political order has meant not 'less state interference and inefficiency,' as Western neoliberal reformers imagined, but simply less order, less peace, and less security" (2006:39). The result: a pervasive sense of crisis, decline, and despair among Africans whose hopes in modernity have been thoroughly scuttled (see Piot 2010).

South Africa may not be the most radical example of neoliberalism, given its high levels of social spending and extensive grants program, but it nonetheless matches the general trend of structural adjustment. Against this backdrop I encountered a widespread sense of foreboding as people watched the fundamental conditions for social reproduction collapse around them. This has fueled a blaze of demonstrations against the state as the swollen ranks of the homeless and underemployed demand better service delivery and a fairer share of the national income. It seems that every year authorities report that the number of protests has reached the highest levels since the end of apartheid. Early in 2014, some 3,000 protests occurred over a 90-day period, involving more than a million people.[2] It's no wonder that South Africa is often described as "the protest capital of the world"—mass strikes, burning tires, rubber bullets, and teargas have become normal subjects of the daily news. Behind the many political demands that get advanced by the drama of the demonstration, fears about the collapse of the conditions for social reproduction often hinge on the idea of the home. Nostalgia gets articulated as a longing to return to a bygone age of moral, ordered homefulness, a time when family values were firm and people knew their places within a predictable social structure. Apartheid is evoked in these discourses as a means of conjuring the image of a well-managed state that enforced morality, order, and the rule of law—everything that they feel the present neoliberal government fails to provide.

In his controversial memoir about growing up in apartheid South Africa, Jacob Dlamini captures the sentiments of "native nostalgia" in a single IsiZulu sentence that he finds frequently on the lips of his elders: "Akusenamthetho; abantu bazenzel' umathanda"—"There is no order anymore; people do as they please" (2009:6). As this sentiment has it, the townships under apartheid were a haven of order, solidarity, and respect for authority. In South Africa, it is not surprising that this long-ing for order—this "hunger for authority" (6)—takes on the dimen-sions of the particular technologies of governance that the apartheid state used for so long to control Africans. The longing is not for apart-heid itself, of course, as in a masochistic desire for racial subjugation and exploitation; everyone recognizes that apartheid was an unjust regime and hails the revolution for breaking its hegemony. Rather, the longing is for the type of order that structured the everyday domestic realities of Africans for so many decades. People value the types of fam-ilies that the colonial state tried to instantiate as tools of governance throughout the twentieth century—namely, the patriarchal families of indirect rule in the rural reserves, and the nuclear families of direct rule in the urban townships. Colonial nostalgia in South Africa is plural; it runs two ways. Like the South African landscape itself, it is divided between rural and urban. Rural citizens' nostalgia and urban citizens' nostalgia refer to the respective domestic orders—and family values— that organized and anchored their social worlds for decades. These two nostalgias are the products, in other words, of long engagement with the bifurcated technologies of a strategy of domination that found its primary object in the domestic structure of the African family.

South Africans just recently gained national independence, and here they are, two decades later, apparently hankering for certain dimen-sions of apartheid. What are we to make of these sentiments? We can read them, as many do, as the misguided musings of people who are too quick to forget the atrocities of apartheid, and who fail to appreciate the gains of a long and difficult revolutionary struggle. Or, as Dlamini suggests, we can take them seriously as a message about contemporary South Africa worth trying to understand. The ideal domestic orders to which nostalgic discourses refer never actually existed, of course. To recapitulate Bissell's insight: the invocation of the past here is a means of establishing a point of critique in the present. I am not interested, ultimately, in determining what the past was *really* like, or how accu-rate people's nostalgic representations of the past happen to be. What matters here is what people *say* about the past. The way that people construct and talk about the past serves as a vessel for their critique of the present—a critique that elucidates the most problematic aspects of late capitalism in South Africa.

The second half of this chapter will show that this dualistic longing for social order and authority has found its mark in a single political figure: Jacob Zuma. I argue that Zuma's immense popularity is partially an accident—the product of a structural moment in South African history quite beyond his agency as a canny political actor—for he embodies a particularly powerful conjuncture on the political landscape. A polyvalent symbol at the confluence of two historical narratives, he simultaneously represents the rural patriarch that Zulu migrants hope will restore their hierarchies and reestablish the conditions for national fruition, as well as the "industrial man" that township residents hope will restore the urban family and the male provider at its center by reversing the injustices of the neoliberal project and securing the substantive rights that the Freedom Charter promised. In other words, the two groups that so recently found themselves locked in a hostile civil war suddenly have found cause for a strange alliance.

REFRAINS ON HOPE AND FAILURE

In 2008, shortly after moving to Durban, I met Abigail, a middle-aged woman from KwaDabeka township. Owing to her congenial, talkative disposition, I quickly grew close to Abigail and often visited her and her small family in KwaDabeka on the weekends. At first blush, Abigail's home life appeared to conform to my expectations of the stereotypical young township family: a working husband and three children living together in a free-standing nuclear family house. Her sitting room had all the accoutrements of a "respectable" modern home, including matching furniture, a doily-covered coffee table, and a cabinet along the wall that proudly displayed the television, the obligatory tea set, and some faded family pictures. But as I got to know Abigail better, I discovered that this apparently ideal order was troubled and unstable. Her story—one of decline, disappointment, and anxiety—poignantly illustrates the collective nightmares that plague those who still struggle to find stability in the wake of colonialism.

Abigail grew up in a rural homestead situated on a sugar plantation near Greytown. She was raised in a multigeneration polygynous family with deep reverence for custom and staunch devotion to Inkatha after it was launched in 1975. During our conversations she would recall, nostalgically, that hers had been a "proper" homestead, with two sides composed of multiple round huts arranged appropriately around a central cattle byre. In the early 1980s Abigail decided to leave her homestead, for after the death of her grandfather it had fallen into fractious disarray, rent by witchcraft accusations. In 1985, Seeking a clean break with the past, she married Joseph, a handsome township youth who had split from what she referred to as his "quarrelsome, drunken family" and abandoned his responsibilities as the eldest son (*inkosana*). The young couple—committed Christians and married in the Western tradition, she in a flowing white gown and he in a slick black suit—purchased a plot of land in the freehold township of KwaDabeka, a little over eighteen miles northwest of Durban's city center, where they built the house in which they still live today. Their home, with a framed and decorated portrait of their wedding day hung prominently in the sitting room, formed a picture of modern domesticity. Given that they were both employed in the booming manufacturing industry at the time, they rode high on their dreams of achieving middle-class respectability.

As the 1990s wore on, however, the hopes upon which Abigail and Joseph had first built their home began to crumble. The manufacturing firms that they had been working for both closed down, forcing them into the ranks of the unemployed, which swelled during that decade in the wake of structural adjustment. Abigail managed to cobble together a few part-time, informal jobs as a domestic servant for white families in Durban, while Joseph found a position as a hospital janitor in a nearby township, which, while more stable than Abigail's piece-work, earned him an even smaller salary. Both jobs were poorly paid, insecure, and lacked benefits—a far cry from their former union jobs. It was not long before financial pressures began to place considerable stress on their marriage. No longer able to command an income sufficient to provide meaningfully for his family, Joseph slipped into depression, lost weight, and became reticent and withdrawn—a shadow of his former self. Abigail found herself filling the gap that he created, taking control of domestic affairs, making decisions and directing the household budget; before long, everyone in the neighborhood recognized her as the head of the home. This made Joseph feel even more emasculated, and, as his resentment festered, he began pursuing affairs with women he met at work, sometimes disappearing for days at a time, as if to assert some modicum of power over his wife.

To make matters worse, Abigail's eldest daughter—already in her early thirties—had been unable to secure either job or husband, and struggled to support a child she had by a boyfriend who had absconded. With the family's misfortunes mounting, Abigail began to wonder whether perhaps they had done something wrong by their ancestors. At around the time of their marriage, Abigail had made a decisive break with her traditional past, joined the UDF, and begun attending a "respectable" Anglican church. Not long afterward, she had become an active and respected COSATU shop steward at her factory—a position that put her in the vanguard of the democratic revolution and trained her in all the values of the liberal ANC. But now she began to wonder if she had been too quick to abandon her past. Recalling her rural family's commitment to the strict observance of sacrificial ritual, she began to think of what she had done wrong. For one, she decided to start saving for her daughter's nubility rites (*umemulo*). But more urgently than that, she needed to make sure that Joseph's ancestors were properly protecting their township house—which, according to a diviner she consulted—they apparently were not. The problem was that Joseph had absolutely no knowledge of ritual. Like many second-generation township youths of his time, Joseph grew up with a distinct distaste for "traditional" custom and ceremony, and his parents—themselves in pursuit of urbane domesticity—did little to correct that deficit.

Abigail asked Joseph to consult a diviner to learn what needed to be done to link his ancestors to their house and secure their aid. As she told it, the diviner advised him to use the *mpafa* branch to "fetch" the spirits of his father and grandfather from their grave sites, to slaughter a goat for each of them, and to use the gallbladder (*inyongo*) and the stomach (*incekwa*)—to root them in the home. Joseph—awkward in his first-time role as ritual celebrant—undertook the ceremony according to the appropriate protocol, and stored the goats' carcasses in the guest room overnight as an offering to the ancestors, with the *mpafa*, the *inyongo*, and the *incekwa* arranged carefully about a makeshift shrine. But then something went terribly wrong. Abigail woke in the middle of the night feeling fiery hot and sweating profusely. Upon checking the meat for mishap, she found it radiating a pestilential heat, and discovered that the room had filled with a nauseating, nightmarish light. Sure that it was a wild ghost she ran out to fetch sea salt and rainwater—two "cooling" agents—which she sprinkled around the room while praying fervently to exorcise the malicious spirit whose presence she sensed. When the same thing recurred the following night, Abigail threw out the *mpafa* and the goats' organs, convinced that Joseph had conducted the procedure improperly and accidentally brought the wrong ancestors to their house. At his father's death, Joseph had buried him—like his grandfather before him—in the township cemetery, a space that forces the spirits of different families and clans into a confused quagmire of mixed-up kinship when custom dictates that they be properly distinguished and buried in their respective rural homesteads. For this reason, the process of "fetching" a spirit from a cemetery is fraught with the possibility that the celebrant might inadvertently coax the wrong one home.

Such was the misfortune that befell Joseph. The ceremony failed dismally, and instead of assuming residence in the new house, Joseph's wild-ghost ancestors continue to wander aimlessly in limbo between homes, maligned, vindictive, and unwilling to grant their protection to his young family. Abigail ascribes this catastrophe to Joseph's ineptitude in ancestral management and the fact that his extended family has long been a tangled mess of disordered relations, a consequence of its early dislocation from homestead to township and consistent neglect of kinship ritual. According to Abigail, this explains why nothing Joseph attempts ever succeeds, and accounts for his failure as a man. Furthering her role as household head, Abigail now invokes her *own* ancestors to provide protection and prosperity for the family in lieu of Joseph's. When Joseph's ancestors desperately need to speak to him, they do so by appearing in dreams to Abigail, more certain of her ritual competence and respect than that of their own descendant, whom they regard with disdain as an irresponsible "absconder" (*isibhunguki*).

Abigail's story provides tragic commentary on the social dislocations that plague postcolonial South Africa. A man's crisis of masculinity in a context of deindustrialization, the inversion of gender roles in the township home, the departure of unemployed youth from legitimate forms of social reproduction, the inability of a hopeful couple to grasp the promises of modernity and development, and the desperate return to traditional cosmologies as a way of explaining persistent misfortune and rendering mundane suffering meaningful—together these threads comprise a telling tapestry of South Africa's tumultuous present. In the narrative of Abigail's life, the dislocations of the past come rushing into consciousness as wild ghosts, telling of a family fragmented by forced removals and strung between townships while the spirits of the dead wander restless and lost across the countryside, unhinged from their homes. The image is one of social chaos in burgeoning urban spaces where individuals have lost not only their kinship moorings, but also the ritual knowledge necessary to recover them. The pestilential heat that attacked Abigail's home the night of the ceremony reflects the chaotic, ill-begotten fecundity that attends this milieu—an image of social reproduction (for that is what the sacrificial meat signifies) gone horribly awry. Abigail's life is one lived navigating the tensions and contradictions between an apartheid past and a postcolonial present, between the roots of her now-abandoned natal homestead and the township in which she planted her dreams.

This renewed interest in culture is happening not only at the level of the family, but also at the level of "clans" (*izibongo*), as I learned in 2008 through a series of extraordinary events in which I was invited to participate. A group of prominent members of the Mkhize clan—such as members of parliament and CEOs—had been noticing for a number of years that things were not well: that their businesses were failing, that their children were not finding good jobs, and that their families were ridden with conflict or falling apart. With the help of the recently founded Mkhize cultural organization, Umbambano Lwabambo, they decided to act on their concerns, publishing ads in the papers to call for Mkhizes around the country to share their experiences of affliction and their ideas about what should be done to bring about restoration. It became something of a national conversation; as the story was told to me, Mkhizes would encounter each other on the street and discuss their misfortunes, agreeing that something significant was afoot in the ancestral realm—something that demanded an organized, national solution. Of those who had sought the advice of diviners, one cause of the Mkhize calamities repeatedly emerged: that an ancient Mkhize king was never properly integrated into the community of clan ancestors, and, tired of wandering in the limbo of the unattached, had turned to afflicting his descendants with misfortunes in order to awaken them to his plight.

The wild ghost that was afflicting the Mkhize clan was nearly two hundred years old. Inkosi Uzihlandlo, the clan's paramount chief in the early nineteenth century, had been a close ally of King Shaka. When Dingane killed Shaka and usurped the throne of the Zulu kingdom, he sought to eliminate Shaka's allies to forestall their trying to avenge the slain king. Hearing of Dingane's preemptive attacks, Uzihlandlo fled toward the kingdom's southern borders, but was ambushed and assassinated by the royal army along the way. That was in 1832, but his grave still lies at the place he was killed, relatively well-maintained and ringed with large stones, at the bottom of a valley near Gcochoyi, just south of the Tukela River deep in the hills of Nkandla. It was this event that the Mkhize people decided to focus on to redress their misfortunes in 2008, 176 years later. After years of planning, the highest-ranking chiefs of the paramount houses of the Mkhize clan convened at Uzihlandlo's grave site to perform a cleansing ritual (*ukugeza*). They arrived with the paradoxical pomp characteristic of such postmodern occasions, emerging

from their gleaming black SUVs clad in the traditional leopard-skin regalia that marks their chiefly status. Removing their sandals, they gathered
around the grave under the direction of an aging Shembe priest. The
acolytes of the priest, who had been dispatched to sacrifice a goat selected
for the occasion, were directed to mix the blood, the gall, and the
umswane (stomach mulch) of the goat in a basin. The priest then sprinkled the mixture over the grave in order to "cleanse" Uzihlandlo's wild
ghost—the first step in the process of reintegrating the spirit of an ancestor who has died a violent death (see chapter 5). This ceremony was
followed by another a few weeks later, during which Mkhize representatives physically traversed the land between the graves of their chiefs,
moving temporally backward from the most recent to the eldest, again
in order to restore harmony with and among the ancestors.

CULTURAL REVIVAL?

What stands out about the Mkhize episode is that it brought an urbane
class of modern elites from the cities to the most "backward" of rural
areas to attend to the mortuary rites of a long-dead king whom they had
spent decades ignoring, all in hopes of redressing what appeared to be
serial misfortunes. Abigail's story bears a similar plot, albeit on a much
smaller scale; she too sought desperately to restore her family's fortunes
by trying—clumsily, falteringly—to reconnect with ancestors she had
long neglected. What do we do with the enigma of people like Abigail
who, even while unsure of their ritual competence, take the risk of
investing in sacrifices that they can scarcely afford for outcomes that
seem so uncertain? How are we to make sense of the cultural revival
that these stories appear to represent?

   These episodes reflect what has become a noticeable trend in Kwa-
Zulu-Natal, which has manifested itself as an uptick in sacrificial ritual
in the townships as people marshal what few resources they have to buy
a goat or a cow for slaughter in hopes of pleasing the ancestors and
improving their fortunes.[3] In 2009 I had a telling conversation with the
IFP councilor of the A Section hostel adjacent to KwaMashu township
in which he pointed to a curious recent convergence between township
residents and rural migrants:

> The people in the urban areas have lost their ancestors. They just do what-
> ever they want. And they cannot do the ritual things that we [rural Zulus]
> do. But they are trying these days to learn. If you compare before and now
> you will see that they are starting, trying to come back. Sometimes on Friday

on Malandela Road you will see township people taking goats back home, and you realize that they are trying now. The difference between us and them is not as stark as it once was. I see that now they are beginning to see what is natural [*imvelo*]. The change started in about 1996. Before they used to say we [rural migrants] were all stupid because we were coming from the farm. They called us idiots [*izilima*]. But now nobody says that. These days they are trying to look back to their ancestors. But it may be too late.

Another longtime resident of KwaMashu township told me: "People these days are becoming more traditional. During the revolution people gave many cultural things up. They never used to do sacrificial ceremonies. But these days there are many!" He also pointed to the fact that today many households feature *izindlu zamadlozi*—separate thatched huts for the ancestors intended to evoke the *indlunkulu* ("great house") of the rural homestead—which were rare even ten years ago. Ritual—once considered by urban Africans to be the insignia of backwardness—is gradually losing its stigma in the townships.

Another instance of this revival of "culture" has appeared in the least likely of places: on Facebook. A number of Facebook groups and pages have sprung up as forums where young IsiZulu speakers ask questions about the details of ritual performance—most popularly the female nubility rite, *umemulo*. Participants express hopes of recovering their ancestors and receiving their blessings in the form of good fortune (*inhlanhla*) and development (*intuthuko*) that will help them secure employment or find a spouse, but are deeply uncertain about how to organize the ritual ceremonies necessary to bring this about. Participants who come from rural backgrounds assume the role of mentors, instructing young urbanites in the nuances of ritual praxis. Similarly, the hostel districts adjacent to urban townships have become crucial resources in this pursuit. Township residents who wish to try their hand at ritual sacrifice increasingly consult with hostel residents about the details of ceremonial procedure. Hostel districts often feature markets where township residents can buy "traditional" artifacts such as calabashes, regalia, skins, spears, and other items that they need in order to pull off an "authentic"—and presumably efficacious—ritual. In other words, in a remarkable inversion, rural hostel residents—who were once considered inveterately backward by township residents—are sought out for their traditional knowledge as part of a collective attempt to recover the past and restore relationships with the ancestors.

For the most part, cultural revival in KwaZulu-Natal townships bears little resemblance to the accounts of revitalization movements that have been explored in the anthropological literature since the publication of Roy Wagner's book *The Invention of Culture* in 1975. Most of the classic studies in this vein—such has Linnekin (1983), Handler (1988), Clifford (1988) and Keesing (1989)—focus on cases where the revitalization of cultural identity dovetailed with some form of nationalist movement or political agenda. These studies show how people with claims to being indigenous—usually minority groups—reify culture as bounded, continuous, and homogeneous according to a logic not dissimilar from that which social scientists have historically used to discuss integrated social units. Such movements tend to objectify culture as a thing with definable characteristics, elevate attachment to the land as a political symbol, fetishize folk pastoralism for its "authenticity," and often commoditize certain symbols of culture such as dress, music, dance, and food.

Umbambano Lwabambo, the Mkhize cultural organization mentioned above, to some extent operates along these lines, as part of its agenda includes gaining recognition from the South African state as a distinct ethnic "nation," albeit without separatist ambitions. But the same cannot be said for Abigail, or for the hundreds like her in townships around Durban, where the performance of sacrificial ritual has been escalating dramatically. They do not have the sense of being a beleaguered minority and are not trying to make any political claims on the modern state. This trend cannot be identified as ethnic nationalism, as separatism, or—to use Spivak's terms—as strategic essentialism; if it were these things, then it would probably focus on Shaka or other key historical symbols of Zulu identity, as Inkatha has done. Indeed, one must keep in mind—as I have been at pains to demonstrate throughout—that most township dwellers have a distinct distaste for the politics of "Zuluness," which they blame their rural counterparts for indulging in. They are not trying to assert their connection with a mythologized past, nor are they trying to reattach to the land, or to construct insider/outsider essentialisms, or to package, sell, and leverage "traditional culture" for economic gain. Never in my long relationship with Abigail, for example, did I hear her express her project in the register of "Zulu culture." Her concerns were much more immediate than that: they focused simply on regaining the favor of her ancestors in order to keep her family from falling apart.

When I initially began to think about the reinvention of tradition in urban areas, I immediately noticed a difference between the semiotics of ritual practice among rural Zulus and that of their urban counterparts.

Rural Zulus appear to perceive no conceptual gap between the signifier—"traditional ritual"—and the things that it signifies, or the things that it is held to accomplish. In other words, ritual practice for them is motivated, efficacious, and has real consequences; it is not just a symbol. If one fails to perform rituals correctly, real consequences ensue. To the extent that rural Zulus represent these practices as "tradition," they do so because the term carries political power and gives them leverage in making certain claims about how they want to organize their world. But "tradition," for them, is not reified as a set of practices separate from everyday life; it is constitutive of everyday life itself. For many township dwellers, in contrast, ritual practice is fenced off as a thing to do in order to conjure the "traditional," to demonstrate to others that they retain the markers of "African identity"—a term that has become increasingly popular in the townships over the past decade (see White 2012). In this context the details of ritual practice appear to be arbitrary instead of motivated—the various actions it entails are not thought to be efficacious in and of themselves. Still, people hope that by at least approximating the practice of tradition they will see real positive effects on their material well-being. This distinction is not absolute, of course—some township dwellers, like Abigail, do pay attention to the details of ritual protocol—but it provides a rough idea of what many migrants see as a key difference between rural and urban.

The revival of culture in the urban townships does not constitute a movement that fundamentally rejects modernity. On the contrary, people continue to cultivate hopes of becoming "modern," or, more accurately, of achieving development. The difference is that they have begun to enlist a different, "older" set of generative strategies and epistemological frameworks to get there. Once again, Abigail's story illustrates this nicely. For people like Abigail, the appeal of "culture" lies, not in the political identity that it supplies, but in the theory of fortune that it offers, which is an alternative to the apparently failed narrative that if you break from the traditional past you will reap the benefits of modernity—both material and symbolic. Neoliberal decay has given the lie to this narrative, and people are looking for ways to explain why development has failed. In the process, they are thinking carefully about the role of ancestors and kinship. And here we have an interesting inversion of the usual trend. In chapter 5 I argued that rural Zulus who inhabit "gift economies" can harness the profits of the capitalist system in order to effloresce their own ideas of the social good; not to become more like Westerners, but to become more like themselves (see Gregory 1982;

Sahlins 1992). In South African townships, it appears that the opposite is true: urban Zulus enamored with capitalist prosperity are turning to the ritual systems of their rural counterparts; not to become more "traditional," but to become more "modern"—to achieve development.

The attempts of township residents to recover traditional ritual practice may appear to flag convergence with the values of the rural population, but that representation is not quite accurate. In invoking the idea of tradition and by performing sacrificial rituals, township residents do not seek to reestablish kinship hierarchies and social differences according to the model of homestead order discussed in chapter 2. On the contrary, they mobilize an entirely different vision of ideal order in the domestic realm. While they seek to recover their connections to their ancestors and regain some semblance—however tenuous—of a long-lost ritual prowess, they also yearn to return to the family forms of the postwar townships during the era before unemployment and crime began to devastate their lives. The only aspect that makes the discourse of rural migrants comparable with that of their urban counterparts is that both evince nostalgic longing for a lost age of social order, specifically the domestic structures used by the colonial state to control Africans differently in rural and urban areas: the hierarchical homestead and the postwar township, respectively.

THE DOMESTIC LIFE OF JACOB ZUMA

The apparent convergence of rural and urban around nostalgia for a bygone era of domestic social order was illustrated quite forcefully during the 2009 national elections, which dramatically changed party politics in KwaZulu-Natal. When South Africans first went to the polls in 1994, the Inkatha Freedom Party won the province handily with 49 percent of the vote, drawn mostly from its rural base. But the party's support waned considerably over the course of the following decade, so that by the 2004 elections, it could claim only 36 percent of the electorate. Unable to arrest this downward trend, the IFP was routed at the ballot box in 2009, and watched its share of the vote reduced to a paltry 23 percent. By contrast, the ANC stormed the province with 63 percent—the first decisive, absolute majority in the history of KwaZulu-Natal, which was one of the few regions in which the party gained popularity during that election cycle.

The media celebrated this drama as it unfolded, rejoicing in the IFP's demise and the downfall of its controversial leader Mangosuthu

Buthelezi, whose reputation remains tainted by his collaboration with the apartheid government, his involvement with the homeland system, and his promotion of violence against the ANC and UDF in the run-up to the 1994 elections. Despite recent attempts to renovate its image, the IFP is still regarded in the national mainstream as hopelessly backward, given its entanglement with the chieftaincy system, its ties to the Zulu kingdom, its support for patriarchal gender politics, its autocratic leadership under president-for-life Buthelezi (whom voters like to compare to Zimbabwe's Robert Mugabe), and its cynical manipulation of ethnic identity. To many, the party's decline represents a triumph of modernity in the national narrative—an evolutionary shift toward the enlightened, postethnic, multicultural urbanity of the ANC.

How did the ANC manage to loosen the IFP's hold on KwaZulu-Natal? In the wake of the 2009 elections, journalists and pundits alike made answering this question something of a national pastime. Some claim that urbanization, improved education, and a demographic shift toward the younger generation have brought voters ineluctably to the ANC, as people break from the darkness of the traditional past and gravitate naturally toward enlightened interests. Others point to the fact that the IFP can no longer manipulate voters through the chieftaincy system, for since the ANC increasingly pays the salaries of the *amakhosi* (chiefs), they are no longer beholden to the IFP as they once were. Still others insist that the IFP's decline reflects the party's inability to deliver the development that rural voters—their primary base—so desperately need. But all agree that the greatest single cause of the IFP's conflagration in 2009 was the presence of the ANC's presidential candidate, Jacob Zuma. Zuma's candidacy fundamentally reorganized the political landscape when he attracted an unstoppable wave of popular support, what the media liked to call the "Zunami." Drawn by his unique appeal, even longtime IFP stalwarts in rural areas switched their allegiance to the ANC—not because they were abandoning the IFP's basic values but because the ANC seemed to be taking them up, and this at a time when the IFP was losing legitimacy and coming to be seen as autocratic and unresponsive to voters' needs.

Rural denizens see in Zuma a man who has not neglected his traditional roots, who—despite rising to the nation's highest office—retains deep ties to his rural home. Known affectionately as "100 percent Zuluboy," Zuma hails originally from Nkandla, the heart of rural Zululand, where he continues to maintain an opulent homestead compound complete with all the essential elements of the orthodox structure: a central cattle byre, ranked sides, and an elaborated *indlunkulu* (great house). Rural Zulus recognize that, despite having lived in exile, Zuma is not an "absconder" (*isibhunguki*), that he has not abandoned his homestead and his responsibilities to his rural relatives; indeed, he has observed all of the duties of a patriarch to his family. His diction, too, registers him as man who has "respect" for *umthetho;* he has an impressive capacity for "deep" IsiZulu oratory and uses carefully measured *hlonipha* language of the sort typically known only to elders. Rural Zulus easily pick up on the indexical iconicity (Silverstein2003:222ff.) of his speech, which flags his fluency in their cultural world. Zuma throws frequent feasts at his Nkandla homestead, to which he extends an open invitation to any who wish to partake of the beasts he sacrifices. When attending traditional ceremonies of this sort—and most notably at his many weddings—Zuma comfortably dons full martial regalia, down to the leopard skin *ibheshu* (loin skirt) and *isicoco* (head ring), and demonstrates profound ease with the embodied nuances of traditional dance. Rural Zulus believe that, as a traditionalist from a poor, rural background with little education, he will sympathize with their suffering and do something to ameliorate it.

In these respects, people draw stark contrasts between Zuma and his predecessor, Thabo Mbeki, who received a graduate education at England's Sussex University and is rarely caught without an immaculate three-piece suit and his favorite pipe—the sartorial accoutrements that earned him the reputation of an elitist technocrat aloof from the concerns of the plebes. But perhaps the most poignant and frequently noted contrast between the two men has to do with their families. While Zuma supports some six wives (the national joke is that no one can be sure) and over twenty children, and—even at the age of seventy-two—has plans to marry yet again, Mbeki has long been committed to his first wife, Zanele, and can claim no progeny from her; hardly the image of a respectable patriarch according to the rural paradigm. In sum, rural Zulus do not perceive in Zuma the same threat that they recognize in other leaders of the liberal, modernist ANC. Instead, they see a man capable of knowing their world and slipping freely in and out of their language game, someone who embodies their ideals of patriarchal masculinity, leadership, and unflagging commitment to rural homestead. Many rural Zulus believe that Zuma will inaugurate an era of national recovery and development because—as one woman I interviewed put it—he is "bringing back culture." An IFP member-turned-Zuma supporter I spoke to said: "Before, the ANC was killing the country. But now Zuma is reviving the culture [*amasiko*]. So maybe the nation will return [*izwe izobuya*] because Zuma is following the culture. Maybe things will get better." This statement refers to the theory of misfortune and fruition described at length in chapter 2. While rural migrants have long regarded the ANC as "killing the country" with an egalitarian project that flattens out social difference, they regard Zuma as restoring ordered hierarchies and therefore reestablishing the conditions for a fruitful national outcome.

It makes sense enough that Zuma holds such appeal among rural voters, given his symbolic (and actual) associations with rural Zuluness; for them, he represents the vindication of the rural, and holds out the promise of redeeming them from their marginalization. Indeed, this is probably the reason for which he was chosen to lead peace negotiations between the ANC and Inkatha during the height of the violence between the two parties.

But how does Zuma manage to garner so much support among voters who have called urban townships home for generations? The voters who long ago abandoned their knowledge of deep IsiZulu, of the *amadlozi,* of homesteads and of ritual? The voters for whom the term *umthetho* has long evoked nothing more than the liberal individual rights enshrined in the Constitution? Zuma's surprising appeal to this demographic became clearest in December 2007, when ANC delegates gathered at Polokwane and elected him to assume the party's presidency in what was widely perceived as a stinging repudiation of Mbeki's leadership. Polokwane is often described as marking a populist insurrection within the ranks of the ANC. Party members and delegates expressed their frustration with the country's neoliberal direction, upset that many of the promises of liberation had been left unrealized. But their choice of Zuma was an odd one, given that his political career had long been dogged with controversy: he was fired from his post as deputy president by Mbeki in 2005 over allegations of corruption and graft, and was charged and tried shortly afterward with raping a thirty-one-year-old HIV-positive woman (see Robins 2008). Both events were subjected to negative scrutiny by liberal pundits, who cast Zuma as a paragon of the backwardness that the new South Africa was trying to escape; he became a symbol of traditionalist chauvinism barring the nation's way to enlightened modernity.

Even though he was acquitted of the charges in 2006, Zuma's rape trial proved to be the most divisive moment of his career, and attracted a storm of international attention. Gender and AIDS activists were outraged at the court's decision to abandon the prosecution, as was the liberal community more broadly, especially in light of Zuma's aspirations to become president of a nation saddled with one of the highest HIV burdens in the world. Zuma—unashamed of his polygynous commitments—was known to have rather "traditional" views about gender in the first place. Moreover, he had spoken out firmly against abortion and premarital pregnancy and had expressed his homophobia in no uncertain terms. But during the rape trial, Zuma's supporters defended him with shocking vehemence. In dramatic scenes around the High Court in Johannesburg, they chanted threatening insults at his accuser and burned images of her. This sort of support was demonstrated not only by men but by women as well—indeed, many of Zuma's most vociferous defenders during protests outside the courts were women (see Hunter 2011).

This same support was mobilized again when, just moments after his election at Polokwane, the National Prosecuting Authority (NPA) recharged Zuma on sixteen counts of corruption, money laundering, and fraud in an attempt to revive the case that had collapsed in 2006. Zuma's supporters—who had grown to constitute a movement of unprecedented force—spent the following months protesting the case as fraudulent. To them, the string of charges against Zuma counted as flagrant persecution, clear evidence that the Mbeki administration was using the courts to hamstring the Zuma movement. September saw thousands of Zuma supporters protesting violently at the door of the NPA in Durban, inviting a storm of police shock bombs and rubber bullets to control the chaos. Addressing the crowds, ANC leaders issued public statements against the judiciary in which they threatened retribution should the NPA continue with the prosecution. In a speech that reflected the fervor of the moment, the firebrand ANC Youth League leader Julius Malema shouted: "Any force that tries to block our way, we will eliminate. We are on a mission here. We will crush you. It doesn't matter who you are . . . we will crush you." On September 12, the High Court in Pietermaritzburg passed judgment on the Zuma case in his favor, which split the country and paved the way for his accession to the nation's presidency in April 2009.

NEOLIBERALISM AND THE CRISIS OF URBAN SOCIAL REPRODUCTION

How do we interpret these events without casting them as a kind of atavistic reversion to the "traditional"? How do we explain the almost magical appeal of Jacob Zuma, and his support among South Africa's underclass in spite of the international condemnation surrounding his trials for rape and graft? Why would people rally around this controversial figure with his patriarchal characteristics that fit so uneasily with the modern, liberal South African Constitution? Certainly, part of the answer has to do with Zuma's apparently leftist views on economic issues and the promise he holds for the beleaguered working class and the vast ranks of the unemployed (see Ceruti 2008; Hunter 2010; Daniel and Southall 2010). In this respect, he appeared poised to reconcile the deepening divide between the ANC and its partners on the left, COSATU and the Communist Party. Yet while serving as Mbeki's deputy president, Zuma participated in the neoliberal project that Mbeki charted, and his presidency has thus far deviated little from this course.[4] Zuma's pro-worker rhetoric alone—which has proven by now to be rather empty, especially in the wake of the Marikana massacre of 2012—cannot explain his appeal to urban township voters. But what is it, then?

We have to begin by understanding the socioeconomic backdrop against which these events began to unfold.

The neoliberal dispensation that has characterized South African capitalism since the 1990s contrasts quite sharply with the type of capitalism that predominated after World War II. The strategy of postwar capitalism in apartheid South Africa was to mitigate "social disorder" and maximize labor productivity by encouraging the development of a stable, docile working class. The hope was that urbanized Africans with family housing, decent social services, and dependable pay would take an interest in their careers and settle into a steady, contented family life that would make them averse to the risks of revolution (Cooper 1996). This shift in Native Policy coincided with a broader global trend toward Fordist-style "embedded liberalism" (Harvey 1989, 2005), a strategy of consent marked by a social compact whereby capital traded stable wages in exchange for productive, domesticated workers who would develop a taste for consumerism. To borrow a phrase used by James Ferguson (1999) to describe a similar historical moment on the Zambian Copperbelt, the postwar era was a time of "socially thick" investment that—despite its racial exclusions—sought to facilitate the social reproduction of urban African families. The paternalistic arrangements of company towns at the time provide an excellent example of this project, where African residents were furnished with family housing, schools, health care, and recreational facilities. As detailed in chapter 3, this experiment in urban social engineering turned on a specific vision of normative family structure, one that placed the heterosexual male breadwinner as head over his domestic wife and nuclear family in a free-standing, four-room township house. The project of urban African modernity was gendered in specific ways, and centered on the mid-century construct of "industrial man" (Cooper 2003).

The system of embedded liberalism first began to unravel in the late 1980s. Influx controls were lifted in 1986, giving Africans formerly relegated to the rural homelands the right to live and work in the cities at will. This led to rapid urbanization as people desperate to escape the poverty of overcrowded reserves sought their fortunes in the city, placing tremendous pressure on township housing at exactly the time when the state was abandoning new developments, resulting in an explosion of informal settlements (Padayachee and Freund 2002). The gradual dismantling of rural-urban segregation coincided with—and was largely driven by—new strategies of capital accumulation that sought novel forms of flexible labor as a cheaper alternative to the expensive, paternalistic social compact of the postwar era. Indeed, the eventual abolition of apartheid was a felicitous moment for South African capitalists.

As the constructs of embedded liberalism began to break down, so too did the conditions for the existence of the urban African family as it was imagined by state planners in the 1950s. Neoliberalism has led to increasing unemployment rates and stagnating wages, which have in turn caused marriage rates to decline precipitously as young men find it impossible to raise the money they need to pay *ilobolo* and establish independent households. Extramarital pregnancies and matrifocal families have both increased in number as a result, as noted in chapter 3. To make matters worse, the postapartheid state has failed to redress the nation's immense housing crisis. The promises of the initial Reconstruction and Development Program (RDP) were undermined by GEAR reforms, so that today the state's attempts at public housing are nothing short of pathetic: cheap, shoddily built structures half the size of the "matchbox houses" that were produced during apartheid and typically located in isolated areas far from the business districts where residents must seek employment. To quote Mark Hunter, "RDP houses are not, in short, *family* houses and yet neither . . . do they represent a discernable alternative vision of how the state should address questions of social reproduction" (2011:1113).

This has led to a serious crisis of masculinity among younger men who cannot access the tight ranks of unionized, relatively high-paying sectors such as mining, milling, and metallurgy. In effect, young men have been expelled from the path to masculinity that was encouraged under apartheid—that of working, marrying, and eventually establishing an independent household in order to become *umnumzana:* a respectable, working-class family man. Instead, young men find themselves unable to pay *ilobolo* and forced to live with their mothers, earning the social derision due an *umnqolo*—a "mamma's boy." Young men in this position are subject to heavy ridicule from their female peers, who jeer at their emasculation and inability to secure jobs and get married, accusing them of being *izahluleki,* "failures" incapable of performing their expected roles. Many of the women I interviewed in the townships complained that their boyfriends—and even sometimes their husbands—were effeminate and weak, incapable of executing the duties of "true men." Beset with these frustrations, young people of both genders evince a deep nostalgia for the antiquated "tradition" of an imagined era of greater moral stability and a clearer order of gendered relations—a scene set in urban townships circa late 1960s. Men hark back to a time when they could command greater respect from women, while women long for a time when they could call on men to marry, support, and provide for them (cf. Hunter 2011).

Of course, this ideal never actually existed in reality; marriages were very often fractious and unstable (Posel 2006), and nuclear families quickly gave way to matrifocal families (see chapter 3). Still, the ideal—which has its source in the discourse of the state's postwar urban planners—holds great sway in the popular imagination. When impoverished South Africans express nostalgia for the days of apartheid—the days when, allegedly, men had stable jobs and could provide for their wives and families—they are mourning the fact that the era of embedded liberalism has given way to a neoliberal dispensation where formal employment is precarious at best and social services are thin. Deindustrialization has made it difficult for many to realize the modern dream of industrial man, and has threatened the gendered edifices that underpin it. The flexibility that neoliberalism demands of its subjects has dismantled the modernist, nuclear family kinship structures around which the townships were initially built. African families in urban townships today are experiencing what Ferguson (1999) has so aptly termed "abjection"—a sense of humiliating expulsion from the new world society and exclusion from the promises of modernity that once appeared so near at hand. With economic decay setting in, people in urban areas have begun to express a deep sense of betrayal, not only by their leaders, but by liberal modernity itself. Modernity, they feel, has failed them.

Enter Jacob Zuma. Even among those who do not support the ANC, his image as a respectable man upholding the gendered ordering of society and providing for his wives resonates with many. This is certainly true for young men, for whom Zuma represents a more ordered world in the realm of gender. But most of the women I interviewed also supported Zuma and heaped praise on him for his "traditional" views and his support for his polygynous family. Many noted with approval the fact that he has offered to pay "damages" and *ilobolo* to the women he has slept with or impregnated outside of wedlock; for many women of this persuasion, *ilobolo* carries the positive valence of a man's sacrifice and commitment—a far cry from the liberal view that denounces the practice as tantamount to the purchase of women. In other words, Zuma represents a re-mooring of gender and generational hierarchies ordered around the domestic realm. Women who I interviewed about Zuma expressed these sentiments in interesting ways:

> He is a womanizer, yes, but women like that he cares for his wives; some hope that there might be a vacancy for themselves!

> He cares for his home. If you can look at his home you'll see it's nice; even the walkways are clean, and there are nice flowers. Zuma makes certain that all of his children are going to school and all his relatives are right. He cares for his wives in a balanced way, so everything is smooth. They all dress beautifully. None of them complain that he is taking more wives. They don't have a problem. Maybe he is lucky from God, because other men are trying to do this but they fail; they cannot balance. So men must take a cue from the president.

Of course, the advantage that Zuma has over other men is that the state funds the maintenance of his homestead, and he provides for his wives and children by drawing on a special budget sourced from public money. Indeed, Zuma's extensive misappropriation of these funds has become a national scandal. Yet his supporters don't seem to care. One woman from KwaDabeka to whom I spoke at length claimed that she "respects Zuma as *uBaba* [father or leader] who like an *inkosi* [chief], has *isizotha* [dignity or gravitas]" and the capacity to fulfill the obligations of masculinity, in contrast to Mbeki, who is "too much like a woman." Zuma's powerful assertions of heteronormative masculinity resonate with many of his supporters—both men and women—who sense that masculinities are under siege and that the conditions for proper social reproduction desperately need to be reasserted. Zuma's opposition to same-sex marriage and new abortion legislation fits within this framework and represent a shift away from liberalism and individual rights (which many people associate with Mbeki) back to an era of more rigid domestic order.

Polokwane signaled much more than just a working-class insurrection within the ANC. It signaled a populist revival of "culture"—a significant departure from Mbeki's vision of the cosmopolitan modernity of the African Renaissance. The massive outpouring of support for Zuma in urban areas arises out of the profound frustration of abjection, a disappointment with modernity, and a messianic hope for the recovery of social well-being—a hope that people have placed in a nostalgic return to 1960s structures of gender and family. People in urban areas today feel as though they have tried liberalism, but it failed them. Now they are harkening back to the past in a desperate attempt to seek solutions to the intractable misfortunes—joblessness, poverty, inability to marry—that they face. In many cases people are turning back to the ancestors for fear that perhaps they left them too hurriedly, in hope that they might recover what they lost when they launched their dreams upon the sea of liberal modernity.

THE POLITICS OF SOCIAL ORDER

One of modernity's permanent laments concerns the loss of a better past, the memory of living in a securely circumscribed place, with a sense of stable boundaries and a place-bound culture with its regular flow of time and a core of permanent relations. Perhaps such days have always been a dream rather than a reality, a phantasmagoria of loss generated by modernity itself rather than its prehistory. But the dream does have staying power.

—Andreas Huyssen, *Present Pasts*

Before assuming the presidency, Jacob Zuma became extremely popular for a series of authoritarian policy remarks, which, while they resonated with much of the population, inspired the outrage of liberal activists. At a Heritage Day celebration in 2006 in Stanger, Zuma stated that same-sex marriage was "a disgrace to the nation and to God," and remarked that, "When I was growing up, an *ungqingili* [homosexual] would not have stood in front of me. I would knock him out."[5] Later, addressing the nation's rising incidence of teen pregnancy, Zuma proposed that the state should confiscate "illegitimate" babies and force the mothers to enroll in college and obtain degrees.[6] On the question of

South Africa's outrageous crime rate, Zuma called for a return to the death penalty and encouraged police to shoot to kill whenever necessary.[7] Since taking office, Zuma has been reined in to some extent by the party's leaders, and has toned down his policy rhetoric on homosexuality, teen pregnancy, and crime to more palatable positions in line with constitutional provisions.

It is in view of perspectives like these that the Zuma movement bears notable resonances with populist movements elsewhere in the world. By populism here I mean a political approach that mobilizes the anger of economically marginalized voters and channels it along socially conservative lines. The conservative movement that grew in the United States beginning in the 1980s provides a good example, where the political agenda of working-class white people had less to do with their class interests than with overriding concerns about religion, abortion, homosexuality, and immigration, and—perhaps most significantly—an eagerness to recuperate the fabled "traditional" family of mid-century America (Coontz 1992). These same concerns lie at the center of conservative Islamic movements. Sayyid Qutb—the intellectual father of Islamic fundamentalism—held that Western liberalism had brought about social degeneration and decay, or *jahiliyyah*. In his landmark treatise *Milestones,* Qutb lamented that "Mankind today is on the brink of a precipice . . . because humanity is devoid of those vital values which are necessary not only for its healthy development but also for its real progress" (cited in Bergesen 2008:35). For Qutb, the health of society hinged on recovering the traditional order of family and gender, with women relegated to the domestic sphere and public responsibilities assigned to men (Calvert 2000:97). These movements lend credence to Hannah Arendt's fear—expressed in *The Origins of Totalitarianism*— that the social anomie brought on by modernity would create the conditions for fascist uprisings as people scramble to reassert moral orders.

The great irony of globalization is that it ends up producing new forms of parochialism. Don Kalb shows that neoliberal globalization has led, not to increased cosmopolitanism and global civil consciousness, but—ironically—to an "upsurge of counter-narratives of nationalism, localism, religion, and tradition" (2005:187). Brigit Meyer and Peter Geschiere (1998) have called this "cultural closure," a process by which popular identities have shifted away from dialectics of cultural flux and have begun to gravitate increasingly toward newly imagined folk communities (cf. Comaroff and Comaroff 2009). In a similar vein, Arjun Appadurai (1996) has shown that in the context of infinitely expanding openness, communities long for belonging and mobilize strong fantasies of home, often along illiberal lines tending toward fascism. In Africanist ethnography, two recent monographs have illustrated similar trajectories. Charles Piot (2010) shows that, responding to the experience of extreme privation in Togo, people are turning to new charismatic religious groups as a way of reestablishing a semblance of order in a context where the state has lost its ability to provide security. Similarly, James Smith (2008) shows that new forms of underemployment and flexible labor in Kenya—and the resultant transformations of gender roles and kinship structure—have aroused deep-seated anxieties and incited violent campaigns against witchcraft.

In South Africa, there is something about this historical moment—the moment where neoliberalism has triumphed—that has led to a crisis of governance and a wave of popular demands for the state to reassert stricter social order. This moment manifests itself, not only in an economic crisis, but in an ontological crisis—a crisis of being. The institutions that the architects of neoliberal capitalism sought to dismantle for the sake of more flexible patterns of production, consumption, and accumulation are now coming back in fashion, as if in resistance to neoliberal modes of governmentality. People want their hierarchies back; they long for a bygone era of domestic social order and of predictable gender relations. Economic liberalism, it seems, has sown the seeds for a popular insurrection against social liberalism. The interesting question becomes: why do people marginalized by economic policy so readily articulate their discontent along noneconomic cleavages, as if social conservatism and the reassertion of domestic order were useful solutions to the problems of neoliberalism?

One way to understand this is as a form of displaced consciousness, though it bears pointing out that if people confuse social liberalism with economic liberalization, they can hardly be blamed, for the two were introduced as a single package by the postapartheid government and the latter draws its justification largely from the principles of the former. But this is only part of the answer, for it falls short of explaining why the return to fundamentalist traditionalism takes on the cultural forms that it does. As William Bissell puts it, "we must pay greater attention to the specific geographies and particular histories of discourses and practices organized around logics of longing and loss" (2008:225). In South Africa, discourses of longing and loss—and expectations for the future—are organized along the lines of apartheid geographies, divided between rural and urban, homestead and township. Given that family form and domestic structure became a key locus of the colonial state's attempts to control Africans over the past century or more, it makes sense that collective nightmares and political aspirations refer to that experience.

Of course, the invocations of the past—or revivals of "culture"—that characterize South Africa today are not at all atavistic. They represent something quite new: an appraisal of present conditions that mobilizes, not the past itself, but conjured images of the past to make its critique. To quote Michael Burawoy and Katherine Verdery, "what may appear as a resurgence of ancient illiberal tradition is something quite different: direct *responses* to the new market initiatives, produced *by* them, rather than remnants of an older mentality. People's responses to a situation may appear as holdovers because they employ a language and symbols adapted from previous orders" (1999:1–2). This use of an older language as the medium of resistance against neoliberal governmentality in South Africa is not altogether surprising, for, as poet Wendell Berry (2001:8) has put it, "It is impossible to prefigure the salvation of the world in the same language by which the world has been dismembered and defaced."

POSTSCRIPT

If the national elections in 2009 spelled doom for the IFP in KwaZulu-Natal, the local elections in 2011 sealed the party's fate. The IFP won only 17 percent of the popular vote and emerged as the outright winner in only two municipalities, down from twenty-six in the 2006 elections—a devastating outcome.[8] One key reason for this is that the IFP's base was split by a breakaway group, the National Freedom Party (NFP), just prior to the elections. The NFP was launched by Zanele Magwaza-Msibi, who had been chosen as the IFP's national chairperson only two years earlier as part of the party's attempts to rejuvenate its image and appeal to younger and female voters. Magwaza-Msibi was ejected from the IFP by the party's leadership when it became clear that she had enough support to supplant Buthelezi and assume the presidency. Going it alone, Magwaza-Msibi's new party captured 11 percent of the vote in KwaZulu-Natal—largely youth and women disaffected with the IFP but not willing to support the ANC—dividing the IFP's share and costing it control of twenty-one municipalities, most of which are now governed by a ANC-NFP coalition.

The ANC emerged as the biggest winner in this drama, as it gained at least partial control of almost all the province's municipalities. Not surprisingly, the IFP leadership has accused Magwaza-Msibi of operating as an ANC proxy, bought out as part of a divide-and-rule strategy intended to consign the IFP to the dustbin of history. This suspicion has generated a good deal of violence in the province between IFP and NFP supporters and has led to dozens of political assassinations.[9] In the 2014 national election things got even worse for the IFP. The party's share of the vote in KwaZulu-Natal slipped to an all-time low of 11 percent.[10]

Yet while the ANC has gained new power in KwaZulu-Natal, the party has actually *lost* support since the 2009 elections that whisked Zuma into the presidency, with its share of the national electorate slipping from 66 percent to 62 percent in the 2014 elections. This drop reflects the changes in political attitudes that have swept across South Africa in the wake of the Marikana massacre in 2012. When members of the COSATU-affiliated National Union of Mineworkers organized a march to protest the union's complicity with the state and employers, union leaders opened fire on their own members, killing two. Later, angry workers staged a wildcat strike that was attacked by the police. Thirty-four people were massacred that day in what many South Africans compare to the Sharpeville massacre in 1960—a comparison that, in a twist redolent of George Orwell's *Animal Farm,* paints the ANC as the heir of the apartheid state, equally ready to suppress dissent with violence. The Marikana massacre has confirmed many workers' suspicions that COSATU's close partnership with the ANC renders it unable to challenge the ruling party on their behalf. Disaffected workers are now abandoning COSATU in favor of independent unions. The Association of Mineworkers and Construction Union (AMCU), initially formed in 1998 to organize primarily IsiZulu-speaking workers who rejected the ANC, now represents a growing portion of the nation's mining workforce, and as much as 70 percent at Marikana.

This discontent with the ruling party is evident in other quarters as well. One example is the powerful Metalworkers Union,[11] which recently broke ranks with the ANC in a historic turn that could open the way for a labor-based opposition to the government for the first time since 1994. Another is the Economic Freedom Fighters (EFF), a party founded by Julius Malema shortly after he was expelled from the ANC in 2012. The EFF has successfully mobilized discontented youth and contested the 2014 elections with more than 6 percent of the national vote, drawing the support of those who celebrate its policy of nationalizing the mines and the banks. Interestingly, the EFF, like AMCU, offers a vision that speaks not only against liberal economic policy, but also against liberal social policy: both groups have a distinctly chauvinistic ethos. The point here is that as anger and disappointment mounts against the ruling party, the political alternative appears as a mix of leftist demands for economic justice and populism with an illiberal bent.

On the Politics of Culture

I opened this book with a set of uncomfortable questions: How do we explain the opposition that so many rural Zulu migrants articulate against the principles of liberal democracy? How can we understand migrants' assertions that democracy is ruining families and bringing about deadly misfortunes? I have argued that this political stance makes sense according to the logic of a moral order that is rooted in the rural homesteads to which migrants are tied. Homesteads inscribe in their spatial layouts a rigorous system of social differentiation through hierarchies arranged according to principles of opposition and encompassment. These hierarchies are considered to be crucial to fruition, good fortune, and social reproduction within the family, and lie at the heart of popular theories of affliction and healing: when people encounter misfortunes—such as unemployment, illness, or even death—they very often interpret them as a sign of breakdown in proper domestic relations or neglect of the rites that produce them. To mitigate these afflictions, people pour themselves into the performance of sacrificial rituals—following the advice of diviners—leveraging the symbolic dimensions of bovine anatomy to recuperate kinship in the mold of an imagined ideal order.

Drawing on this cosmology of misfortune, many migrants are wary of the liberal polices promoted by the ANC—policies that have to do with abortion, sexuality, marriage, public housing, child support grants, the rights of women and youth, and autonomous individualism in general. They see these policies—which they lump together under the rubric of "democracy"—as threatening normative hierarchies and equalizing individuals across boundaries of gender and generation, producing a kind of sterile sameness that threatens to undermine the conditions for good fortune, well-being, and even development. This fear of impending misfortune has found traction in South Africa's recent economic history, as neoliberal structural adjustment has eroded the livelihoods of South Africa's working class and wrought devastating harm on rural families in particular. Migrants have experienced this tragedy as a crisis of social reproduction, eroding their ability to pay bridewealth, secure marriages, and build up their families and homesteads in the manner to which they aspire. But instead of blaming the ANC's brand of liberal *economic* policy, they point the finger at the party's platform of liberal *social* policy, articulating a critique of liberal democracy set against the foil of the homestead.

In the process of formulating this critique, migrants reify the homestead through a kind of structural nostalgia, minimizing the complexities of domestic worlds that are in fact fraught with conflict and in many cases fragile and crumbling—a reality that only further fuels their devotion to the ideal. Migrants contrast this caricature of the rural homestead with another equally inaccurate caricature: that of the urban township, and of the ANC as a quintessentially liberal institution (which it is not; indeed, it is deeply patriarchal and autocratic). For migrants, township houses invert the moral order of the homestead, and stand as the material embodiment of all that is wrong with liberal democracy. What we have here is a set of powerful moral ideals built on a symbolic opposition between homestead and township. Much of this book has dwelt on how these ideals have been constructed. I have argued that these caricatures are in large part a consequence of how colonial governance shaped the social field, manipulating hierarchical homesteads in rural areas and engineering nuclear families in urban areas, and entrenching the migrant labor system that continues to circulate people between these two spaces. Indeed, the particular variety of indirect rule deployed in rural Natal may explain why that region became the seat of resistance to the liberation movement in the 1980s and 1990s, while other rural regions in South Africa proved willing to support the ANC.

In their representations of ideal homestead life, middle-aged men tend to celebrate the patriarchal and gerontocratic dimensions of hierarchy by invoking rules once enshrined in the Natal Code of Native Law—rules that do not necessarily operate in lived reality. Women and younger migrants, for their part, subscribe to a more dynamic conception of gendered and generational hierarchies that more closely approximates the actual distribution of power in most homesteads. But there is also a great deal of common ground between these views: both uphold the value of hierarchy, the importance of *hlonipha* and *umthetho,* and the centrality of ritual practice to the ancestor cult and its theory of misfortune.

What is the status of these beliefs? On the one hand, we can see migrants' fetishization of rural homestead culture as a form of ideology (a political vision organized around a particular ideal), not terribly unlike how conservative politicians in the United States marshal an inaccurate representation of the so-called Golden Age of the American family in their call for a certain kind of moral order. In light of this, it might be tempting to see migrants' representations of the homestead as nothing more than an "officializing strategy"—to use Pierre Bourdieu's (1977) term—that they leverage to justify the more cynical interests of realpolitik. But there is another possibility that we must take seriously, namely, that migrants sincerely believe in the value of the ritual processes of social differentiation that they hold to be so crucial to fruition.

This is not only a belief, not simply a representation. This is a matter of life and death. Families across the Zululand countryside invest a tremendous amount of their meager incomes toward purchasing livestock for sacrifice in a desperate bid to reorder their families and solicit the protection of their ancestors against a world of mounting misfortune. To Western observers this seems insane—a clear instance of false consciousness that prevents people from recognizing and addressing the true sources of their suffering. One might retort, of course, that it is no less insane than attending church or turning to prayer in times of personal crisis. But there is something else worth saying here; something more substantial. To rural Zulus, this kind of practice makes sense because of their conceptions about personhood and relatedness. For them, the person is not conceived as finally bounded, but rather as coterminous with specific others and sharing in a common substance according to the logic of encompassment. This is not a metaphor; it has real entailments for people's life courses. It means that individuals spend a great deal of time and large amounts of money attempting to heal the bodies and relationships of relatives whose fortunes determine and constrain their own, even when those relatives have been dead for generations.

Rural migrants are aware that this habitus appears as backward—or even as evil—according to the logic of liberalism, which celebrates individual autonomy and personal responsibility as moral imperatives. In liberal thought, the kind of interdependence that characterizes rural Zulu personhood and kinship figures as a form of bondage, as the very opposite of freedom. Yet in rural Zululand interdependence and even hierarchical relationships are thought to enable the individual's flourishing rather than constrain it. Indeed, it is the absence or breakdown of such relationships that most worries them. In a recent article titled "Declarations of Dependence," James Ferguson (2013) argues that this kind of system provides people not only with a rich sense of value and social membership, but also with protective buffers against economic instability. Without them, individuals—particularly impoverished ones—are left at the mercy of the market. As Ferguson puts it, "It seems that for poor South Africans it is not dependence but its absence that is really terrifying—the severing of the thread, and the fall into the social void." Migrants' critique of liberalism, then, comes from two angles: as a repudiation of the neoliberal subject who is left to sink or swim in the brave new world of the market, and as a rejection of the autonomous, self-realizing individual disembedded from kinship and cut loose from the ancestors.

None of this is to say that relationships of hierarchy and dependence are not contested, or even sometimes abusive. They are. And this appears to be particularly true when families lack the resources necessary for social reproduction. As scholars of South Africa have pointed out again and again, crises of social reproduction often spur crises of masculinity, and women and children often bear the brunt of the anger and frustration that this generates (Waetjen 1999; Hunter 2010).[1] By arguing that we should take culture seriously I am not saying that we should simply accept these issues as part of some kind of relativist project. That is not what is at stake here. Rather, the stakes have to do with, first, our capacity to understand the desires and motivations of people who are considered subaltern (for this I would invoke Geertz's [1984] lecture on anti anti-relativism), and, second, how we end up representing them (and for this I would invoke the insights of the subaltern studies group). Projecting the assumptions of Western social scientific models not only compromises the accuracy of our analysis but also claims recruits to a particular (Eurocentric) way of being human who actually object to the very premise of it.

THE CONUNDRUM OF CULTURE

This brings me to reflect on one of this book's key arguments. I have sought to question the claim that migrants' politics are intelligible according to some generic human nature, as an interest in accumulating resources and labor power, for example. Instead, I have argued that migrants' interests, utilities, and motivations derive from their cultural schemes, frameworks of meaning that establish the parameters for reason and action, such as ideas about what causes misfortunes, what is required for fruition and collective well-being, and what makes a ritual efficacious. I have attempted to use anthropological insights as a corrective to some of the Eurocentric assumptions that find their way into the literature on anti-liberal politics in South Africa, which ultimately tell us more about ourselves than about the people whose lives we seek to understand. As Marshall Sahlins has put it, without some idea of culture "our accounts are reduced to the indeterminacies of a generic human nature or the implicit common sense of [our] own tribe—the ethnocentricity of the latter, in the form of rational self-interest, often taken for the universality of the former" (2004:124).

This is a tricky argument to make in anthropology today, and in South Africa in particular, for the reasons that I laid out at the end of chapter 2. Since the so-called "writing culture" moment in the 1980s, anthropologists have learned—thankfully—that we can no longer innocently propagate an image of the world as a mosaic of bounded cultures with clear traits that play out in everyday life in predictable ways. Propelled by this critique, trends in anthropology have bended toward exploring the processes by which the *idea* of local culture gets *produced,* and looking at how statements about culture arise and circulate in any given field—be they by anthropologists, politicians, marketers, or activists. William Mazzarella's monograph *Shoveling Smoke* (2003) provides a clear example of this kind of approach, focusing as it does on how the global advertising industry manufactures representations of "local culture" in order to whip up brand identification. In South Africa, Jean and John Comaroff's *Ethnicity, Inc.* (2009) explores the commodification, exchange, and consumption of cultural identity and how these processes reconfigure people's lived sense of collective belonging. Even closer to the subject matter of this book, Donald Donham (2011) has used a similar kind of approach to show how key episodes of violence during South Africa's transition only became ethnically charged after the fact, as perpetrators invoked "ethnicity" as a way of explaining the violence in retrospect; in other words, ethnic identity was not a cause of the conflict but an outcome.

Focusing on how representations of cultural difference get produced and circulated allows a useful way around the conundrum of culture.

This is an important move to be sure—and one that offers significant analytical traction—but it runs the risk of reducing culture to a utility function, a tactical claim to entitlement or a means of profit maximization, and therefore risks obscuring the possibility of actual cultural difference, by which I mean differences in the substantive ideas that inform the everyday lives of the people who inhabit the worlds that get essentialized or branded by politicians or profiteers. We need to be able to appreciate the difference between culture as a sign and culture as a set of signs, or, to use Clifford Geertz's terms, as webs of significance that furnish parameters of meaning through which people understand and interpret the world. Culture is more than just representation. It is also real. This is an important analytical point, not just a relativist position. My claim in this book has been that if we want to explain the anti-liberal stance of rural Zulu migrants in South Africa, then we need to be able to understand culture as more than just instrumental interest, and that a crucial first step toward this is to step outside the Western paradigm of interest itself.

This is not the same thing as claiming that culture is static, bounded, uncontested, or "authentic" (see Bashkow 2004). To make such a claim in South Africa would be to reproduce the logic of colonialism and apartheid, and, indeed, to be complicit with racist politics (cf. Adam Kuper 1999). It seems to me that we need some way of thinking about cultural coherence, in the sense that Ruth Benedict and Daniel Rosenblatt have described, without implying some sort of racial theory. To do this, I have attempted to *historicize* culture in South Africa—not only the culture of rural Zulu migrants (i.e., their homestead ideology and their ideas about moral order), but also the culture of the urban townships and the politics of National Democratic Revolution. I have argued that we have to understand both of these cultural worlds as emerging from 150 years of engagement with colonialism and capitalism—with segregation, the migrant labor system, customary law, forced removals, and an intense form of colonial nostalgia that has taken root in the present neoliberal context. I have argued, in other words, that culture is always more global than itself.

At first glance, such an argument seems to skirt close to a theory of colonial determination, which is politically problematic inasmuch as it threatens to eclipse the agency of the colonized. Emphasizing the power of colonialism means relegating the colonized to the role of acting out their lives in a world whose parameters have been established by Europeans—a perspective that carries problematic racial undertones. But the politics of this position run both ways. Strands of this argument are often advanced by politically concerned scholars eager to prove that Africa's social pathologies, such as ethnic conflict, dictatorship, and state corruption, are in fact products of colonial power, which reified "tribes," propped up proxy dictators, and created networks of political patronage through indirect rule. From this perspective, pointing to the surfeit agency of colonialism is crucial to denouncing the colonial project itself, and to dismantling the common racist belief that Africans are bound to produce failed states by dint of their presumed cultural inferiority. Each of these angles has important points to add to the project of progressive politics, but both run the risk of reproducing problematic racial assumptions. This is why Africanists so frequently tack back and forth between the two positions depending on the audience they are trying to persuade.

One way to resolve this conundrum is to make the obvious point that the initial condition was not determined by colonialism, that there was *something there* that preceded the colonial encounter—not just a tabula rasa—and that the agents of colonialism had to work with what they found. The policy of indirect rule, the codification of customary law, the manipulation of kinship hierarchy and so on only worked because there was already something there to act upon. Culture—or "tradition," in Terence Ranger's terms—was not invented out of whole cloth. Recognizing this, Ranger (1993) himself ended up revising his previous position and suggesting the term "imagination" in place of the more determinate "invention." In the case of rural Natal, the project of indirect rule sought to exaggerate and reify dimensions of already-existing social systems, and with only partial success at that. In other words, culture determined the trajectory of colonialism as much as colonialism determined culture. Theophilus Shepstone, the architect of indirect rule, provides the perfect example of this dialectic. The policies that he devised for governing Natal Africans came out of a life-long exchange of ideas with precisely the people he sought to govern; indeed, the very idea of indirect rule was borrowed in large part from Shaka himself, whom Shepstone sought to emulate. Shepstone's legacy of indirect rule is as much a product of the imagination of the colonized as of the imagination of the colonizers. We cannot emphasize one to the exclusion of the other; the important thing is to underscore the dynamic between them.

In Natal, the colonial government did not have the privilege of over-determining the culture of Africans—it never enjoyed such unilateral power. It could never control Africans to the degree that it may have wished, and it could never hope to totalize its hegemony. As the subaltern studies group has famously asserted, there were certain domains of human life that lay outside the reach of the colonial state (see, e.g., Chatterjee 1993). What the colonial government *did* do, however, was influence culture in certain directions, as in through the organization of indirect rule in rural areas and the development of modernist townships in urban areas. And this influence was not one-off; it was a long-term project that spanned decades, a constant pushing. This process resulted in the bifurcation of moral orders that marks KwaZulu-Natal today. Of course, the tensions that persist between rural and urban Africans in the province could never have been predicted by colonial administrators. Their present form has nothing at all to do with European design. Rural Zulu migrants have interacted with the idea of National Democratic Revolution in a manner that no European could have invented and few could have understood.

THE PARADOX OF MULTICULTURAL DEMOCRACY

As one might expect, the conundrum of culture is not confined to the arena of scholarly debate in South Africa. It has also become a crucial policy issue in the making of the postapartheid nation. South Africa's new Constitution was constructed with the intent of departing radically from the country's long history of legally coded racial and ethnic differences. The end product was a document "founded on the most comprehensive, the most liberal, most enlightened notions of democratic pluralism" (Comaroff and Comaroff 2005:34), which is particularly attentive to universal enfranchisement and human rights. As part of this package, the Constitution also explicitly accommodates the claims of culture in an effort to dismantle the apartheid-era idea that certain cultural groups are lesser than others. This presents a problem when the particular claims of culture bump up against the universal claims of human rights. The solution, outlined in chapter 2 of the Bill of Rights, works as follows:

Section 31. Cultural, religious and linguistic communities
    1. Persons belonging to a cultural, religious or linguistic community may not be denied the right, with other members of that community
        a. to enjoy their culture, practice their religion and use their language; and

   b. to form, join and maintain cultural, religious and linguistic
     associations and other organs of civil society.
  2. The rights in subsection (1) may not be exercised in a manner
    inconsistent with any provision of the Bill of Rights.

The Constitution repeatedly emphasizes that, while citizens are permitted to practice "their" culture and "their" religion (note the language of possession), they may do so only to the extent that these *particular* cultural practices do not violate the *universal* rights of the generic individual (see Mokgoro 1999). This policy comes as standard fare in international political theory. For example, the United Nations' Declaration on minority rights states that any cultural prerogatives recognized in the Declaration "shall not prejudice the enjoyment of all persons of universally recognized human rights and fundamental freedoms" (Article 8.2). According to the political theorist Will Kymlicka, "every international declaration and convention on these issues makes the same point—the rights of minorities and indigenous people are an inseparable part of a larger human rights network, and *operate within its limits*" (2007:7; emphasis mine). Cultural difference gets encompassed—and trumped— by the universalizing principles of Western individualism.

In other words, while the new Constitution appears to permit a radical accommodation of cultural difference, it actually departs very little from the nationalist ideology of the old regime. The apartheid state defined national being according to the illiberal principle of unequal, segregated, and internally homogeneous cultural groups. In contrast, the founders of the new nation sought to formulate a nationalist ideology that would encompass and unify the many subgroups of the population; in other words, they sought to depart from standard, Herderian notions of nationalism (Wilson 1973) in order to formulate a nationalist ideology that did not rely on notions of cultural homogeneity. But while claiming to accept cultural difference, the new nationalism still demands a form of cultural homogeneity. National homogeneity is maintained insofar as individual persons, regardless of how they may differ, share essential ontological attributes. Under multicultural democracy, the essential shared attributes are those of the cosmopolitan, rights-bearing individual inscribed in the Constitution and presumed in much mass-mediated discourse: the generic citizen, patterned after Enlightenment assumptions about reason and human nature. "Sameness overrides difference" in the new postsegregation nationalism (Handler 1988:6). "Culture" is allowed to exist, but it must take the form of a democratic association consistent with the logic of Western-style civil society, namely, a voluntary collection of free, autonomous individuals.

The nation maintains the veneer of homogeneous unity by carefully managing and organizing diversity, insisting that all cultural distinctiveness be expressed according to a single logic—what Richard Wilk (1995) calls a "structure of common difference." Unlike the logic of apartheid nationalism, the new South Africa does not require common cultural *content* among its citizens. But it does require a common set of *formats and structures* for the expression of difference, so that every culture is different in a safe, intelligible, and standardized way. Culture is reduced to individual identity and confined to a set of accoutrements that colorfully adorn an otherwise homogeneous mass of similar persons. The new hegemony of the nation, therefore, is located in the structures of common difference that it enforces, which "celebrate particular kinds of diversity while submerging, deflating or suppressing others" (Wilk 1995:118). At base, this ideology provides the rationalization for the state's subject-making project. Under the rhetorical veil of "multiculturalism," the liberal state compels its citizens to conform to the Eurocentric mold of the individual. They are permitted to bear their "culture" only as a possession—one kept from permeating their subjectivity—and only insofar as they do so within the overriding logic of modern personhood.

This illuminates a contradiction at the very center of the multicultural project. Multiculturalism masquerades as a relaxed tolerance of the other, but in actuality partakes of deeply racist violence. As Slavoj Žižek has pointed out, tolerance of the other "passes imperceptibly into a destructive hatred of all Others who do not fit into our idea of tolerance; in short, against all actual Others" (2002:225). Liberal multiculturalism seeks an experience of the other completely deprived of its actual otherness, meaning anything that departs from the principles of egalitarian multiculturalism. To this extent, multiculturalism blurs into a kind of racism such that respect for the other is premised on agreement. As Jodi Dean has put it, "The other with deep fundamental beliefs, who is invested in a set of unquestionable convictions, whose enjoyment is utterly incomprehensible to me, is not the other of multiculturalism" (2005:167). While multiculturalism claims to denounce violent fundamentalisms and adopts the veneer of neutral, disembodied universalism, it actually has a hard kernel of violent fundamentalism at its center. The multicultural state insists that all others must conform to the contours of a "generic" human subjectivity—while disavowing the cultural particularity of this position—and is prepared to enforce this conformity with the violence of arrest and imprisonment, effectively purging the others of their otherness.

Taking its mandate from Section 31 of the Bill of Rights, South Africa's Department of Arts and Culture provides regular forums for the expression of safe, standardized cultural difference. The quintessential example of such a forum is the National Arts Festival held annually in Grahamstown, which hosts a "vibrant celebration of South Africa's rich and multi-faceted" cultures reminiscent of Disney's "Small World," college courses in "World Music," and other controlled expressions of difference. Such festivals render South Africa's cultural diversity safe by organizing, objectifying, and commodifying various expressions of music, dance, cuisine, and architecture. By contrast, decidedly dangerous—and constitutionally unallowable—forms of cultural expression include practices such as compulsory circumcision, divination and witch-prosecution, and rituals of birth, marriage, and death that violate the liberties of minors and women; cultural practices which push up against what Comaroff and Comaroff (2004) call "the limits of liberalism" in accommodating difference. This becomes an issue each year in KwaZulu-Natal during the annual "reed dance" (*uMkosi WoMhlanga*) of the Zulu kingdom, when many of the 25,000 participating maidens undergo "traditional" virginity testing. Virginity testing has become a lightning rod in the politics of culture in South Africa. Proponents insist that it falls within the boundaries of "cultural rights," and that it protects girls' honor and helps stem the HIV crisis, while critics consider it to be a violation of individual liberties and a marker of hierarchy, chauvinism, and everything anti-modern about culture.

The difficulty is that these heterodox practices are widely popular within the communities that claim them. For example, 60 to 70 percent of IsiZulu-speaking girls and their mothers support the practice of virginity testing (Taylor et al. 2002). If one were to put the legality of this and other illiberal cultural practices to a vote, in most cases they would pass with majority support. Similarly, if the liberal-democratic principles enshrined in the Constitution were put to national referendum today, we might find the values of rights-based individualism overturned by a landslide—a possibility that causes a great deal of anxiety among South African liberals. This is the paradox of democracy: that its key mechanism (universal franchise) can undermine its basic principle (liberalism). As Partha Chatterjee has put it, "modernity is facing an unexpected rival in the form of democracy" (2004:41). We have to ask ourselves the difficult question: How democratic is the new South Africa, really? How democratic can any postcolonial nation be that foists a modernizing project on its citizens and forces conformity to the legal categories of liberal, multicultural personhood? This is what Stephanos Nhleko—the leader of National Union I quoted earlier—was getting at when he criticized the ANC for "trying to put everyone in one pot by force," for "subjecting everyone to the same law," and thereby "rubbishing the idea of the rainbow nation." He recognized that liberal, multicultural democracy is a thin ruse for a sometimes violent project of cultural homogenization. He called for a more radical form of multiculturalism—a form of multiculturalism true to its stated claims and willing to accept actual cultural difference. And, as others like him, he was ready to reflect favorably on the apartheid past as a time when the state permitted—indeed, even encouraged—radical alterity.

By reducing cultural diversity to mere "structures of common difference," the Constitution obscures the subaltern subjectivities that constitute the majority of the nation's population and juridically eliminates alternative ways of imagining personhood, community, and value. This is hardly a model that allows for cultural pluralism in any substantive sense. But it is difficult to imagine inverting the formula of Section 31 to allow culture to trump individual rights, so enshrined is the construct of the individual at the center of the modern nation-state. The only way such an arrangement would be thinkable—without slipping into new forms of segregation and apartheid—is if individuals could retain the right to choose whether or not they would subject themselves to the dictates of culture. But even this presumes the autonomous individual: a pure agent who stands apart from all orientations in order to make a totally free choice unencumbered by any sense of obligation or belonging. This is exactly the assumption that rural Zulu migrants want to challenge. From their point of view, the neoliberal maxim, attributed to Margaret Thatcher, that "There is no society; only individuals" reeks of absolute non-being. As the new Constitution seeks to deconstruct old forms of hierarchy and authority in the name of freedom, many migrants see this as stripping the world down to bare life and reducing personhood to a brutish form of animal existence. For them, there is nothing freeing about individual freedom.

The colonial state maintained a distinction between the realm of civil law (direct rule) and the realm of customary law (indirect rule) as a strategy for precluding rural, black South Africans from accessing the rights of citizenship under the ruse of promoting "cultural difference."

After 1994, the ANC began to dismantle this dual legal system and set the country under the rule of a single constitution under the banner "One Law for One Nation." The goal was to gradually abolish the rule of customary law, which the ANC saw as a vestige of segregation and colonial domination (see Mokgoro 1996). But it had the additional effect of creating a "neutral" framework within which cultural difference could be negotiated according to a single set of rules—much like the notion of multiculturalism itself. As Comaroff and Comaroff put it, "In policultural nation-states, the language of legality affords an ostensibly neutral medium for people of difference to make claims on each other and on the state, to transact unlike values, to enter into contractual relations, and to deal with their conflicts. In so doing, it produces an impression of consonance amidst contrast" (2004:192). But the modern legal system is far from "neutral" in its assumptions, for it relies on concepts of "reasonable man," "individual responsibility," "agency," "interest," and "motivation" patterned—once again—after a Eurocentric model of personhood tacitly assumed to be universal.

This creates problems when it comes to assessing culpability across cultural divides. Take, for example, the cases of rural migrants who used violence against what they perceived to be the dangerously anti-social agenda of township activists. In courts of law, they defended their actions under the sign of culture, just as Jacob Zuma did during his rape trial when he invoked the rights and responsibilities of Zulu masculinity, and as the virginity testers continue to do today. The court system has had difficulty reconciling the assumptions of legal universalism with people's claims to cultural difference, in other words, bridging subsections 1 and 2 of Section 31. For the system to remain intact, legal universalism—and the assumptions of "reasonable man" theory—must be upheld over relativist heterodoxy, but some residual, subordinate space must be found within this framework for the claims of culture to have some purchase, however limited. According to Comaroff and Comaroff, the strategy of many judges has been to let defendants off the hook by treating culture as a form of madness, as "a source of diminished responsibility, of temporary loss of reason on par with intoxication" (2004:194). Just as defendants who can prove that they committed any given crime while drunk, insane, or in the grip of passion can have their sentences commuted from, say, first-degree murder to culpable homicide, so too the denizens of custom can plead "cultural belief" as a regrettable lapse of reason.

This observation brings me circling back to where I began this book, for the equation of culture with unreason resonates with the assumptions that form the center of most social scientific accounts of rural Zulu migrants' political motivations. As shown in previous chapters, scholars tend to explain the migrant insurrection in one of two ways: either by casting culture as a form of irrational false consciousness cynically encouraged by the colonial state and manipulated by opportunistic leaders; or by casting migrants as rational individuals interested in maximizing utility and securing control over resources, power, and territory by instrumentalizing the idea of culture. Both approaches assume a model of capitalist, Euro-American personhood that relies on a basic dichotomy between individual and society, or reason and culture. Not coincidentally, this same assumption underpins the liberal conception of freedom, which sees freedom as the ability to reason for oneself outside the "constraints" of culture. Throughout this book I have been at pains to demonstrate that reason and culture should not—indeed, cannot—be considered separately. There is no such thing as human reason independent of culture. Reason is always culturally constituted; that of Western social scientists as much as that of rural Zulu migrants (cf. Sahlins 1976). This point goes a long way not only toward explaining anti-liberal politics from an emic perspective, but also toward exposing the assumptions about personhood that lie at the heart of the twin institutions of social science and liberal democracy.

Notes

1. The *New York Times,* for instance, featured headlines such as "Tribal Feuds Won't Let Up in South Africa's East" and characterized the conflict as "an ethnic divide" pitting "the Zulus versus the Xhosas" (August 20, 1990).

2. Migrancy is difficult to define in KwaZulu-Natal. Under apartheid, the term "migrant" was used to refer to African workers who lacked the legal right to reside permanently in white urban areas, regardless of how far away they lived or whether they identified with rural or urban lifeways. Today the term is used more loosely to refer to people from rural areas who travel to work in urban areas. I use the term with a slight twist: in this book, "rural migrants" refers to migrants who define themselves specifically in reference to their residence in rural homesteads.

3. I spoke with female migrants whenever possible, and I highlight their voices in chapters 4 and 6.

4. The Democratic Alliance for Egypt (led by the Muslim Brotherhood) won 37.5 percent of the vote in Egypt's post-uprising elections, and the Islamist Bloc (led by the Salafist Al-Nour Party) won 27.8 percent.

5. William Joseph Goode's *World Revolution and Family Patterns* (1963) provides a good example of this kind of thinking.

6. There is an extensive literature on kinship ties and clientelism in the political realm generating corruption and cronyism in Africa. International institutions such as the World Bank and the IMF see these relationships as obstacles to democracy and target them for reform through structural adjustment programs.

7. For Marx, the individual is controlled by society in the form of ruling-class ideology; false consciousness prevents individuals from understanding the objective conditions of their existence and developing class solidarity. That

said, true consciousness for Marx is always a consciousness that leads to social solidarity rather than individual isolation. For Freud, the individual (ego) is repressed by social norms and expectations (the superego), which are imagined as external constraints or impositions. The ego is at its most free when it has maximum latitude with respect to the superego (see Taylor 1989:33).

8. Scholars have drawn attention to how the idea of autonomy relies on assumptions about personhood that derive from a masculinist, white middle-class context and emphasizes the rational, bounded, and atomistic characteristics of the individual at the expense of its embodied, relational, and socially embedded dimensions (see Mahmood 2005:13–14).

9. On corruption in the ANC, see Feinstein 2010.

10. Known as the SACP.

11. This idea has a long history in revolutionary theory. In *The Eighteenth Brumaire,* Marx himself characterizes the peasantry as "superstitious" and unenlightened, living in "stupefied bondage" to the old order. Lacking unity of interests, the peasantry, to Marx, constitutes nothing more than a "homogenous multitude," a "sack-full of potatoes" without political organization (Marx 1998:608–9).

12. Similar theories of affliction have been found to drive political movements like the Mau Mau uprising in Kenya, the Maji Maji rebellion in German East Africa, and the Kamajors in Sierra Leone, as well as the guerrilla movement in Zimbabwe (Lan 1985), the Hutu-led genocide in Rwanda (Taylor 1999), and the Lord's Resistance Army in Uganda (Allen and Vlassenroot 2010).

13. Details of the IMF deal can be found in Nowak and Ricci 2005.

14. Unemployment rose from 13 percent in 1994 to a peak of 30.3 percent in 2001 (Banerjee et al. 2007). The Stats SA Labour Force Survey for Q1 2013 announced unemployment at 25.2 percent. The 37.7 percent figure, from the same source, represents the "broad" definition of unemployment that includes people who have given up searching for work.

15. These statistics come from the Living Conditions Survey 2008/9 by Statistics South Africa.

16. These forces include the efforts of Shaka to subordinate the region's many chiefdoms and clans to the Zulu kingdom in the early nineteenth century; the efforts of missionaries and ethnographers who codified and standardized "Zulu" customs and language; and the efforts of mission-educated intellectuals who sought to mobilize Natal Africans around a common cultural identity (and around the figure of Shaka) as a form of resistance against imperialism (see Marks 1986; Hamilton 1998; Vail 1989).

17. Healy-Clancy and Hickel 2014 is based on this claim.

18. This school of thought attempts to see terrorists as rational actors with predictable interests and economic motives (see, e.g., Berman 2009; Cronin 2009; Moyar 2009; Pape 2006; Perry 2010; United States, Department of the Army 2007).

19. Rorty 1989 resolves this conundrum by suggesting that we recognize the contingency of our claims about the political good, ironizing the projects we espouse.

20. See Hickel and Khan 2012.

CHAPTER 1

1. Inkatha was initially founded in the 1920s by Zulu King Solomon kaDinuzulu. Buthelezi revived the organization in 1975 (see Cope 1990).

2. Gevisser 2007:338 offers a compelling narrative of how this rupture unfolded.

3. For more on the Durban Strikes, see Institute for Industrial Education 1974.

4. These early trade unions were led largely by the Trade Union Advisory and Coordinating Council (TUACC) (see Ulrich 2007). They sought to avoid the fate of their predecessor, SACTU (the South African Congress of Trade Unions), whose association with resistance politics led to its banning in 1961.

5. Most notably Richard Turner.

6. Interview with Jay Naidoo.

7. For the general outlines of this history, see Baskin 1991; Steven Friedman 1987; Luckhardt and Wall 1980; Lambert and Webster 1988. For the debate about workerism versus popularism, see Cronin 1987.

8. Cited in Middleton 1984.

9. The alternative to the two-stage policy was Leon Trotsky's theory of permanent revolution. Trotsky argued that workers in developing countries should create alliances with the peasantry rather than with the indigenous bourgeoisie, given that the latter would never willingly cede power. This perspective was suppressed in the Soviet Union under Stalin.

10. Interview with Alan Govinsamy, an elder shop steward of the Food and Allied Workers Union.

11. "National Union" is short for National Sugar Refining and Allied Industries Union, or NASARAIEU.

12. Known as UWUSA.

13. Today there are a number of other well-known examples of such unions: in the mining sector, for instance, the Association of Mineworkers and Construction Union (AMCU) emerged in 1998 to organize mostly IsiZulu-speaking workers disaffected with the COSATU-affiliated National Union of Mineworkers (NUM), setting off the conflict that eventually led to the massacre of thirty-four people during a strike in Marikana in 2012.

14. For a more detailed account of how these tensions developed between unions in KwaZulu-Natal's sugar industry, see Hickel 2012.

15. Known as COSAS.

16. In addition to these high-profile events, more everyday acts of terror were perpetrated by armed gangs. The A-Team and the AmaSinyora, both of which supported Inkatha, remain the most infamous.

17. The best-known warlords include Harry Gwala (ANC), who operated near Pietermaritzburg, and Mandla Shabalala (Inkatha), who operated out of Lindelani near Durban.

18. The following year Nelson Mandela stated that he had authorized the use of lethal force in defense of Shell House.

19. The events that I have recounted here comprise a mere sampling of those recorded in Aitchison 1993, Jeffrey 1997, Greenstein 2003, and the final report of the Truth and Reconciliation Commission.

20. Volume 3 of the Truth and Reconciliation Report attributes nearly four thousand killings to Inkatha members and over one thousand to ANC members during the transitional violence in KwaZulu-Natal (p. 325). It is not clear whether the second figure includes killings attributed to the UDF.

21. For examples that rely to varying degrees on ethnic nationalism as an explanatory device, see Sitas 1996; Horowitz 1991; Minnaar 1991, 1992; Sutcliffe and Wellings 1988; Aitchison 1989, 1993; Giliomee 1990.

22. The *Weekly Mail* and the *Guardian* first broke news of this conspiracy in 1991.

23. Bill Keller, "Island of Fear: Inside a Soweto Hostel," *New York Times*, September 10, 1992.

24. This according to an influential 1993 report titled *Fortresses of Fear* by the Independent Board of Inquiry, a local human rights organization.

25. This was the narrative that the Truth and Reconciliation Commission preferred: papering over real political differences was crucial to the illusion of reconciliation that was necessary for unified nationhood.

26. I conducted about three dozen personal interviews with people of this demographic.

27. For Marx, proletarianization generated a crucial cultural transformation, dissolving the bonds that constitute kinship and clan and creating demystified individuals ready to act in their own interests (see Poulantzas 1978). This theory does not work well in the case of South Africa, where apartheid used the migrant labor system to *prevent* individualization ("detribalization," in the language of the time) and to forestall a revolutionary movement of demystified people eager to partake of Enlightenment political freedoms. In other words, South Africa presents a situation where capitalism and wage labor do not overdetermine a particular culture or consciousness: rural Africans have long been deeply integrated into the capitalist economy, yet they do not operate according to the logic of secular political modernity as such.

28. A number of National Union leaders that I interviewed alleged that they had been pursued by COSATU agents sent as hit men during the height of the conflict in the late 1980s.

29. See Worsely 1956 for an early example of this kind of critique.

30. See Illich 1982:11. Note that Marx and Locke made the same assumptions about the ownership of labor power, which run through the accounts of Left and Right alike.

31. Not all Europeans in colonial South Africa wanted this, of course. Missionaries were a clear exception. So were settler farmers, who wanted to outlaw polygyny because it allowed African producers to outcompete them.

32. Barney Nyameko Pityana, a founder of South Africa's Black Consciousness movement along with Steve Biko, notes that Hegelian thought influenced the movement's conception of freedom (Pityana 2012).

33. For a good example of this kind of thinking applied to southern Africa, see van Onselen 1973.

CHAPTER 2

1. The migrant labor system changed the division of labor as women had to take charge of previously male tasks, such as tilling the fields. It undermined the authority of homestead heads over their sons because young men gained access to wages, which meant that they could decide for themselves when they wanted to marry: they could pay for bridewealth without waiting for their fathers to help them. As part of this transformation, bridewealth came to be paid increasingly in cash rather than in cows.

2. For comparative perspectives on money, morality, and fertility, see Taussig 1977; Parry and Bloch 1989; Shipton 1989.

3. A number of other vernacular terms are less commonly used to designate the *umndeni,* including *umlibo* (lit. shoots of a gourd), *usendo* (group of people sharing the same male ancestor), and *uzalo* (progeny, mouth of a river, female genitalia, womb, origin).

4. Adam Kuper's (1982b) comparative study of homesteads across the region found sufficient evidence to suggest a single common symbolic structure that underlay temporal and geographical variations.

5. *Isibayesikhulu:* lit., the great byre. It is also sometimes referred to as *kwesokudla:* of the right hand; of the food-eating hand.

6. *Ikhohlwa:* lit., the forgotten. It is also sometimes referred to as *uhlangothi:* lit., side.

7. *Umnawekosana:* lit., the brother of *inkosona* (the eldest son of the eldest wife).

8. *Umnawekhohlwa:* lit., the brother of *ikhohlwa.*

9. Rafters: *amabibi*

10. Tribute: *etula*

11. *Umndeni wesisu;* lit., family of the stomach/womb.

12. People in rural areas say great houses must be thatched because the ancestors cannot pass through a tin roof. There is much speculation about how township dwellers—whose roofs are rarely thatched—must have lost their ancestors long ago. Township dwellers, for their part, generally dismiss this notion, although some are anxious about it: it is becoming increasingly common for people to construct small thatched huts in their yards specifically to house ancestral spirits.

13. The right/left distinction in the house is not a rigid one. The gender of the sides can change depending on family custom: in some cases the left side might be designated male and senior to the right.

14. Bachelor houses: *amalawu*

15. We might say that the difference between male and female has less to do with genitalia than the capacity for fertility; sterile and postmenopausal females enjoy many of the privileges otherwise reserved for males.

16. Shepstone held the position of chief liaison for Africans in Natal from 1845. Later this position was formalized as that of secretary of native affairs, which Shepstone held from 1856 until 1877.

17. The 1878 Natal Code of Native Law was drafted by a board that was established by the Natal Administration Law (1874), which was written by Shepstone. The code was signed by J.C.C. Chadwick, the secretary of native

affairs after Shepstone, but was written largely by one Sir Henry Conner. The 1891 version was many times longer than the 1878 version and rendered its general principles into rigid laws.

18. I have relied here on the 1932 version of the code (see Natal Code of Native Law 1943).

19. I should be clear that Shepstone was not directly responsible for the codification of customary law—that happened the year after he left office—but he laid down the principles that made it possible.

20. It would be easy to assume that Shaka instrumentalized social hierarchy to control his vassals and shore up his own power, but if the elaboration of hierarchy has to do with fertility and fortune, as I suggest, then there is reason to believe that he was motivated also by more mystical concerns. See Webb and Wright 1976.

21. It was only after the institutionalization of the code that the first serious ethnographies of Natal Africans were written. Rarely—if ever—did these accounts of "Zulu culture" acknowledge that the social structures they described existed in direct interaction with the dictates of colonial indirect rule. Today, many ethnographic accounts of Zulu customs and beliefs draw on those early publications in attempts to reach back in time to a pristine, unsullied tradition. In this pursuit of an authentic past, the role of colonial power in the making of Zulu culture tends to get erased.

22. For a detailed account of *hlonipha* rules see Raum 1973.

23. Ash heap: *imlotha*

24. Praise songs: *izitakazelo*

25. For sociolinguistic analysis of the language of respect (*IsiHlonipho*) see Rudwick and Shange 2006. Doke and Vilakazi 1958 provides a dictionary of *IsiHlonipho* language.

26. *Ukubonga*: praise speech.

27. On "women left behind" in rural areas operating differently—and with more autonomy—than they do when migrant men are at home with them, see Archambault 2010.

28. In this respect the ritual return of migrants to rural homesteads recalls Marcel Mauss's study of Eskimo social morphology, which shows that during the summer, Alaskan Eskimos live in dispersed, nuclear-family tent settlements and give very little attention to religious practice or ritual protocol, but during the winter they concentrate in multifamily houses and engage in "a state of continuous religious exaltation"—they participate in collective ritual, consolidate the kinship system by invoking lineage ancestors, pay especially close attention to the observation of taboos, and whip up a general spirit of "wholeness." As Mauss puts it, "at this time, the group not only regains its unity but sees itself reformed . . . as an ideal group" (1979:59).

29. Catherine Bell (1992:102–3) discusses the role of ritual in creating social differences, citing Gregory Bateson's (1933) notion of "schizmogenesis" and Lévi-Strauss's notion of "parceling," the process of making minute distinctions (Lévi-Strauss 1981). Bell points out that these differences are usually asymmetrical and entail hierarchical relationships of dominance and subordination, as Robert Hertz ([1909] 1973) and Terence Turner (1977, 1984) have shown. For

Turner, the ritual process of differentiation produces a hierarchical form of unity, which Bourdieu (1977:163) describes as a strategy of "integration in and through division."

30. As elsewhere in Africa (Evans-Pritchard 1956; Heusch 1985).

31. For detailed accounts of female rites of passage in Zululand, see du Toit 1987 and Scorgie 1998.

32. This cluster of associations—between piercing, separation, and fertility—appears repeatedly in Zulu folklore (e.g., Berglund 1976:33). Similar logic also operates in the secretive royal ritual known as *Umkosi Wokweshwama,* the annual ceremony of the firstfruits (Webb and Wright 1976; Gluckman 1938; Beidelman 1966; Lincoln 1987).

33. A plural noun often rendered as "bad luckies" in English. Misfortune is also variously termed *amabhati* or *amashobolo.*

34. Ironically, such remedies are all incredibly expensive, especially given that the people who most earnestly seek them are by definition beset with financial woes—the very sign of their misfortune in the first place.

35. Diviners wield a great deal of power when it comes to deciding what counts as normative. In this sense, we might say that diviners invent kinship norms as much as they reflect them.

36. This theme emerges in the regional ethnographies (Berglund 1976; Ngubane 1976, 1977, 1981; Comaroff 1980), as well as elsewhere in Africa (Evans-Pritchard 1937; Jackson 1982; Riesman 1986).

37. This is particularly true for women, who have precarious access to land and inheritance under customary law. Some of these imbalances are being challenged in South Africa's courts, largely by the Commission for Gender Equality (see Mokgoro 2003). Yet even where laws are changing, misogynistic attitudes often remain entrenched. As a result, women in rural KwaZulu-Natal experience high rates of violence and forced sex in intimate relationships, which leaves them at heightened risk of HIV infection (Hoque et al. 2009). Gender-based violence in this region is no more prevalent than in the rest of the country, but women who fall under the remit of customary law often have a difficult time appealing for the rights that the Constitution provides. The same thing can be said for children and for gay men and women. This is unsurprising, given that customary law was designed by elite European males in conjunction with elite African males in what Guy 1997 calls an "accommodation of patriarchs," shot through with heteronormative principles.

CHAPTER 3

1. On these movements, see Carton 2000; Delius 1989, 1990; Kepe and Ntsebeza 2012; Marks 1970; Mbeki 1964; Van Kessel 1993.

2. The inconsistency within this model was, of course, that both missionaries and colonial agents accepted African women working in European homes as paid domestic workers.

3. These projects were sustained by the proceeds of the Native Beer Act of 1908, which allowed the city to monopolize the production and sale of sorghum beer to Africans for the purpose of generating the money necessary to

finance the Native Administration bureaucracy. This model, known as "the Durban system," was replicated by colonial governments across the continent.

4. KCF94, PNAB Microfiche, Killie Campbell Africana Library, Durban. I draw heavily on data from this series, which includes rare information on domestic organization and kinship structure in Umkhumbane.

5. According to the Native (Urban Areas) Act of 1923.

6. Cato Manor Heritage Center, Durban. Informal settlements developed a dynamic cultural character in some ways analogous to the Harlem Renaissance in the United States. Alan Paton immortalized the rich tradition of jazz, poetry, and general urban effervescence of the era in his play *Umkhumbane*.

7. KCF94, PNAB Microfiche, Killie Campbell Africana Library, Durban.

8. For early perspectives on the illicit beer trade, see Hellmann 1934.

9. I hesitate to use the term "public sphere" here because I want to emphasize that informal settlements like Umkhumbane did not in fact sustain a rigid, modernist contrast between public and private domains.

10. A similar tradition developed equally on the mission stations, where many of the ANC's leaders received their early education in accordance with liberal European values.

11. When women protestors in Umkhumbane were asked who their chiefs were, they responded, "We have none!" (Welsh 1971:30).

12. Natal Public Health Acts—which were specific to the province—were passed earlier in 1903, 1906, and 1914.

13. The apartheid state's view that the lack of nuclear families among urban Africans posed a threat to national stability resonates with the Moynihan Report in the United States, which was influential at roughly the same time (Moynihan 1965).

14. See the election manifesto of the National Party, 1948. This flew in the face of the Fagan Report of 1948, which criticized the migrant labor system for its destructive effects on African families and advocated for policies that would encourage the permanent stabilization of African families in urban areas.

15. KwaMashu had to be situated well away from white areas as per the rules of the Group Areas Act of 1950.

16. As an instance of massive black resettlement under the Group Areas Act, the elimination of Umkhumbane rivals that of District 6 in Cape Town and Sophiatown in Johannesburg for prominence in South Africans' historical imagination. Forced removals in South Africa attracted international attention with the 1983 clearance of the Crossroads settlement outside of Cape Town, where "police were filmed using teargas, rubber bullets, attack dogs, and baton charges to drive people out of their homes . . . [and] followed up by confiscating the sorry sheets of plastic that the newly homeless victims tried to use for shelter, and even the clothing of mothers and babies, in order to force residents to leave the destroyed neighborhood" (Ferguson 2007; see also Platzky and Walker 1985).

17. The team was, however, concerned that individualism and the close quarters of flat life might lend itself to immorality and an increase in children born out of wedlock.

18. These aims were adapted from the Native Economic Commission's suggestions on Native Education.

19. Bourquin's tenure in this office lasted from 1950 to 1979. After 1948 the name of the department was changed from the Department of Native Affairs to the Department of Bantu Administration, and then later (during Bourquin's tenure as director) to the Port Natal Administration Board.

20. KCM 55166–55232, Killie Campbell Africana Library, Durban.

21. The Durban area was restructured in accordance with the mandates for segregation dictated by the Group Areas Act after 1950.

22. The Bantu Men's Social Center in Durban provides a telling example of such a controlled public sphere. The state and European society sought to keep Africans "off the street" and forestall rebellious activity by providing institutions that fostered public sociality through the promotion of civilized docility.

23. The Commission worked in consultation with the Department of Native Affairs and the National Building Research Institute to compile technical procedures for the construction of African housing. The legislation that deals with Housing Schemes and their layouts is comprised of the Housing Act 35/1920 and the Housing (Emergency Powers) Act 45/1945. In Natal, relevant legislation is contained in the Natal Housing Ordinance of 1945. Part of the Commission's mission was "To ensure effective segregation of races i.e., effective buffer strips, zoning, etc. [by drawing attention] to the provisions of the Group Areas Act 41/1950, and the Native (Urban Areas) Consolidation Act 25/1945."

24. This legislation was produced under the aegis of Section 38(3) of the Native (Urban Areas) Consolidation Act no. 25 of 1945.

25. They also had to be qualified to live in urban areas according to Section 10 of the Natives Laws Amendment Act of 1945.

26. The Slums Act of 1934 called for 100 cubic feet of free air space and 40 square feet of floor space for persons over the age of ten and half that for younger children.

27. Data from the 1960s show that up to 69 percent of township families were of the simple-nuclear type; see Pauw 1973; Reader 1966; Schlemmer and Stopforth 1974; Marwick 1978. The Surplus People's Project also bears this transformation out clearly: compare survey results in files 6 and 38 of the Surplus People's Project Data housed in the Killie Campbell Africana Library, Durban.

28. Such transformations are well documented in the literature, where a range of studies speak to changes in bridewealth and marriage patterns in urban areas (Brandel 1958; Krige 1936; Mathewson 1959; Verster 1965), and to kinship and culture change as a consequence of urbanization more generally (Amoateng and Heaton 2007; Beinart 1980; Dubb 1974; Hellmann 1937, 1971, 1974; Monica Hunter 1932; Mayer 1961; Murray 1981; Phillips 1938; Preston-Whyte 1973; Schapera 1947; Spiegel and McAllister 1991; Vilakazi [1962] 1965; Wilson and Wilson 1945).

29. Drawing on data collected in East London in the 1960s, B. A. Pauw (1973) concluded that as many as 37 percent of households were headed by women, and that most of the male-headed multigeneration households consisted of a married couple with husbandless daughters and their children. Pauw proposed that the typical household structure comprised two basic types: a major type, based on a male-headed elementary family during its earlier phase of growth, and a minor type, based on the group consisting of an unmarried

mother and her children (1973:154). Marwick 1978 demonstrates that, in the case of extended families, if the extension involves the head of the household's generation, it is likely to be through a male, while if the extension involves the children of the household, it is likely to be through a female—a pattern attributable to the greater frequency with which "illegitimate" children of daughters are included in the household as opposed to those of sons. Like Pauw, Marwick reiterates the growing incidence of matrifocality and shows that matrifocality operates as the primary organizing principle among a significant proportion of households.

30. In the case of KwaMashu, this happened after the township's incorporation into the KwaZulu homeland, once residents were allowed to own their houses and the land on which they were situated.

31. Hammond-Tooke 1970 concluded that urbanized Africans were more likely than rural Africans to attribute misfortune to nonmystical causes rather than to witchcraft or ancestral wrath.

CHAPTER 4

1. Sibley 1995, Goode and Ben-Yehuda 1994, and Thompson 1998 use the term "moral panic" to suggest a perceived threat to values or ideals held to be crucial to social order, which justifies the erection of boundaries between upstanding insiders and the insidious outsiders who threaten to undermine society.

2. The negotiations began under the Convention for a Democratic South Africa (CODESA). CODESA broke down after the Boipatong Massacre in 1992, and negotiations resumed later under the Multiparty Negotiating Platform.

3. According to a 2000 report by the National Labour and Economic Development Institute.

4. Banerjee et al 2007; Stats SA Labour Force Survey for Q1 2013.

5. "Sad South Africa: Cry, the Beloved Country," *The Economist,* October 20, 2012.

6. This despite a dramatic increase in the number of black millionaires, spurred largely by the Black Economic Empowerment program. In 2013, there were reportedly 7,800 black millionaires in South Africa (Theresa Taylor, "Huge Spike in SA Black Millionaires," *BusinessReport,* November 15, 2013).

7. Statistics South Africa, Census 2011.

8. These figures come from "Living Conditions Survey 2008/9," Statistics South Africa. The poverty line I use here is R577 per person per month, the "upper-bound" poverty line.

9. On this tension between neoliberalism and welfare in South Africa, see Ferguson.

10. Bridewealth "prices" were fixed by Natal's colonial administrators in 1869 and set at ten cows (for commoners). The price remains roughly the same today, at between ten and twelve cows, depending on which animals are counted. Many people opt for a cash equivalent of R15,000–R25,000. To settle for less than this is often considered shameful.

11. The Termination of Pregnancy Act took effect in early 1997 and remains the most liberal abortion law in Africa.

12. Homosexuality became a particularly hot topic with the introduction of the Civil Unions law in 2006, which legalized same-sex unions (see Robins 2008). It is worth pointing out that there is one expression of homosexuality that is generally acceptable in rural KwaZulu-Natal, namely, diviners who are possessed by opposite-gendered spirits.

13. But nearly 60 percent of people in rural KwaZulu-Natal believe that abortion is justified in the case of rape, incest, or if continued pregnancy would endanger a woman's health.

14. This is also why many rural migrant workers find the principle of social grants—a founding premise of the ANC's platform—so vile; "nothing should be received for free," they often say.

15. For more on the medical anthropology of HIV/AIDS in KwaZulu-Natal, see LeClerc-Madlala (1996, 1999, 2001, 2002, 2008).

16. Ntokozo Mfusi and Sibusiso Mboto, "Women: Don't Dare Wear Trousers in Umlazi," *The Mercury,* July 25, 2007.

17. Mpanza's assailants were finally convicted in December 2010 and sentenced in May 2011.

18. I have paraphrased the second sentence here for the sake of clarity.

19. Note the resonance here with competing feminisms in the United States. Ginsburg 1989 reported that both pro-life and pro-choice advocates considered themselves feminists: pro-life advocates saw themselves as defending the uniqueness of womanhood and motherhood, protecting women from being reshaped into "structural men," while pro-choice advocates saw themselves as defending women's rights and battling sexual discrimination. The former emphasized the moral value of difference, while the latter emphasized the moral value of sameness.

20. It bears noting that the first perspective, that of evolutionary thought, relies on a spatial metaphor—an imaginary line, with rural Zulus depicted, literally, as "behind," or to the left (with the axis of progress moving from left to right). But rural Zulus do not use a similar spatial metaphor, since they do not espouse the same grand historical metanarrative.

21. "Foreign" and "global" typically register as effeminate in this discourse and contrast with the masculinity of the "local." For comparison, see Freeman 2001.

22. Volume 3 of the Truth and Reconciliation Commission report claims that arson "was by far the most common type" of violence used during the political transition in KwaZulu-Natal, "with nearly 4,000 cases reported" (p. 324).

23. Specifically "female" lightning, which is said to be "red."

24. "Blazing bird from the heavens" is my translation of *umbumbulo wezulu,* or *inyoni yezulu.*

25. Many say that witches cannot be cut (because they embody the principle of anti-differentiation), so arson is the most effective way to eliminate them.

26. Many rural Zulus lament the fact that the liberal rights enshrined in the Constitution preclude the accusation and punishment of suspected witches,

which—for them—is one of the reasons for South Africa's precipitous moral decline (Ashforth 2005). Since the modern state refuses to prosecute witches, but willingly prosecutes people who *kill* witches (e.g., the organizers of witch-hunts), some see it as colluding with witches.

27. This interpretation departs from the accounts of Shula Marks (1970) and Mark Lambert (1995), who—importing more familiar social-scientific categories—read the rebellion as a struggle of peasants against the forces of colonial proletarianization, a proto-Marxist expression of resistance against the incursions of capitalism.

28. This is the same union discussed in chapter 1. Once again, "National Union" is short for National Sugar Refining and Allied Industries Union.

29. Many National Union members express displeasure with COSATU's practice of promoting well-educated youth to positions of power over their elder colleagues; certificates and degrees appear to upend generational rankings.

CHAPTER 5

1. South African Department of Health study, 2009.

2. According to the World Bank's World Development Indicators as of 2008.

3. *Umkhuphulo* is also known as an "unveiling ceremony."

4. According to Giorgio Agamben in his brief discussion of funeral rites (1995:98) death releases a vague, structurally ambivalent being ("matter out of place") that needs to be ritually transformed into a proper ancestor, someone who clearly belongs to the world of the dead, thus moving the dead from being dangerous to being powerful and protective.

5. In IsiZulu, this thorn tree, *Zizyphus mucronata,* or buffalo thorn in English, is called *umphafa* or *umlahlankosi,* literally, "that which buries the chief." Its zigzaggy branches and hooked thorns are ideal for "catching" wild spirits. See Palmer and Pitman 1972.

6. See also Ngwane 2001 and White 2001.

7. A reality television show called *Kumbul'ekhaya* (Remember Home) was enormously popular while I was doing fieldwork in South Africa. Each episode follows the story of a different rural family that has been searching for a long-lost relative who never returned from the city after leaving to find employment. The producers of the show find the lost relative for the family and arrange for their reunion, which each time dramatizes the ambivalence of the returnees, who are torn between loyalty to their rural family and commitment to their urban lifestyle.

8. According to my interlocutors, one way this can be accomplished is by sneaking at night to the grave of a person who has just been buried and using *umuthi* to draw the spirit away before it can be rooted back in its home. Ancestor theft can also happen at any time after this sensitive liminal period if the family fails to perform the necessary integration ritual, or performs it incorrectly. This ever-present risk means that people can never be certain as to whether their ancestors have been stolen or not. It is up to diviners to say.

9. Bile: *inyongo.*

10. See Evans-Pritchard 1956 and Heusch 1985 on the significance of sacrificial meat in other African contexts.

11. The gendered distinction is expressed in the spatial layout of the great house, where the right side is coded male and the left is coded female.

12. IsiZulu speakers employ the terms *abafazi* and *omama* to designate both the wives and mothers of the homestead head as well as the wives and mothers of the homestead head's brothers and sons (i.e., married women).

13. Technically called *imihlubulo*, the rib cage can also be called *uhlangoti*, the same term used to designate the "side" of a homestead, corroborating the analogue between the homestead and the sacrificial cow.

14. I witnessed this most often during weddings, where the marriage epitomizes kinship and the prospects for legitimate social reproduction.

15. Note that the homesteads of chiefs are known as *amakhanda*, "the heads," as were the barracks of the former Zulu kings.

16. An additional note about the gender of meat cuts: male cuts of meat are designated according to the generational statuses of elder men (*amakehla, amadoda*), young men (*izinsizwa*), and boys (*abafana*)—a military-political scale—while female cuts of meat are designated according to affinal relations (wives, or *omama*) and agnatic relations (daughters, or *amadodakazi*)—a kinship scale.

17. The feminine valence of the homestead is historically recent. The advent of migrant labor displaced the masculine element from the homestead and externalized it to the workplace.

18. The term *isithebe* can also be used to refer to a piece of the meat distributed during this process.

19. Some families devolve this responsibility onto the eldest daughter of the first wife of the homestead head—the *umafunwase,* the female equivalent of the male heir, *inkosana.* For house-specific ceremonies, the woman associated with the sponsoring house assumes responsibility for cutting and distribution.

20. The IsiZulu term is *ethula,* which also refers to the practice by which lesser chiefs offer their daughters as wives to the paramount chief.

21. See parallels in McKinnon 1991.

22. Stick fighting is known as *ukuqatha.*

23. For more on stick-fighting in Zululand, see Coetzee 1996; Schoeman 1982; Msimang 1975.

24. Praise poetry: *izibongo*

25. Evans-Pritchard 1956 shows the same for the Nuer.

26. This affliction is known as *izibobo.* People say that "traditionally" cows were pierced through the front flank instead of through the spine—a practice that prolonged the cow's agony in order to get it to bellow, thereby "calling" the ancestors. The shift to the spine method happened recently in response to animal rights campaigns.

27. Including John Langalibalele Dube, the first president of the ANC.

CHAPTER 6

1. During the 1960s and 1970s, per capita income in sub-Saharan Africa grew at a modest rate of 1.6 percent. But when structural adjustment was

applied to the continent, beginning with Senegal in 1979, per capita income began to *fall* by 0.7 percent per year. The GNP of the average African country *shrank* by around 10 percent during the 1980s and 1990s (see Chang 2007:28).

2. Max du Preez, "Our Protest Culture is Far from Dead," *Pretoria News,* February 11, 2014.

3. People will often elect to spend their meager resources on sacrifice instead of, say, bridewealth, since it promises the possibility of improved fortunes in the future. In other words, the sacrifice of one animal might bring about fortune good enough to supply enough animals for bridewealth.

4. Zuma's signature National Development Plan (NDP)—South Africa's new macroeconomic policy—has been criticized by the unions for further advancing the neoliberal policies of GEAR.

5. "Profile: Jacob Zuma," *Johannesburg Sunday Times,* December 23, 2007.

6. Jackie May, "Jacob Zuma, Boarding Schools, and Our Teachers," *Times Live,* November 24, 2008.

7. "South Africa's Zuma Urges Police to Shoot to Kill Amid Fears Crime Will Put Fans Off Attending World Cup," *Mail Online,* September 29, 2009.

8. There are a total of fifty-one municipalities in KwaZulu-Natal.

9. The NFP claims that twenty-one of its members were killed within the first two years of the party's founding ("Another NFP member killed," *IOLNews,* July 18, 2012); the IFP claims that ten of its members were killed during the same period (Genevieve Quintal, "South Africa: Political Murders—It's About the Dough," *All Africa,* July 29, 2012).

10. The NFP, for its part, ended up with 7 percent in KwaZulu-Natal in the 2014 national elections, somewhat lower than it achieved in the 2011 local elections. The ANC's support went up to 65 percent.

11. The National Union of Metalworkers of South Africa (NUMSA)

CONCLUSION

1. Yet we should not lose sight of the fact that the culture of liberalism has been no less problematic, and no less violent. The extension of neoliberal capitalism, the project of individual self-realization through consumerism, so-called development programs run by institutions like the World Bank, and a number of wars in the Middle East have all been organized under the banner of liberal individualism, with very destructive consequences for many people. Lila Abu-Lughod (2002) and Saba Mahmood (2001) have pointed out that they are constantly pressed to denounce the Islamic movements that they study or else be labeled as apologists, but that "there never seems to be a parallel demand for those who study secular humanism and its projects, despite the terrible violences that have been associated with it over the last couple of centuries" (Abu-Lughod 2002:788).

Glossary of IsiZulu Words

This list includes IsiZulu words that appear repeatedly throughout the book. Words and terms that appear only a few times are defined at each use.

AMADLOZI (sing. *idlozi*): ancestors, spirits

AMALUNGELO (sing. *ilungelo*): liberal rights; or, duties, roles, responsibilities (the root *–lunga* connotes correctness, good behavior, right order, membership of a body, anatomical joint)

AMASHWA: misfortune, affliction, bad luck

HLONIPHA (inf. *ukuhlonipha*, n. *inhlonipho*): respect, discipline, decorum, honor; system of taboo and avoidance; system of respectful speech

ILOBOLO (v. *ukulobola*): bridewealth

INCEKWA: inner stomach of an animal

INDLU: house; hut within a homestead

INDLUNKULU: lit. great house; the main house of a homestead; ancestral house; chief's house; royal family

INHLAWULO: fine imposed on a man for impregnating a woman outside of marriage

INSONYAMA: special cut of meat from a cow that belongs to elders

INYONGO: gallbladder; bile

IPHAPHU (p. *imiphaphu*): lung; event where young boys gather to fight over the lungs of a sacrificed cow

MPAFA: special branch used to attract wandering spirits

UBEDU: sausage-like cut of meat that usually includes part of a cow's trachea, the tip of the heart, and the fat that covers the upper portion of the lungs

UKUGIYA: to dance in the manner of a warrior

UMEMULO: coming of age ceremony for girls

UMGANGELA: organized stick-fighting battle

UMKHUPHULO: ceremony for incorporating a deceased relative into the community of ancestors

UMNDENI: family

UMSAMO: shrine, space of ancestral significance, usually at the back of the great house in a homestead

UMSWANE: partially digested material inside an animal's stomach

UMTHETHO (pl. *imithetho*): law, rule, traditional code of conduct; sometimes used to refer to the Natal Code of Native Law; sometimes used to refer to the Constitution

UMUZI: homestead; the family that inhabits a homestead

References

Abu-Lughod, Lila. 1990. "The Romance of Resistance: Tracing Transformations of Power Through Bedouin Women." *American Ethnologist* 17(1):41–55.

———. 2002. "Do Muslim Women Really Need Saving? Anthropological Reflections on Cultural Relativism and Its Others." *American Anthropologist* 104:783–790.

Adam, Heribert, and Kogila Moodley. 1992. "Political Violence, 'Tribalism', and Inkatha." *Journal of Modern African Studies* 30(3):485–510.

Agamben, Giorgio. 1995. *Homo Sacer: Sovereign Power and Bare Life*. Stanford, CA: Stanford University Press.

Aitchison, John. 1989. "The Civil War in Natal." In *South African Review* 5, ed. G. Moss and I. Obery. Johannesburg: Ravan Press.

———. 1993. *Numbering the Dead: The Course and Pattern of Political Violence in the Natal Midlands, 1987–1989*. Pietermaritzburg: University of Natal.

———. 2003. "The Origins of the Midlands War." In *The Role of Political Violence in South Africa's Democratisation*, ed. Ran Greenstein Johannesburg: Community Agency for Social Enquiry.

Allen, Tim, and Koen Vlassenroot. 2010. *The Lord's Resistance Army: Myth and Reality*. London: Zed Books.

Amoateng, Acheampong, and Tim B. Heaton. 2007. *Families and Households in Post-apartheid South Africa: Socio-demographic Perspectives*. Cape Town: HSRC Press.

Amselle, Jean-Loup. 1998. *Mestizo Logics: Anthropology of Identity in Africa and Elsewhere*. Stanford, CA: Stanford University Press.

Appadurai, Arjun. 1996. "Disjuncture and Difference in the Global Cultural Economy." In *Modernity at Large: Cultural Dimensions of Globalization*. Minneapolis: University of Minnesota Press.

Apter, A. 1987. "Things Fell Apart? Yoruba Responses to the 1983 Elections in Ondo State, Nigeria." *Journal of Modern African Studies* 25(3): 489–503.

Archambault, Caroline. 2010. "Women Left Behind? Migration, Spousal Separation, and the Autonomy of Rural Women in Ugweno, Tanzania." *Signs: Journal of Women in Culture and Society* 35(4).

Arendt, Hannah. 1951. *The Origins of Totalitarianism.* New York: Harcourt, Brace.

———. 1969. *On Violence.* New York: Harcourt, Brace & World.

Argyle, J. 1992. "Faction Fights, Feuds, Ethnicity and Political Conflict in Natal: A Comparative View." Paper presented to the Project on Contemporary Political Conflict in Natal Conference "Ethnicity, Society and Conflict in Natal," University of Natal, Pietermaritzburg, 14–16 September.

Asad, Talal. 1973. *Anthropology and the Colonial Encounter.* London: Athlone.

———. 2003. *Formations of the Secular: Christianity, Islam, Modernity.* Stanford, CA: Stanford University Press.

Ashforth, Adam. 2002. "An Epidemic of Witchcraft? The Implications of AIDS for the Post-apartheid State." *African Studies* 61(1).

———. 2005. *Witchcraft, Violence, and Democracy in South Africa.* Chicago: University of Chicago Press.

Atkins, Keletso. 1993. *The Moon is Dead! Give Us Our Money! The Cultural Origins of an African Work Ethic, Natal, South Africa, 1843–1900.* Portsmouth, NH: Heinemann.

Auslander, Mark. 1993. "Open the Wombs! The Symbolic Politics of Modern Ngoni Witchfinding." In *Modernity and Its Malcontents: Ritual and Power in Postcolonial Africa* ed. Jean Comaroff and John Comaroff. Chicago: University of Chicago Press.

Austin, John L. 1962. *How to Do Things with Words.* Cambridge, MA: Harvard University Press.

Bakhtin, M. M. 1981. "Discourse in the Novel." In *The Dialogic Imagination,* ed. Michael Holquist, trans. Caryl Emerson and Michael Holquist. Austin: University of Texas Press.

Banerjee, Abhijit, et al. 2007. *Why Has Unemployment Risen in the New South Africa?* Cambridge, MA: National Bureau of Economic Research.

Bank, Leslie. 1999. "Men with Cookers: Transformations in Migrant Culture, Domesticity and Identity in Duncan Village, East London." *Journal of Southern African Studies* 25:393–416.

Barchiesi, Franco. 2010. "Episode 39: South Africa—Precarious Liberation: Workers, the State, and Contested Social Citizenship." Audio file, http://works.bepress.com/franco_barchiesi/32.

———. 2011. *Precarious Liberation: Workers, the State, and Contested Social Citizenship in Postapartheid South Africa.* New York: State University of New York Press.

Barnett, Steve, and Martin Silverman. 1979. *Ideology and Everyday Life: Anthropology, Neomarxist Thought, and the Problem of Ideology and the Social Whole.* Ann Arbor: University of Michigan Press.

Barry, A., T. Osborne, and N. Rose, eds. 1996. *Foucault and Political Reason: Liberalism, NeoLiberalism and Rationalities of Government.* Chicago: University of Chicago Press.

Bashkow, Ira. 2004. "A Neo-Boasian Conception of Cultural Boundaries." *American Anthropologist* 106:443–58.

Baskin, Jeremy. 1991. *Striking Back: A History of the Congress of South African Trade Unions (COSATU).* Johannesburg: Ravan Press.

Bateson, Gregory. 1933. *Naven: A Survey of the Problems Suggested by a Composite Picture of the Culture of a New Guinea Tribe Drawn from Three Points of View.* Cambridge: Cambridge University Press.

Beidelman, T. O. 1966. "Swazi Royal Ritual." *Africa: Journal of the International African Institute* 36(4):373–405.

Beinart, William. 1980. "Labor Migrancy and Rural Production: Pondoland c. 1900–1950." In *Black Villagers in an Industrial Society,* ed. Philip Mayer. Cape Town: Oxford University Press.

Bell, Catherine. 1992. *Ritual Theory, Ritual Practice.* Oxford: Oxford University Press.

Benedict, Ruth. 1934. *Patterns of Culture.* New York: Penguin.

Bergeson, Albert, ed. 2008. *The Sayyid Qutb Reader: Selected Writings on Politics, Religion, and Society.* London: Routledge.

Berglund, Axel-Ivar. 1976. *Zulu Thought Patterns and Symbolism.* London: C. Hurst.

Berman, Eli. 2009. *Radical, Religious, and Violent: The New Economics of Terrorism.* Cambridge, MA: MIT Press.

Berry, Wendell. 2001. *Life is a Miracle: An Essay Against Modern Superstition.* Washington, DC: Counterpoint Press.

———. 2005. *Standing by Words.* Washington, DC: Counterpoint Press.

Bezuidenhout, Andries, and Khayaat Fakier. 2006. "Maria's Burden: Contract Cleaning and the Crisis of Social Reproduction in Post-apartheid South Africa." *Antipode* 38:462–85.

Bhabha, Homi. 1994. *The Location of Culture.* New York: Routledge.

Bissell, William. 2008. "Engaging Colonial Nostalgia." *Cultural Anthropology* 20(2).

Bjerk, Paul. 2006. "They Poured Themselves into the Milk: Zulu Political Philosophy Under Shaka." *Journal of African History* 47.

Bloch, Maurice. 1992. *Prey into Hunter: The Politics of Religious Experience.* New York: Cambridge University Press.

Bond, Patrick. 2000. *Elite Transition: From Apartheid to Neoliberalism in South Africa.* Sterling, VA: Pluto Press.

———. 2006. *Talk Left, Walk Right: South Africa's Frustrated Global Reforms.* Scottsville, South Africa: University of KwaZulu-Natal Press.

Bonner, Philip, and Vusi Ndima. 2009. "The Roots of Violence and Martial Zuluness on the East Rand." In *Zulu Identities: Being Zulu, Past and Present,* ed. Benedict Carton et al. New York: Columbia University Press.

Borges, Jorge Luis. 1964. *Labyrinths: Selected Stories and other Writings.* New York: New Directions.

Bourdieu, Pierre. 1977. *Outline of a Theory of Practice*. New York: Cambridge University Press.

———. 1979. *Algeria 1960: The Disenchantment of the World: The Sense of Honour: The Kabyle House or the World Reversed: Essays*. New York: Cambridge University Press.

Boym, Svetlana. 2001. *The Future of Nostalgia*. New York: Basic Books.

Bozzoli, Belinda. 1983. "Marxism, Feminism and South African Studies." *Journal of Southern African Studies* 9(2): 139–71.

Bradford, H. 1987. "'We are now the men': Women's Beer Protests in the Natal Countryside, 1929." In *Class, Community, and Conflict*, ed. Belinda Bozzoli. Johannesburg: Ravan Press.

Brandel, M. 1958. "Urban Lobolo Attitudes." *African Studies* 27:34–51.

Braudel, Fernand. 1980. "History and Sociology." In id., *On History*. Chicago: University of Chicago Press.

Brewer, John D. 1985. "The Membership of Inkatha in Kwamashu." *African Affairs* 84(334):111–35.

Bryant, A.T. 1948. *The Zulu People: As They Were Before the White Man Came*. New York: Negro Universities Press.

Burawoy, Michael, and Katherine Verdery, eds. 1999. *Uncertain Transition: Ethnographies of Change in the Postsocialist World*. Lanham, MD: Rowman & Littlefield.

Burchell, Graham, C. Gordon, and P. Miller, eds. 1991. *The Foucault Effect: Studies in Governmentality*. Chicago: University of Chicago Press.

Burke, Tim. 1996. *Lifebuoy Men, Lux Women: Commodification, Consumption, and Cleanliness in Modern Zimbabwe*. Durham, NC: Duke University Press.

Burrows, John. 1959. *The Population and Labor Resources of Natal*. Natal Town and Regional Planning Reports, vol. 6. Pietermaritzburg: Town and Regional Planning Commission.

Calderwood, D.M. 1953. "Native Housing in South Africa." PhD diss., University of the Witwatersrand, Johannesburg.

Calvert, John. 2000. "'The World Is an Undutiful Boy!' Sayyid Qutb's American Experience." *Islam and Christian-Muslim Relations* 11(1).

Carrier, J.G. 1991. "Emerging Alienation in Production: A Maussian History." *Man* 27:539–58.

Carton, Benedict. 2000. *Blood from Your Children: The Colonial Origins of Generational Conflict in South Africa*. Charlottesville: University of Virginia Press.

Certeau, Michel de. 1992. *The Mystic Fable*. Vol. 1, *The Sixteenth and Seventeenth Centuries*. Chicago: University of Chicago Press.

Ceruti, Claire. 2008. "African National Congress Change in Leadership: What Really Won It for Zuma?" *Review of African Political Economy* 35(115).

Chakrabarty, Dipesh. 1989. *Rethinking Working-Class History: Bengal, 1890–1940*. Princeton, NJ: Princeton University Press.

———. 2008. *Provincializing Europe: Postcolonial Thought and Historical Differences*. Princeton, NJ: Princeton University Press.

Chang, Ha-Joon. 2007. *Bad Samaritans: The Myth of Free Trade and the Secret History of Capitalism*. New York: Bloomsbury Press.

Chatterjee, Partha. 1993. *The Nation and Its Fragments: Colonial and Postcolonial Histories*. Princeton, NJ: Princeton University Press.

———. 2004. *The Politics of the Governed*. New York: Columbia University Press.

Chibber, Vivek. 2013. *Postcolonial Theory and the Specter of Capital*. London: Verso.

Chipkin, Ivor. 2003. "The South African Nation." *Transformation: Critical Perspectives on Southern Africa* 51.

———. 2004. "Nationalism as Such: Violence During South Africa's Political Transition." *Public Culture* 16(2):315–35.

———. 2007. *Do South Africans Exist? Nationalism, Democracy, and the Identity of the People*. Johannesburg: Witwatersrand University Press.

Clegg, Jonathan. 1981. "Ukubuyisa Isidumbu—'Bringing Back the Body': An Examination into the Ideology of Vengeance in the Msinga and Mpofana Rural Locations, 1882–1944." In *Working Papers in Southern African Studies*, vol. 2, ed. P. Bonner. Johannesburg: Ravan Press.

Clifford, James. 1988. *The Predicament of Culture: Twentieth-Century Ethnography, Literature, and Art*. Cambridge, MA: Harvard University Press

———. 1992. "Travelling Cultures." In *Cultural Studies*, ed. Lawrence Grossberg, Cary Nelson, and Paula A Treichler. New York: Routledge.

Clifford, James, and George E. Marcus. 1986. *Writing Culture: The Poetics and Politics of Ethnography*. Berkeley: University of California Press.

Cock, Jacklyn. 1980. *Maids and Madams: A Study of the Politics of Exploitation*. Johannesburg: Ravan Press.

Coetzee, M. H. 1996. *Playing the Sticks: An Exploration of Zulu Stick Fighting as Performance*. Pietermaritzburg: University of Natal.

Comaroff, Jean. 1980. "Healing and the Cultural Order: The Case of the Barolong Boo Ratshidi of Southern Africa." *American Ethnologist* 7(4).

———. 1985. *Body of Power, Spirit of Resistance: The Culture and History of a South African People*. Chicago: University of Chicago Press.

Comaroff, Jean, and John L. Comaroff. 1990. "Goodly Beasts, Beastly Goods: Cattle and Commodities in a South African Context." *American Ethnologist* 17(2):195–216.

———. 2006. *Law and Disorder in the Postcolony*. Chicago: University of Chicago Press.

———. 1992. *Ethnography and the Historical Imagination*. Boulder, CO: Westview Press.

———. 1997. "Mansions of the Lord." In Jean Comaroff and John Comaroff, *Of Revelation and Revolution*. Chicago: University of Chicago Press.

———. 2000. "Millennial Capitalism: First Thoughts on a Second Coming." *Public Culture* 12(2):291–343.

Comaroff, John L., and Jean Comaroff. 2004. "Criminal Justice, Cultural Justice: The Limits of Liberalism and the Pragmatics of Difference in the New South Africa." *American Ethnologist* 31(2).

———. 2009. *Ethnicity, Inc.* Chicago: University of Chicago Press.

Connell, P. H., C. Irvine-Smith, and K. Jonas. 1939. *Native Housing: A Collective Thesis*. Johannesburg: Witwatersrand University Press.

Connerton, Paul. [1989]. 1998. *How Societies Remember*. New York: Cambridge University Press.

Cooper, Frederick. 1996. *Decolonization and African Society*. New York: Cambridge University Press.

———. 2003. "Industrial Man Goes to Africa." In *Men and Masculinities in Modern Africa*, ed. Lisa A. Lindsay and Stephan Miescher, 128–37. Portsmouth, NH: Heinemann.

Coontz, Stephanie. 1992. *The Way We Never Were: American Families and the Nostalgia Trap*. New York: Basic Books.

Cope, Nicholas. 1990. "The Zulu Petit[e] Bourgeoisie and Zulu Nationalism in the 1920s: Origins of Inkatha." *Journal of Southern African Studies* 16:431–51.

Coquery-Vidrovitch, Catherine. 1994. *African Women: A Modern History*. Boulder, CO: Westview Press.

Cronin, Audrey Kurth. 2009. *How Terrorism Ends: Understanding the Decline and Demise of Terrorist Campaigns*. Princeton, NJ: Princeton University Press.

Cronin, Jeremy. 1987. "Errors of Workerism." *South African Labour Bulletin*. 12(3).

Crush, J. S., Alan Jeeves, and David Yudelman. 1991. *South Africa's Labor Empire: A History of Black Migrancy to the Gold Mines*. Boulder, CO: Westview Press.

Cutten, A. J. 1951. "The Planning of a Native Township." *Race Relations Journal* 18(2):74–95.

Daniel, John, and Roger Southall, eds. 2010. *Zunami! The 2009 South African Elections*. Auckland Park, South Africa: Jacana.

Darrow, Margaret H. 1979. "French Noblewomen and the New Domesticity, 1750–1850." *Feminist Studies* 5:41–65.

Das, Veena. 1997. "Language and Body: Transactions in the Construction of Pain." In *Social Suffering*, ed. Arthur Kleinman, Veena Das, and Margaret Lock. Berkeley: University of California Press.

Davidoff, Leonore, and Catherine Hall. 1987. *Family Fortunes: Men and Women of the English Middle Class, 1780–1850*. Chicago: University of Chicago Press.

Davis, Fred. 1979. *Searching for Yesterday: A Sociology of Nostalgia*. New York: Free Press.

Dean, Jodi. 2005. "Zizek Against Democracy." *Law, Culture and the Humanities* 1:154–77.

De Haas, Mary, and Paulus Zulu. 1994. "Ethnicity and Federalism: The Case of KwaZulu/Natal." *Journal of Southern African Studies* 20(3).

Delius, Peter. 1989. "Sebatakgomo: Migrant Organization, the ANC and the Sekhukhuneland Revolt." *Journal of Southern African Studies* 15(4):581–615.

———. 1990. *A Lion Amongst the Cattle: Reconstruction and Resistance in the Northern Transvaal*. Portsmouth, NH: Heinemann.

Dlamini, Jacob. 2009. *Native Nostalgia*. Auckland Park, South Africa: Jacana.

Doke, Clement M., and B. W. Vilakazi. [1948] 1958. *Zulu-English Dictionary*. 2nd ed. Johannesburg: Witwatersrand University Press.

Doke, C. M., M. Malcolm, and J. Sikakana. 1990. *English-Zulu, Zulu-English Dictionary.* Johannesburg: Witwatersrand University Press.

Donham, Donald L. 2011. *Violence in a Time of Liberation: Murder and Ethnicity at a South African Gold Mine, 1994.* Durham, NC: Duke University Press.

Douglas, Mary. 1966. *Purity and Danger: An Analysis of Concepts of Pollution and Taboo.* London: Routledge & Kegan Paul.

Drew, Allison. 2000. *Discordant Comrades: Identities and Loyalties on the South African Left.* Aldershot, UK: Ashgate.

Du Bois, J. W. 1986. "Self-evidence and Ritual Speech." In *Evidentiality: The Linguistic Coding of Epistemology,* ed. Wallace L. Chafe, and Johanna Nichols. Norwood, NJ: Ablex.

Du Toit, B. 1987. "Menarche and Sexuality Among a Sample of Black South African Schoolgirls." *Social Science and Medicine* 24(7):561–71.

Dubb, A. A. 1974. "The Impact of the City." In *The Bantu-Speaking Peoples of Southern Africa,* ed. W. D. Hammond-Tooke. London: Routledge.

Dumont, Louis. [1966] 1980. *Homo Hierarchicus: The Caste System and Its Implications.* Rev. ed. Chicago: University of Chicago Press.

Durkheim, Émile. [1912] 1995. *The Elementary Forms of the Religious Life.* New York: Free Press.

Edwards, Richard. 1979. *Contested Terrain: The Transformation of the Workplace in the Twentieth Century.* New York: Basic Books.

Eglash, Ron. 1999. *African Fractals: Modern Computing and Indigenous Design.* New Brunswick, NJ: Rutgers University Press.

Elder, Glen. 2003. "Malevolent Traditions: Hostel Violence and the Procreational Geography of Apartheid." *Journal of Southern African Studies* 29(4):921–35.

Engels, Frederick. 1884. *The Origin of the Family, Private Property, and the State.* Hottingen, Zurich.

Englund, Harri. 2006. *Prisoners of Freedom: Human Rights and the African Poor.* University of California Press.

Epprecht, Marc. 2000. *'This matter of women is getting very bad': Gender, Development and Politics in Colonial Lesotho.* Pietermaritzburg: University of Natal Press.

Evans-Pritchard, E. E. 1937. *Witchcraft, Oracles, and Magic Among the Azande.* London: Oxford University Press.

———. 1956. *Nuer Religion.* London: Oxford University Press.

Evans, Ivan Thomas. 1997. *Bureaucracy and Race: Native Administration in South Africa.* Berkeley: University of California Press.

Everatt, David. 1992. "Alliance Politics of a Special Type: The Roots of the ANC/SACP Alliance, 1950–1954." *Journal of Southern African Studies* 18(1).

Fakier, Khayaat, and Jacklyn Cock. 2009. "A Gendered Analysis of the Crisis of Social Reproduction in Contemporary South Africa." *International Feminist Journal of Politics* 11:353–71.

Feinstein, Andrew. 2010. *After the Party: Corruption, the ANC, and South Africa's Uncertain Future.* London: Verso.

Ferguson, James. 1985. "The Bovine Mystique: Power, Property and Livestock in Rural Lesotho." *Man* 20(4).

———. 1999. *Expectations of Modernity: Myths and Meanings of Urban Life on the Zambian Copperbelt.* Berkeley: University of California Press.

———. 2006. *Global Shadows: Africa in the Neoliberal World Order.* Durham, NC: Duke University Press.

———. 2007. "Formalities of Poverty: Thinking About Social Assistance in Neoliberal South Africa." *African Studies Review* 50(2).

———. 2013. "Declarations of Dependence: Labour, Personhood, and Welfare in Southern Africa." *Journal of the Royal Anthropological Institute* 19:223–42.

Fortes, Myer, and E. E. Evans-Pritchard, eds. 1940. *African Political Systems.* London: Oxford University Press.

Foster, J. 1982. "The Workers' Struggle: Where Does FOSATU Stand?" *South African Labour Bulletin* 7(8).

Foster, Robert. 1991. "Making National Cultures in the Global Ecumene." *Annual Review of Anthropology* 20.

Foucault, Michel. [1975] 1995. *Discipline and Punish: The Birth of the Prison.* New York: Vintage Books.

———. 1984. "Space, Knowledge, and Power." In *The Foucault Reader,* ed. Paul Rabinow. New York: Pantheon Books.

———. 1991. "Governmentality." In *The Foucault Effect: Studies in Governmentality,* ed. G. Burchell, Collin Gordon, and Peter Miller. Chicago: University of Chicago Press.

Frank, Thomas. 2004. *What's the Matter with Kansas? How Conservatives Won the Heart of America.* New York: Metropolitan Books.

Fraser, Nancy. 1990. "Rethinking the Public Sphere: A Contribution to the Critique of Actually Existing Democracy." *Social Text* 25–26:56–80.

Freeman, Carla. 2001. "Is Local:Global as Feminine:Masculine? Rethinking the Gender of Globalization." *Signs* 26(4): 1007–37.

Freud, Sigmund. [1926] 1959. *Inhibitions, Symptoms, and Anxiety.* In *The Standard Edition of the Complete Psychological Works of Sigmund Freud,* vol. 20. London: Hogarth Press.

Friedman, Andrew. 1977. *Industry and Labor: Class Struggles at Work and Monopoly Capitalism.* London: Macmillan.

Friedman, Jonathan. 2002. "From Roots to Routes: Tropes for Trippers." *Anthropological Theory* 2(1).

Friedman, Steven. 1987. *Building Tomorrow Today: African Workers in Trade Unions, 1970–1984.* Johannesburg: Ravan Press.

Gaitskell, Deborah. 1983. "Housewives, Maids, or Mothers: Some Contradictions of Domesticity for Christian Women in Johannesburg, 1903–1939." *Journal of African History* 24.

Geertz, Clifford. 1973. *The Interpretation of Cultures.* New York: Basic Books.

———. 1984. "Distinguished Lecture: Anti Anti-relativism." *American Anthropologist* 86:263–278.

Gevisser, Mark. 2007. *Thabo Mbeki: The Dream Deferred.* Johannesburg: Jonathan Ball.

Gibbs, Timothy. 2014. *Mandela's Kinsmen: Nationalist Elites and Apartheid's First Bantustan.* New York: Boydell & Brewer.

Gilbert, Roger. 1991. *Walks in the World: Representation and Experience in Modern American Poetry.* Princeton, NJ: Princeton University Press.

Giliomee, Hermann. 1990. "Explaining the Slaughter." *Star* (Johannesburg), August, 24.

Ginsburg, Faye. 1989. *Contested Lives: The Abortion Debate in an American Community.* Berkeley: University of California Press.

Gledhill, John. 1994. *Power and Its Disguises: Anthropological Perspectives on Politics.* Sterling, VA: Pluto Press.

Gluckman, Max. 1938. "Social Aspects of the First Fruits Ceremonies Among the South-Eastern Bantu." *Africa* 11:25–41.

———. 1940a. "Analysis of a Social Situation in Modern Zululand." *Bantu Studies* 14:1–30, 147–74.

———. 1940b. "The Kingdom of the Zulu of South Africa." In *African Political Systems*, ed. Meyer Fortes and E. E. Evans-Pritchard. London: Oxford University Press.

———. 1950. "Kinship and Marriage of the Lozi of Northern Rhodesia and the Zulu of Natal." In *African Systems of Kinship and Marriage*, ed. A. R. Radcliffe-Brown. London: Oxford University Press.

———. 1975. "Anthropology and Apartheid: The Work of Social Anthropologists." In *Studies in African Social Anthropology*, ed. M. Fortes and S. Patterson. London: Academic Press.

Godehart, Susanna. 2006. *The Transformation of Townships in South Africa: The Case of kwaMashu, Durban.* Dortmund: SPRING Centre.

Goode, Erich, and Ben-Yehuda, Nachman. 1994. *Moral Panics: The Social Construction of Deviance.* Oxford: Blackwell.

Goode, William Joseph. 1963. *World Revolution and Family Patterns.* New York: Free Press of Glencoe.

Goodman, Jane, and Paul Silverstein. 2009. *Bourdieu in Algeria: Colonial Politics, Ethnographic Practices, Theoretical Developments.* Lincoln: University of Nebraska Press.

Gordon, Robert, and Andrew Spiegel. 1993. "Southern Africa Revisited." *Annual Review of Anthropology* 22:83–105.

Graeber, David. 2004. *Fragments of an Anarchist Anthropology.* Chicago: Prickly Paradigm Press.

———. 2013. *The Democracy Project.* London: Allen Lane.

Gray, J.N. 1980. "On Negative and Positive Liberty." *Political Studies* 28(4):507–26.

Greaves, Adrian. 2005. *Crossing the Buffalo: The Zulu War of 1879.* London: Cassell Military.

Greenstein, Ran, ed. 2003. *The Role of Political Violence in South Africa's Democratization.* Johannesburg: Community Agency for Social Inquiry.

Gregory, C.A. 1982. *Gifts and Commodities.* London: Academic Press.

Guha, Ranajit. 1983. *Elementary Aspects of Peasant Insurgency in Colonial India.* Delhi: Oxford University Press.

———, ed. 1997. *A Subaltern Studies Reader: 1986–1995.* Minneapolis: University of Minnesota Press.

Gupta, Akhil, and James Ferguson. 1997. "Culture, Power, Place: Ethnography at the End of an Era." In *Culture, Power, Place: Explorations in Critical Anthropology*, ed. Akhil Gupta and James Ferguson, 1–29. Durham, NC: Duke University Press.

Gutmann, M. C. 2002. *The Romance of Democracy: Compliant Defiance in Contemporary Mexico*. Berkeley: University of California Press.

Guy, Jeff. 1987. "Analyzing Pre-Capitalist Societies in Southern Africa." *Journal of Southern African Studies* 14(1):18–37.

———. 1994. *Destruction of the Zulu Kingdom: The Civil War in Zululand, 1879–1884*. Pietermaritzburg: University of Natal Press.

———. 1997. "An Accommodation of Patriarchs: Theophilus Shepstone and the Foundations of the System of Native Administration in Natal." Unpublished paper, University of Natal.

———. 2013. *Theophilus Shepstone and the Forging of Natal: African Autonomy and Settler Colonialism in the Making of Traditional Authority*. Scottsville, South Africa: University of KwaZulu-Natal Press.

Gwala, Nkosinathi. 1989. "Political Violence and the Struggle for Control in Pietermaritzburg." *Journal of Southern African Studies* 15(3).

Habermas, Jürgen. 1998. *The Structural Transformation of the Public Sphere: An Inquiry into a Category of Bourgeois Society*. Cambridge, MA: MIT Press.

Habib, Adam, and Vishnu Padayachee. 2000. "Economic Policy and Power Relations in South Africa's Transition to Democracy." *World Development* 28:245–63.

Hall, Catherine. 1985. "Private Persons Versus Public Someones: Class, Gender and Politics in England, 1780–1850." In *Language, Gender, and Childhood*, ed. C. Steedman, C. Urwin, and V. Walkerdine. London: Routledge & Kegan Paul.

Hall, Martin. 1984. "The Myth of the Zulu Homestead: Archeology and Ethnography." *Africa: Journal of the International African Institute* 54(1): 65–79.

Hamilton, Carolyn. 1986. "Ideology, Oral Traditions, and the Struggle for Power in the Early Zulu Kingdom." MA thesis. University of the Witwatersrand, Johannesburg.

———. 1998. *Terrific Majesty: The Powers of Shaka Zulu and the Limits of Historical Invention*. Cambridge, MA: Harvard University Press.

Hammond-Tooke, W. D. 1970. "Urbanization and the Interpretation of Misfortune: A Quantitative Analysis." *Africa: Journal of the International African Institute* 40(1):25–39.

———. 1977. "Lévi-Strauss in a Garden of Millet: The Structural Analysis of a Zulu Folktale." *Man* 12(1).

———. 1984. "In Search of the Lineage: The Cape Nguni Case." *Man* 19(1): 77–93.

———. 1997. *Imperfect Interpreters: South Africa's Anthropologists, 1920–1990*. Johannesburg: Witwatersrand University Press.

Handler, Richard. 1988. *Nationalism and the Politics of Culture in Quebec*. Madison: University of Wisconsin Press.

———. 1994. "Is 'Identity' a Useful Cross-Cultural Concept?" In *Commemorations: The Politics of National Identity*, ed. John Gillis. Princeton, NJ: Princeton University Press.

Handler, Richard, and Jocelyn Linnekin. 1984. "Tradition, Genuine or Spurious?" *Journal of American Folklore* 97(385):273–90.

Hanretta, Sean. 1998. "Women, Marginality and the Zulu State: Women's Institutions and Power in the Early Nineteenth Century." *Journal of African History* 39(3):389–415.

Hansen, Karen Tranberg. 1981. "Family and Role Divisions: The Polarization of Sexual Stereotypes in the 19th Century." In *The German Family*, ed. R. Evans and W. Lee. Totowa, NJ: Barnes & Noble.

———. 1989. *Distant Companions: Servants and Employers in Zambia*. Ithaca, NY: Cornell University Press.

———. 1992. *African Encounters with Domesticity*. New Brunswick, NJ: Rutgers University Press.

Harries, Patrick. 1993. "Imagery, Symbolism, and Tradition in a South African Bantustan: Mangosuthu Buthelezi, Inkatha, and Zulu History." *History and Theory* 32(4).

Harrison, Abigail, et al. 2000. "Barriers to Implementing South Africa's Termination of Pregnancy Act in Rural KwaZulu/Natal." *Health Policy and Planning* 15:424–31.

Hart, Gillian. 2002. *Disabling Globalization: Places of Power in Post-apartheid South Africa:* University of California Press.

Harvey, David. 1989. *The Condition of Postmodernity*. Oxford: Basil Blackwell.

———. 2005. *A Brief History of Neoliberalism*. Oxford: Oxford University Press.

Hassim, S. 1993. "Family, Motherhood and Zulu Nationalism: The Place and Politics of the Inkatha Women's Brigade." *Feminist Review* 43.

Healy-Clancy, Meghan, and Jason Hickel. 2014. *Ekhaya: The Politics of Home in KwaZulu-Natal*. Pietermaritzburg: University of KwaZulu-Natal Press.

Hellmann, Ellen. 1934. "The Importance of Beer-Brewing in an Urban Native Yard." *Bantu Studies* 8(1).

———. 1935. "Native Life in a Johannesburg Slum Yard." *Africa* 8(1).

———. 1937. "The Native in the Towns." In *Bantu-Speaking tribes of South Africa*, ed. I. Schapera. London: Routledge.

———. 1971. "Social Change Among Urban Africans." In *South Africa: Sociological Perspectives*, ed. H. Adam. Cape Town: Oxford University Press.

———. 1974. "African Townsmen in the Process of Change." *South African International* 5:14–22.

Helms, Mary. 1998. *Access to Origins: Affines, Ancestors, and Aristocrats*. Austin: University of Texas Press.

Héritier-Augé, F. 1989. "De l'engendrement à la filiation." *Topique* 44:173–85.

Herskovitz, Melville. 1926. "The Cattle Complex in East Africa." *American Anthropologist* 28(1–4).

Hertz, Robert. [1909] 1973. "The Pre-eminence of the Right Hand: A Study in Religious Polarity." In *Right and Left: Essays on Dual Symbolic Classification*, ed. Rodney Needham. Chicago: University of Chicago Press.

Heusch, Luc de. 1985. *Sacrifice in Africa*. Bloomington: Indiana University Press.

Hickel, Jason. 2009. "Not So Sweet History of Sugar Unions in South Africa." *South African Labour Bulletin* 33(3).

———. 2012a. "Social Engineering and Revolutionary Consciousness: Domestic Transformations in Colonial South Africa." *History and Anthropology* 23(3).

———. 2012b. "Subaltern Consciousness in South Africa's Labor Movement: 'Workerism' in the KwaZulu-Natal Sugar Industry." *South African Historical Journal* 64(3).

Hickel, Jason, and Arsalan Khan. 2012. "The Culture of Capitalism and the Crisis of Critique." *Anthropological Quarterly* 85(1):203–27.

Hobbes, Thomas. [1651] 2005. *Leviathan*. Whitefish, MT: Kessinger.

Hobsbawm, E. J. [1959] 1978. *Primitive Rebels: Studies in Archaic Forms of Social Movement in the 19th and 20th Centuries*. Manchester: Manchester University Press.

Holston, James. 1999. "The Modernist City and the Death of the Street." In *Theorizing the City: The New Urban Anthropology Reader*, ed. Setha M. Low. New Brunswick, NJ: Rutgers University Press.

Horowitz, Donald L. 1991. *A Democratic South Africa? Constitutional Engineering in a Divided Society*. Berkeley: University of California Press.

Hoque, M. E., M. Hoque, and S. B. Kader. 2009. "Prevalence and Experience of Domestic Violence Among Rural Pregnant Women in KwaZulu-Natal, South Africa." *Southern African Journal of Epidemiology and Infection* 24(4):34–37.

Hubert, Henri, and Marcel Mauss. 1964. *Sacrifice: Its Nature and Function*. Chicago: University of Chicago Press.

Huffman, Thomas N. 1986. "Archaeological Evidence and Conventional Explanations of Southern Bantu Settlement Patterns." *Africa* 56(3).

———. 2001. "The Central Cattle Pattern and Interpreting the Past." *Southern African Humanities* 13.

Hunt, Nancy R. 1990. "Domesticity and Colonialism in Belgian Africa: Usumbura's *Foyer Social, 1946–1960*." *Signs* 15:447–74.

Hunter, Mark. 2010. *Love in the Time of AIDS: Inequality, Gender, and Rights in South Africa*. Bloomington: Indiana University Press.

———. 2011. "Beneath the 'Zunami': Jacob Zuma and the Gendered Politics of Social Reproduction in South Africa." *Antipode* 43(4).

Hunter, Monica. 1932. "Results of Culture Contact on the Pondo and Xhosa Family." *South African Journal of Science* 29:681–86.

Huntington, Richard, and Peter Metcalf. 1979. *Celebrations of Death: The Anthropology of Mortuary Ritual*. Cambridge: Cambridge University Press.

Huntington, Samuel. 1996. *The Clash of Civilizations and the Remaking of World Order*. New York: Simon & Schuster.

Huyssen, Andreas. 2000. "Present Pasts: Media, Politics, Amnesia." *Public Culture* 12(1):21–38.

———. 2003. *Present Pasts: Urban Palimpsests and the Politics of Memory*. Stanford, CA: Stanford University Press.

Illich, Ivan. 1982. *Gender*. New York: Pantheon Books.

Independent Board of Inquiry. 1993. *Fortresses of Fear*. Johannesburg: The Board.

Institute for Industrial Education. 1974. *The Durban Strikes, 1973: "Human Beings with Souls"* Johannesburg: Institute for Industrial Education.

Irvine, Judith T. 2010. "Ideologies of Honorific Language." *Pragmatics* 2(3): 251–62.

Isaacs, Nathaniel. 1836. *Travels and Adventures in Eastern Africa: A Description of the Zoolus, Their Manners, Customs, etc.* London: E. Churton.

Jackson, Michael. 1982. *Allegories of the Wilderness*. Bloomington: Indiana University Press.

Jackson, Michael, and Ivan Karp, eds. 1990. *Personhood and Agency: The Experience of Self and Other in African Cultures*. Washington, DC: Smithsonian Institution Press.

Jeffrey, Anthea. 1997. *The Natal Story: Sixteen Years of Conflict*. Johannesburg: South African Institute of Race Relations.

Kalb, Don. 2005. "From Flows to Violence: Politics and Knowledge in the Debates on Globalization and Empire." *Anthropological Theory* 5(2): 176–204.

Kapferer, Bruce. 1988. *Legends of People, Myths of State: Violence, Intolerance, and Political Culture in Sri Lanka and Australia*. Washington, DC: Smithsonian Institution Press.

———. 1989. "Nationalist Ideology and a Comparative Anthropology." *Ethnos* 54(3–4):161–99.

Karlstrom, M. 1996. "Imagining Democracy: Political Culture and Democratisation in Buganda." *Africa* 66(4):485–505.

Keane, Webb. 2007. *Christian Moderns: Freedom and Fetish in the Mission Encounter*. Berkeley: University of California Press.

Keesing, Roger. 1989. "Creating the Past: Custom and Identity in the Contemporary Pacific." *Contemporary Pacific* 1(1–2):19–42.

Kepe, T., and L. Ntsebeza. [2011] 2012. *Rural Resistance in South Africa: The Mpondo Revolt After Fifty Years*. Cape Town: UCT Press.

Kidd, Dudley. 1904. *The Essential Kafir*. London: A. and C. Black.

Kiernan, J.P. 1978. "Saltwater and Ashes: Instruments of Curing Among Some Zulu Zionists." *Journal of African Religion* 9(1).

———. 1988. "The Other Side of the Coin: The Conversion of Money to Religious Purposes in Zulu Zionist Churches." *Man* 23(3).

———. 1990. *The Production and Management of Therapeutic Power in Zionist Churches within a Zulu City*. Lewiston, NY: Edwin Mellen Press.

Klein, Naomi. 2008. "Democracy Born in Chains: South Africa's Constricted Freedom." In *The Shock Doctrine: The Rise of Disaster Capitalism*. New York: Picador Press.

Krämer, Mario. 2007. *Violence as Routine: Transformations of Local-Level Politics and the Disjunction Between Center and Periphery in KwaZulu-Natal*. Cologne: Rudiger Köppe.

Krige, Eileen Jensen. 1936. "Changing Conditions in Marital Relations and Parental Duties Among Urbanized Natives." *Africa* 2:1–23.

Kuklick, Henrika. 1991. *The Savage Within: The Social History of British Anthropology, 1885–1945*. New York: Cambridge University Press.

Kuper, Adam. 1979. "Zulu Kinship Terminology over a Century." *Journal of Anthropological Research* 35(3):373–86.

———. 1982a. "Lineage Theory: A Critical Retrospect." *Annual Review of Anthropology* 11:71–95.

———. 1982b. *Wives for Cattle: Bridewealth and Marriage in Southern Africa.* London: Routledge.

———. 1993. "The 'House' and Zulu Political Structure in the Nineteenth Century." *Journal of African History* 34(3):469–87.

———. 1999. *Culture: The Anthropologists' Account.* Cambridge, MA: Harvard University Press.

Kuper, Leo. 1965. *An African Bourgeoisie: Race, Class, and Politics in South Africa.* New Haven, CT: Yale University Press.

Kymlicka, Will. 1995. *Multicultural Citizenship: A Liberal Theory of Minority Rights.* Oxford: Oxford University Press.

———. 2007. *Multicultural Odysseys: Navigating the New International Politics of Diversity.* Oxford: Oxford University Press.

La Hausse, Paul. 1988. *Brewers, Beerhalls and Boycotts: A History of Liquor in South Africa.* Johannesburg: Ravan Press.

———. 1997. "Alcohol, The Ematsheni and Popular Culture in Durban, 1902–1936." In *The People's City: African Life in Twentieth-Century Durban*, ed. P. Maylam and I. Edwards. Pietermaritzburg: University of Natal Press.

Lambert, Mark. 1995. *Betrayed Trust: Africans and the State in Colonial Natal.* Scottsville, South Africa: University of Natal Press.

Lambert, Michael. 1993. "Ancient Greek and Zulu Sacrificial Ritual: A Comparative Analysis." *Numen* 40(3):293–318.

Lambert, Rob, and Eddie Webster. 1988. "The Re-emergence of Political Unionism in Contemporary South Africa?" In *Popular Struggles in South Africa*, ed. William Cobbett and Robin Cohen. London: James Currey.

Lan, David. 1984. *Guns and Rain: Guerillas and Spirit Mediums in Zimbabwe.* Berkeley: University of California Press.

Latour, Bruno. 1993. *We Have Never Been Modern.* Cambridge, MA: Harvard University Press.

Leclerc-Madlala, Suzanne. 1996. "Crime in an Epidemic: The Case of Rape and AIDS." *Acta Criminologica* 9(2).

———. 1999. "Demonising Women in the Era of AIDS: An Analysis of the Sociocultural Construction of HIV/AIDS in KwaZulu-Natal." PhD diss., Department of Anthropology, University of Natal.

———. 2001. "Virginity Testing: Managing Sexuality in a Maturing HIV/AIDS Epidemic." *Medical Anthropology Quarterly* 15(4):533–52.

———. 2002. "On the Virgin Cleansing Myth: Gendered Bodies, AIDS and Ethnomedicine." *African Journal of AIDS Research* 1:87–95.

———. 2008. "AIDS in Zulu Idiom: Etiological Configurations of Women, Pollution, and Modernity." In *Zulu Identities: Being Zulu, Past and Present*, ed. Benedict Carton, John Laband, and Jabulani Sithole. Scottsville, South Africa: University of KwaZulu-Natal Press.

Lefebvre, Henri. 1974. *La production de l'espace*. Paris: Éditions Anthropos. Trans. Donald Nicholson-Smith as *The Production of Space* (Cambridge, MA: Blackwell, 1991).

Leibbrandt, Murray, Arden Finn, and Ingrid Woolard. 2012. "Describing and Decomposing Post-apartheid Income Inequality in South Africa." *Development Southern Africa* 29(1):19–34.

Lévi-Strauss, Claude. 1969. *The Raw and the Cooked*. Chicago: University of Chicago Press.

———. 1981. *The Naked Man: Introduction to a Science of Mythology*. New York: Harper & Row.

———. 1984. *Anthropology and Myth: Lectures 1951–1982*. Translated by Roy Willis. Oxford: Basil Blackwell.

Lincoln, Bruce. 1987. "Ritual, Rebellion, Resistance: Once More the Swazi Ncwala." *Man* 22(1):132–56.

Linnekin, Jocelyn. 1983. "Defining Tradition: Variations on the Hawaiian Identity." *American Ethnologist* 10(2).

Locke, John. [1689] 1999. *Two Treatises of Government*. London: Dent.

Luckhardt, Ken, and Brenda Wall. 1980. *Organize or Starve: The History of the South African Congress of Trade Unions*. New York: International Publishers.

Lukes, S. 1973. *Individualism*. Oxford: Basil Blackwell.

Maasdorp, Gavin, and A. S. B. Humphreys. 1975. *From Shantytown to Township: An Economic Study of African Poverty and Rehousing in a South African Township*. Cape Town: Juta.

Mack, Kathleen, Tim Maggs, and Dana Oswald. 1991. "Homesteads in Two Rural Zulu Communities: An Ethnoarchaeological Investigation." *Natal Museum Journal of Humanities* 3:79–129.

Macpherson, C. B. 1962. *The Political Theory of Possessive Individualism: Hobbes to Locke*. Oxford: Clarendon Press.

Mahmood, Saba. 2001. "Feminist Theory, Embodiment, and the Docile Agent: Some Reflections on the Egyptian Islamic Revival." *Cultural Anthropology* 16(2):202–35.

———. 2005. *Politics of Piety: The Islamic Revival and the Feminist Subject*. Princeton, NJ: Princeton University Press.

Maine, Henry. 1861. *Ancient Law*. London: John Murray.

Malinowski, Bronislaw. 1945. *The Dynamics of Culture Change: An Inquiry into Race Relations in Africa*. New Haven, CT: Yale University Press.

Mamdani, Mahmood. 1996. *Citizen and Subject: Contemporary Africa and the Legacy of Late Colonialism*. Princeton, NJ: Princeton University Press.

Mare, Gerhard, and Georgina Hamilton. 1987. *An Appetite for Power: Buthelezi's Inkatha and South Africa*. Johannesburg: Ravan Press.

Marks, Shula. 1970. *Reluctant Rebellion: The 1906–8 Disturbances in Natal*. Oxford: Clarendon Press.

———. 1986. *The Ambiguities of Dependence in South Africa: Class, Nationalism, and the State in Twentieth Century Natal*. Johannesburg: Ravan Press.

Marwick, Max. 1978. "Household Composition and Marriage in a Witwatersrand African Township." In *Social System and Tradition in Southern*

Africa: Essays in Honour of Eileen Krige, ed. John Argyle and Eleanor Preston-Whyte. Cape Town: Oxford University Press.

Marx, Karl. [1867] 1990. *Capital: A Critique of Political Economy.* London: Penguin Books.

———. 1998. "The Eighteenth Brumaire of Louis Bonaparte." In *The Marx-Engels Reader,* ed. Tucker. New York: Norton.

Mathewson, J. E. 1957. "The Establishment of an Urban Bantu Township." PhD diss., University of the Witwatersrand, Johannesburg.

Mathewson, J. E. 1959. "Impact of Urbanization on Lobolo." *Journal for Racial Affairs.* 10:72–76.

Mauss, Marcel. 1979. *Seasonal Variations of the Eskimo: A Study in Social Morphology.* London: Routledge. Translation of *Essai sur les variations saisonnières des sociétés Eskimos,* originally published in 1936 as pt. 7 of *Sociologie et anthropologie.*

Mayer, Philip. 1961. *Townsmen or Tribesmen: Conservatism and the Process of Urbanization in a South African City.* Cape Town: Oxford University Press.

Mazzarella, William. 2003. *Shoveling Smoke: Advertising and Globalization in Contemporary India.* Durham, NC: Duke University Press.

Mbeki, Govan. 1964. *South Africa: The Peasants' Revolt.* London: Penguin Books.

McAllister, Pat. 1985. "Beasts to Beer Pots—Migrant Labour and Ritual Change in Willowvale District, Transkei". *African Studies* 44(2): 121–35.

McCaul, Colleen. 1984. "Inkatha's New Labour Wing." *Work in Progress* (32):34–35.

McKinnon, Susan. 1991. *From a Shattered Sun: Hierarchy, Gender, and Alliance in the Tanimbar Islands.* Madison: University of Wisconsin Press.

———. 2005. *Neo-liberal Genetics: The Myths and Moral Tales of Evolutionary Psychology.* Chicago: Prickly Paradigm Press.

McKinnon, Susan, and Fenella Cannell, eds. 2013. *Vital Relations: Modernity and the Persistent Life of Kinship.* Sante Fe, NM: SAR Press.

McKnight, J. D. 1967. "Extra-Descent Group Ancestor Cults in African Societies." *Africa* 37(1):1–21.

Mda, Zakes. 2002. *Ways of Dying: A Novel.* New York: Picador.

Mdluli, Praisley. 1987. "Ubuntu-Botho: Inkatha's 'People's Education.'" *Transformation* 5.

Meillassoux, Claude. 1981. *Maidens, Meal, and Money: Capitalism and the Domestic Community.* New York: Cambridge University Press.

Meyer, Brigit, and Peter Geschiere, eds. 1999. *Globalization and Identity: Dialectics of Flow and Closure.* Malden, MA: Blackwell.

Middleton, Jean. 1984. "Unity of Democratic Forces: The Transvaal Stayaway." *Sechaba.* ANC online archives, www.anc.org.za/show.php?id=2908.

Minnaar, Anthony. 1991. *Conflict and Violence in KwaZulu-Natal.* Pretoria: Human Sciences Research Council.

———. 1992. "Undisputed Kings: Warlordism in Natal." In *Patterns of Violence,* ed. id. Pretoria: Human Sciences Research Council.

———, ed. 1993. *Communities in Isolation: Perspectives on Hostels in South Africa*. Pretoria: Human Sciences Research Council.

Mitchell, T. 1991. "The Limits of the State: Beyond Statist Approaches and Their Critics." *American Political Science Review* 85:77–96.

Mokgoro, Yvonne. 1996. "Traditional Authority and Democracy in the Interim South African Constitution." *Review of Constitutional Studies* 3:60.

———. 1999. "The Protection of Cultural Identity in the Constitution and the Creation of National Unity in South Africa: A Contradiction in Terms." *SMU Law Review* 52(4):1549.

———. 2003. "Constitutional Claims for Gender Equality in South Africa: A Judicial Response." *Albany Law Review* 67(2):565.

Moodie, T. Dunbar. 1994. *Going for Gold: Men, Mines, and Migration*. Berkeley: University of California Press.

Morgan, David H.J. 1985. *The Family, Politics, and Social Theory*. London: Routledge & Kegan Paul.

Morgan, Lewis H. [1870] 1997. *Systems of Consanguinity and Affinity of the Human Family*. Lincoln: University of Nebraska Press.

———. [1877] 2000. *Ancient Society*. New Brunswick, NJ: Transaction Publishers.

Morrell, Robert. 1996. *Political Economy and Identities in KwaZulu-Natal: Historical and Social Perspectives*. Durban: Indicator Press.

Morris, Mike, and Doug Hindson. 1992. "South Africa: Political Violence, Reform and Reconstruction." *Review of African Political Economy* 53:43–59.

Moyar, Mark. 2009. *A Question of Command: Counterinsurgency from the Civil War to Iraq*. New Haven, CT: Yale University Press.

Moynihan, Daniel Patrick. 1965. *The Negro Family: The Case for National Action*. Washington, DC: U.S. Department of Labor, Office of Policy Planning and Research.

Msimang, C. 1975. *Kusadliwa Ngoludala*. Pietermaritzburg: Shuter & Shooter.

Mudimbe, V. 1988. *The Invention of Africa: Gnosis, Philosophy, and the Order of Knowledge*. Bloomington: Indiana University Press.

Mueggler, Erik. 2001. *The Age of Wild Ghosts: Memory, Violence, and Place in Southwest China*. Berkeley: University of California Press.

Murray, Colin. 1981. *Families Divided: The Impact of Migration Labor in Lesotho*. Johannesburg: Ravan Press.

Myers, Jason Conard. 2008. *Indirect Rule in South Africa: Tradition, Modernity, and the Costuming of Political Power*. Rochester, NY: University of Rochester Press.

Nandy, Ashis. 1983 *The Intimate Enemy: Loss and Recovery of Self Under Colonialism*. Delhi: Oxford University Press.

Nash, Andrew. 1999. "The Moment of Western Marxism in South Africa." *Comparative Studies of South Asia, Africa, and the Middle East* 19(1).

Natal Code of Native Law. 1943. *African Studies* 2(1):1–26. Originally passed in 1891.

National Housing and Planning Commission. 1951. *A Guide to the Planning of Non-European Townships*. Pretoria: National Housing and Planning Commission.

Ndlovu, Sifiso. 2008. "A Reassessment of Women's Power in the Zulu King-dom." In *Zulu Identities: Being Zulu, Past and Present,* ed. Benedict Carton, John Laband, and Jabulani Sithole. University of KwaZulu-Natal Press.

Ngubane, Harriet. 1976. "Some Notions of 'Purity' and 'Impurity' Among the Zulu." *Africa: Journal of the International African Institute* 46(3):274–84.

———. 1977. *Body and Mind in Zulu Medicine: An Ethnography of Health and Disease in Nyuswa-Zulu Thought and Practice.* London: Academic Press.

———. 1981. "Marriage, Affinity, and the Ancestral Realm." In *Essays on African Marriage in Southern Africa,* ed. Eileen Jensen Krige and John L. Comaroff. Cape Town: Juta.

Ngwane, Zolani. 2001. "'Real Men Awaken Their Fathers' Homesteads, The Educated Leave Them in Ruins': The Politics of Domestic Reproduction in Post-apartheid Rural South Africa." *Journal of Religion in Africa* 31(4).

Niehaus, Isak, with Eliazaar Mohlala and Kally Shokane. 2001. *Witchcraft, Power and Politics: Exploring the Occult in the South African Lowveld.* Sterling, VA: Pluto Press.

Nowak, Michael, and Luca Antonio Ricci. 2005. *Post-apartheid South Africa: The First Ten Years.* Washington, DC: International Monetary Fund.

Nyamanga, Peter, Collette Suda, and Jens Aagaard-Hansen. 2006. "Similarities Between Human and Livestock Illness Among Luo in Western Kenya." *Anthropology & Medicine* 13(1):13–24.

Oakly, Ann. 1974. *Women's Work: The Housewife, Past and Present.* New York: Pantheon Books.

Obeyesekere, Gannanath. 1992. *The Apotheosis of Captain Cook: European Mythmaking in the Pacific.* Princeton, NJ: Princeton University Press.

Offe, Claus, and Hans Wiesenthal. 1980. "Two Logics of Collective Action: Theoretical Notes on Social Class and Organizational Form." In *Political Power and Social Theory I,* ed. Maurice Zeitlin. Greenwich, CT: JAI Press.

Olivier, Johan L. 1992. "Political Conflict in South Africa: A Resource Mobili-zation Approach," In *Capturing the Event: Conflict Trends in the Natal Region, 1986–1992,* ed. Simon Bekker. Durban: Center for Social and Development Studies.

Padayachee, Vishnu. 2013. "The Reserve Bank in Post-apartheid South Africa." Unpublished paper, University of Pretoria.

Padayachee, Vishnu, and Bill Freund, eds. 2002. *(D)urban Vortex: South Afri-can City in Transition.* Scottsville, South Africa: University of KwaZulu-Natal Press.

Paley, Julia. 2001. *Marketing Democracy: Power and Social Movements in Post-dictatorship Chile.* Berkeley: University of California Press.

———. 2002. "Toward an Anthropology of Democracy." *Annual Review of Anthropology* 31.

Palmer, Eve, and Nora Pitman. 1972. *Trees of Southern Africa.* Vol. 2. Cape Town: Balkema.

Pape, Robert Anthony. 2006. *Dying to Win: The Strategic Logic of Suicide Ter-rorism.* New York: Random House.

Parry, Jonathan, and Maurice Bloch. 1989. *Money and the Morality of Exchange.* New York: Cambridge University Press.

Pauw, B.A. 1973. *The Second Generation: A Study of the Family Among Urbanized Bantu in East London.* Cape Town: Oxford University Press.

———. 1980. "Recent South African Anthropology." *Annual Review of Anthropology* 9:315–38.

Pennington, M.V. 1978. "Urban Black Housing." MA thesis, University of Natal.

Perin, Constance. 1980. *Everything in Its Place: Social Order and Land Use in America.* Princeton, NJ: Princeton University Press.

Perry, Mark. 2010. *Talking to Terrorists: Why American Must Engage with Its Enemies.* New York: Basic Books.

Phillips, Ray Edmund. 1930. *The Bantu Are Coming: Phases of South Africa's Race Problem.* Lovedale, South Africa: Student Christian Movement Press.

———. 1938. *The Bantu in the City: A Study of Cultural Adjustment on the Witwatersrand.* Lovedale, South Africa: Lovedale Press.

Piot, Charles. 1999. *Remotely Global: Village Modernity in West Africa.* Chicago: University of Chicago Press.

———. 2010. *Nostalgia for the Future: West Africa After the Cold War.* University of Chicago Press.

Pityana, Barney Nyameko. 2012. "Black Consciousness, Black Theology, Student Activism and the Shaping of the New South Africa." Steve Biko Memorial Lecture at the London School of Economics.

Platzky, Laurine, and Cherryl Walker. 1985. *The Surplus People: Forced Removals in South Africa.* Johannesburg: Ravan Press.

Polanyi, Karl. 1944. *The Great Transformation.* New York: Rinehart.

Posel, Deborah. 2006. "Marriage at the Drop of a Hat: Housing and Partnership in South Africa's Urban African Townships, 1920s-1960s." *History Workshop Journal* 61:57.

Poulantzas, Nicos. 1978. *State, Power, Socialism.* Translated by Patrick Camiller. New York: Verso.

Preston-Whyte, E.M. 1973. "The Making of a Townswoman: The Process and Dilemma of Rural-Urban Migration Amongst African Women in Southern Natal." In *Sociology, Southern Africa, 1973: Papers from the First Congress of the Association for Sociologists in Southern Africa.* Durban: University of Natal.

Radcliffe-Brown, A.R. 1950. *African Systems of Kinship and Marriage.* London: Oxford University Press.

———. 1952. "The Mother's Brother in South Africa." In id., *Structure and Function in Primitive Society.* Glencoe, IL: Free Press.

———. 1964. *The Andaman Islanders.* New York: Free Press.

Radhakrishnan, R. 1996. *Diasporic Mediations: Between Home and Locations.* Minneapolis: University of Minnesota Press.

Ranger, Terence. [1983] 1984. "The Invention of Tradition in Colonial Africa." In *The Invention of Tradition,* ed. Eric Hobsbawm and Terence Ranger. New York: Cambridge University Press.

———. 1993. "The Invention of Tradition Revisited: The Case of Colonial Africa." *Legitimacy and the State in Twentieth-Century Africa* 62–111.

Raum, O.F. 1973. *The Social Functions of Avoidances and Taboos Among the Zulu.* Berlin: Walter de Gruyter.

Reader, D.H. 1966. *Zulu Tribe in Transition: The Makhanya of Southern Natal.* Manchester: Manchester University Press.

Ricœur, Paul. 1990. *Time and Narrative.* Chicago: University of Chicago Press.

Riesman, Paul. [1974] 1977. *Freedom in Fulani Social Life.* Chicago: University of Chicago Press.

———. 1986. "The Person and the Life Cycle in African Social Life and Thought." *African Studies Review* 29(2):71–138.

Robbins, Joel. 2004. *Becoming Sinners: Christianity and Moral Torment in a Papua New Guinea Society.* Berkeley: University of California Press.

Robins, Steven. 2008. "Sexual Politics and the Zuma Rape Trial." *Journal of Southern African Studies* 34(2).

Robinson, Jennifer. 1992. "Power, Space, and the City: Historical Reflections on Apartheid and Post-apartheid Urban Orders." In *The Apartheid City and Beyond: Urbanization and Social Change in South Africa,* ed. David Smith. London: Routledge.

Rorty, Richard. 1989. *Contingency, Irony, and Solidarity.* New York: Cambridge University Press.

Rose, Nikolas. 1996. "Governing 'advanced' Liberal Democracies." In *Foucault and Political Reason: Liberalism, Neo-liberalism and Rationalities of Government,* ed. Andrew Barry, Thomas Osborne, and Nikolas Rose. Chicago: University of Chicago Press.

———. 1999. *Powers of Freedom: Reframing Political Thought.* New York: Cambridge University Press.

Rosenblatt, Daniel. 2003. "Houses and Hopes: Urban *Marae* and the Indigenization of Modernity in New Zealand." PhD diss., University of Chicago.

———. 2004. "An Anthropology Made Safe for Culture: Patterns of Practice and the Politics of Difference in Ruth Benedict." *American Anthropologist* 106(3): 459–72.

Rousseau, Jean-Jacques. [1754] 1999. *Discourse on the Origin of Inequality.* New York: Oxford University Press.

Rudwick, Stephanie, and Magcino Shange. 2006. "Sociolinguistic Oppression or Expression of 'Zuluness'? *IsiHlonipho* Among isiZulu-speaking Females." *Southern African Linguistics and Applied Language Studies* 24(4): 473–82.

Rybczynski, Witold. 1986. *Home: A Short History of an Idea.* New York: Viking Penguin.

Sahlins, Marshall. 1976. *Culture and Practical Reason.* Chicago: University of Chicago Press.

———. 1985. *Islands of History.* Chicago: University of Chicago Press.

———. 1992. "The Economics of Develop-Man in the Pacific." *Res* 21.

———. 2004. *Apologies to Thucydides: Understanding History as Culture and Vice Versa.* Chicago: University of Chicago Press.

———. 2008. *The Western Illusion of Human Nature.* Chicago: Prickly Paradigm Press.

Said, Edward. 1978. *Orientalism.* New York: Pantheon Books.

Schaffer, F.C. 1997. "Political Concepts and the Study of Democracy: The Case of *Demokaraasi* in Senegal." *PoLAR: Political Legal Anthropology Review* 20(1):40–49.

Schapera, Isaac. 1947. *Migrant Labor and Tribal Life: A Study of Conditions in the Bechuanaland Protectorate*. London: Oxford University Press.

Schlemmer, L., and P. Stopforth. 1974. *Poverty, Family Patterns and Material Aspirations Among Africans in a Border Industry Township*. Durban: Institute for Social Research, University of Natal.

Schoeman, H.S. 1982. *Spel in die kultuur van sekere Natalse Nguni*. Pretoria: Universiteit van Suid-Afrika.

Scorgie, Fiona. 1998. "Zulu Women's Experiences and Recollections of the Menarche: A Qualitative Study of Gender, Pollution Beliefs and Puberty Rites in a Rural Community in KwaZulu-Natal." MA thesis, University of Natal, Durban.

Scott, David. 1999. *Refashioning Futures: Criticism After Postcoloniality*. Princeton, NJ: Princeton University Press.

Scott, James. 1998. *Seeing Like a State: How Certain Schemes to Improve the Human Condition Have Failed*. New Haven, CT: Yale University Press.

Seekings, Jeremy. 2000. *The UDF: A History of the United Democratic Front in South Africa 1983–1991*. Cape Town: David Phillip.

Segal, Lauren. 1992. "The Human Face of Violence: Hostel Dwellers Speak." *Journal of Southern African* Studies 18(1):197–98.

Shipton, Parker. 1989. *Bitter Money: Cultural Economy and Some African Meanings of Forbidden Commodities*. Washington, DC: American Anthropological Association.

Sibley, David. 1995. *Geographies of Exclusion: Society and Difference in the West*. London: Routledge.

Silverstein, Michael. 1976. "Shifters, Linguistic Categories, and Cultural Description." In *Meaning in Anthropology*, ed. K.H. Basso and H. Selby. Albuquerque: University of New Mexico Press.

———. 1981. "Metaforces of Power in Traditional Oratory." Lecture, Department of Anthropology, Yale University, New Haven, CT.

———. 1992. "Metapragmatic Discourse and Metapragmatic Function." In *Reflexive Language*, ed. J.A. Lucy. New York: Cambridge University Press.

———. 2003. "Indexical Order and the Dialectics of Sociolinguistic Life." *Language & Communication* 23:193–229.

Silverstein, Paul. 2009. "Of Rooting and Uprooting: Kabyle *Habitus,* Domesticity, and Structural Nostalgia." In *Bourdieu in Algeria: Colonial Politics, Ethnographic Practices, Theoretical Developments*, ed. Jane Goodman and Paul Silverstein. Lincoln: University of Nebraska Press.

Simkins, Charles. 1986. "Household Composition and Structure in South Africa." In *Growing up in a Divided Society*, ed. S. Burman and P. Reynolds. Johannesburg: Ravan Press.

Sitas, Ari. 1996. "The New Tribalism: Hostels and Violence." *Journal of Southern African Studies* 22(2).

Smith, Adam. [1776] 1999. *The Wealth of Nations*. New York: Penguin Books.

Smith, James. 2008. *Bewitching Development: Witchcraft and the Reinvention of Development in Neoliberal Kenya*. Chicago: University of Chicago Press.

Soni, Dhiru. 1992. "The Apartheid State and Black Housing Struggles." In *The Apartheid City and Beyond: Urbanization and Social Change in South Africa*, ed. David Smith. London: Routledge.

South African Democracy Education Trust. 2004. *The Road to Democracy in South Africa*. Cape Town: Zebra Press.

Southall, Roger. 1986. "A Note on Inkatha Membership." *African Affairs* 85(341):573–88.

Spiegel, Andrew, and Patrick McAllister, eds. 1991. *Tradition and Transition in Southern Africa*. New Brunswick, NJ: Transaction Publishers.

Spivak, Gyatri C. 1987. *In Other Worlds: Essays in Cultural Politics*. New York: Routledge.

Strathern, Marilyn. 1988. *The Gender of the Gift*. Berkeley: University of California Press.

Sutcliffe, Michael, and Paul Wellings. 1985. "Worker Militancy in South Africa: A Sociospatial Analysis of Trade Union Activism in the Manufacturing Sector." *Environment and Planning D: Society and Space* 3(3).

———. 1988. "Inkatha Versus the Rest." *African Affairs* 87(348).

Tambiah, Stanley. 1969. "Animals Are Good to Think and Good to Prohibit." *Ethnology* 8(4).

Taussig, Michael. 1977. "The Genesis of Capitalism Amongst a South American Peasantry: Devil's Labor and the Baptism of Money." *Comparative Studies in Society and History* 19:130–55.

Taylor, Charles. 1989. *Sources of the Self: The Making of Modern Identity*. Cambridge, MA: Harvard University Press.

Taylor, Christopher. 1992. *Milk, Honey, and Money: Changing Concepts in Rwandan Healing*. Washington, DC: Smithsonian Institution Press.

———. 1999. *Sacrifice as Terror: The Rwandan Genocide of 1994*. Oxford: Berg.

Thompson, Kenneth. 1998. *Moral Panics*. London: Routledge.

Tocqueville, Alexis de. [1835–40] 2000. *Democracy in America*. New York: Bantam Dell.

Turner, Richard. 1973. *The Eye of the Needle: An Essay on Participatory Democracy*. Johannesburg: Special Programme for Christian Action in Society.

Turner, Terence. 1977. "Transformation, Hierarchy and Transcendence: A Reformulation of Van Gennep's Model of the Structure of Rites of Passage." In *Secular Ritual,* ed. Sally F. Moore and Barbara G. Myerhoff, 53–70. Assen: Van Gorcum.

———. 1984. "Dual Opposition, Hierarchy, and Value: Moiety Structure and Symbolic Polarity in Central Brazil and Elsewhere." In *Différences, valeurs, hiérarchie: Textes offerts à Louis Dumont*, ed. J.-C. Galey, 335–70. Paris: École des Hautes Études en Sciences Sociales.

United States. Department of the Army. 2007. *The U.S. Army/Marine Corps Counterinsurgency Field Manual*. Foreword by David H. Petraeus and James F. Amos. Chicago: University of Chicago Press.

Vail, Leroy. 1989. "Introduction: Ethnicity in Southern African History." In *The Creation of Tribalism in Southern Africa*, ed. id. Berkeley: University of California Press.

Van Dijk, Rijk, Ria Reis, and Marja Spierenburg. 2000. *The Quest for Fruition Through Ngoma: Political Aspects of Healing in Southern Africa*. Athens: Ohio University Press.

Van Gennep, Arnold. 1909. *Les rites de passage*. Paris: Émile Nourry.

Van Holdt, Karl. 2003. *Transition from Below: Forging Trade Unionism and Workplace Change in South Africa*. Pietermaritzburg: University of Natal Press.

Van Kessel, Ineke. 1993. "'From Confusion to Lusaka': The Youth Revolt in Sekhukhuneland." *Journal of Southern African Studies* 19(4):593—614.

Van Onselen, Charles. 1973. "Worker Consciousness in Black Miners: Southern Rhodesia, 1900–1920." *Journal of African History* 14.

Van Warmelo, N. J. 1931. *Kinship Terminology of the South African Bantu*. Pretoria: Government Printer.

Vásquez, Manuel. 2011. *More Than Belief: A Materialist Theory of Religion*. Oxford: Oxford University Press.

Verdery, K. 1996. *What Was Socialism, and What Comes Next?* Princeton, NJ: Princeton University Press.

Verster, J. 1965. "The Trend and Pattern of Fertility in Soweto: An Urban Bantu Community." *African Studies* 24(3–4):131–98.

Vilakazi, Absolom. [1962] 1965. *Zulu Transformations: A Study of the Dynamics of Social Change*. Pietermaritzburg: University of Natal Press.

Von Holdt, Karl, and Edward Webster. 2005. "Work Restructuring and the Crisis of Social Reproduction: A Southern Perspective." In *Beyond the Apartheid Workplace: Studies in Transition*, ed. id., 3–40. Durban: University of KwaZulu-Natal Press.

Waetjen, Thembisa. 1999. "The 'Home' in Homeland: Gender, National Space, and Inkatha's Politics of Ethnicity." *Ethnic and Racial Studies* 22(4): 653–78.

———. 2004. *Workers and Warriors: Masculinity and the Struggle for Nation in South Africa*. Urbana: University of Illinois Press.

Wagner, Roy. 1975. *The Invention of Culture*. Chicago: University of Chicago Press.

———. 1977. "Analogic Kinship." *American Ethnologist* 4(4).

———. 1991. "The Fractal Person." In *Great Men and Big Men: Personifications of Power in Melanesia*, ed. Maurice Godelier and Marilyn Strathern, 159–73. Cambridge: Cambridge: University Press.

Walker, Cherryl. 1991. *Women and Resistance in South Africa*. Cape Town: David Philip.

———, ed. 1990. *Women and Gender in Southern Africa to 1945*. Cape Town: David Philip.

Walshe, Peter. 1971. *The Rise of African Nationalism in South Africa*. Berkeley: University of California Press.

Watson, R. G. T. 1960. *Tongaati: An African Experiment*. London: Hutchinson.

Webb, Colin de B., and John B. Wright, eds. 1976–. *The James Stuart Archive of Recorded Oral Evidence Relating to the History of the Zulu and Neighbouring Peoples*. Pietermaritzburg: University of Natal Press.

Weber, Max. 1946. "Politics as Vocation." In *From Max Weber: Essays in Sociology*, trans. and ed. H.H. Gerth and C. Wright Mills. New York: Oxford University Press.

Weir, Jennifer. 2000. "'I Shall Need to Use Her to Rule': The Power of 'Royal' Zulu Women in Pre-colonial Zululand." *South African Historical Journal* 43:3–23.

———. 2006. "Chiefly Women and Women's Leadership in Pre-colonial Southern Africa." In *Women in South African History: Basus'imbokodo, Bawel'imilambo/They Remove Boulders and Cross Rivers*, ed. Nomboniso Gasa. Cape Town: HSRC Press.

Wells, J. 1993. *We Now Demand! The History of Women's Resistance to Pass Laws in South Africa*. Johannesburg: Witwatersrand University Press.

Welsh, D. 1971. *The Roots of Segregation: Native Policy in Colonial Natal, 1845–1910*. Oxford: Oxford University Press.

West, Harry. 1998. "Traditional Authorities and the Mozambican Transition to Democratic Governance." In *Africa's Second Wave of Freedom: Development, Democracy, and Rights*, ed. Lyn S. Graybill and Kenneth W. Thompson. Lanham, MD: University Press of America.

West, M.E. 1979. *Social Anthropology in a Divided Society*. Cape Town: University of Cape Town.

White, Hylton. 2001. "Tempora et Mores: Family Values and the Possessions of a Post-apartheid Countryside." *Journal of Religion in Africa* 31(4).

———. 2004. "Ritual Haunts: The Timing of Estrangement in a Post-apartheid Countryside." In *Producing African Futures: Ritual and Reproduction in a Neoliberal Age*, ed. Brad Weiss. Boston: Brill.

———. 2010. "Outside the Dwelling of Culture: Estrangement and Difference in Postcolonial Zululand." *Anthropological Quarterly* 83:497–518.

———. 2012. "A Post-Fordist Ethnicity: Insecurity, Authority, and Identity in South Africa." *Anthropological Quarterly* 85:397–427.

Wilk, Richard. 1995. "Learning to Be Local in Belize: Global Systems of Common Difference." In *Worlds Apart: Modernity through the Prism of the Local*, ed. Daniel Miller. London: Routledge.

Wilson, Godfrey, and Monica Wilson. 1945. *The Analysis of Social Change*. New York: Cambridge University Press.

Wilson, William. 1973. "Herder, Folklore, and Romantic Nationalism." *Journal of Popular Culture* 6(4).

Wolpe, Harold. 1972. "Capitalism and Cheap Labor Power in South Africa: From Segregation to Apartheid." *Economy and Society* 1(4).

Worsely, Peter M. 1956. "The Kinship System of the Tallensi: A Reevaluation." *Journal of the Royal Anthropological Institute* 86:37–75.

Wylie, Dan. 1991. "Who's Afraid of Shaka Zulu?" *Southern African Review of Books*. May–June.

———. 1992. "Textual Incest: Nathaniel Isaacs and the Development of the Shaka Myth." *History in Africa* 19:411–33.

———. 1993. "A Dangerous Admiration: E.A. Ritter's *Shaka Zulu*." *South African Historical Journal* 22:98–118.

———. 2000. *Savage Delight: White Myths of Shaka.* Pietermaritzburg: University of Natal Press.

———. 2006. *Myth of Iron: Shaka in History.* Scottsville, South Africa: University of KwaZulu-Natal Press.

Zibechi, Raúl. 2005. "Subterranean Echos: Resistance and Politics 'desde el sótano.'" *Socialism and Democracy* 19(3):13–39.

Žižek, Slavoj, ed. 2002. *Selected Writings of Lenin from 1917.* London: Verso.

Zulu, Paulus. 1993. "Durban Hostels and Political Violence: Case Studies in KwaMashu and Umlazi." *Transformation* 21.

Index

abortion: comparison with United States, 198; in South African law, 227n11; Jacob Zuma's position on, 192, 197; migrants' concerns about, 10, 125, 203, 227n11, 227n13

Agamben, Giorgio: on the state of exception, 138–139, 228n4

agency: critique of, 20, 22, 24–25, 55–56; in liberal theories of freedom, 5–8, 12, 43–44, 49

ANC: *See* Inkatha; migrants

apartheid: *See* "indirect rule" and "labor migration system"

Bambatha Rebellion, 89; comparison with migrants' politics, 140; spurred urbanization, 95

beer: in South African law, 223n3; ritual distribution of, 132, 135; role in urban sociality, 96–97, 105, 224n8; women's production of, 50, 78, 82, 96–97, 131

Benedict, Ruth: on reason, 55–56; theory of culture, 208

bile/gallbladder (*inyongo*), 153, 157, 160, 181, 228n9

Bill of Rights, 210; migrants' resistance to, 3

Bloch, Maurice: on money and morality, 221n2; on the body, 88; theory of rebounding violence in ritual, 170–171

Boipatong massacre, 36, 226

Botha, P. W.: collaboration with Inkatha, 39

Bourdieu, Pierre: on houses, 17, 63; theory of culture, 48, 101; socialization in homesteads, 70; officialising strategy, 205; critique of his representation of Kabyl houses, 80; township planners prefigure his theory of practice, 101; on ritual and hierarchy, 222n9

Bourquin, Sighart: role in forced removals to KwaMashu, 103–104, 107–108, 225n19

bridewealth (*ilobolo*), 78; and misfortune, 86–87, 127, 148, 150, 230n3; changes to, 61, 139, 221n1, 225n28, 226n10; creating kinship, 134–163; gender symbolism, 162; in social theory, 47–48; masculinity, 126–127; men unable to pay, 11, 96, 110, 204

British Social Anthropology: role in culture theory in South Africa, 153–154

burning of houses, 30, 36, 130, 137–140

Buthelezi, Mangosuthu: collaboration with apartheid state, 39, 189; conflict with National Freedom Party, 200; founding of United Workers Union of South Africa, 35; role in Inkatha, 30–31, 38–39, 219n1; use of Zulu symbolism, 20

Calderwood, D. M.: theory of township planning, 102–13, 107

Cato Manor: *See* "Umkhumbane"